THE EDUCATED CITIZEN'S GUIDE

TO ESSENTIAL

AMERICAN HISTORY

TOM ROUSH

*This book is dedicated to my fellow travelers
who thirst for knowledge in a complex and
difficult world, where information is plentiful,
but knowledge and wisdom are still scarce.*

ADVANCE PRAISE FOR

The Educated Citizen's Guide to Essential American History

"Many thanks, Tom Roush, for creating an eloquently written, excellent book which makes the story of the US accessible to those of us who have not had the benefit of studying US history as part of our formal education. There are many of us from other parts of the world who have chosen to make America our home and who really appreciate the opportunities this country has to offer. We are grateful to now have at our disposal a compact volume which really helps us understand the essential milestones on a journey which has created this remarkable nation." —Robin MacMillan, retired Executive at National Oilwell Varco.

"This is one of the most comprehensive and complete books on the history of the United States that I have ever read. Not only does it give the major factors which make America and American what and who they are, it provides the information leading up to the events, a thorough understanding of the event and the aftermath and how it leads to the next historical event. As a former teacher at university level, this book should be required reading in every history class from middle school through college." —LTC Paul Sinor USA (Ret)

"Tom Roush loves his country. This book is a "must read" for anyone that feels the same way. The timeline of our nation's growth is extremely important and Tom has done an excellent job of narrating the complex, winding story." —David Anthony, Spring Forest Middle School History Teacher

"After decades of "critical" histories of the United States, it is refreshing to have a compact volume that takes a less antagonistic view of our history. This book makes an interesting companion for the frankly unsatisfactory US History textbooks found in school classrooms today. Happy to have my children read it when they reach school age!" —Lt. William Fox, CEO at Data Gumbo

"Author and historian Tom Roush has performed the near-impossible. His essential U.S. history book distills the essence of American lore, legend, and legacy into less than 300 pages, giving readers an abbreviated, thorough education of the must-knows for the many key players, politics, battles, and important events that occurred on U.S. soil. I highly recommend this book for anyone who wants to familiarize themselves with U.S. history with interesting, digestible bites of information." —Denise Dorman, CEO Right Brain Media

TABLE OF CONTENTS

ACKNOWLEDGMENTS

I am forever grateful to my parents, Tom and Neta Roush, who indulged my early interest in visiting historic places, to Mr. Thomas Wentworth who operated a small museum in Pensacola where I spent many hours looking at his collection of historic artifacts, and to my many friends and co-workers, principal among them Mr. Bruce Bullock, who told me stories, shared their lives, and explained to me how the world works.

PREFACE

———

The past is the country you are from to which you may never return. I've thought this for a long time. This statement is the bastardization of a phrase from an old British novel that reads: "The past is a foreign country; they do things differently there." Both statements are true.

Your knowledge of the past is critical to understanding the great story of human life. A mind that is a blank historical slate is not a good thing. It's like walking into a movie halfway through and trying to backfill the story while you watch the rest of the film. To live effectively in the present, you need to know that back story. Understanding history gives you the ability to decipher the current world and its politics, economics, culture, and foreign affairs in the proper context.

I've always had a strong interest in history. I grew up in Florida, but my Dad is from West Virginia. Each year when we visited my grandparents, we had to drive through territory that witnessed many battles of the Civil War. I would read about these battles and then consult maps to see where the battle sites lay relative to our driving route. Sometimes, much to the consternation of my sister, I could get my parents to detour and stop at a historical site or battlefield. I saw the places with my own eyes that I had been reading about and those places became more than a historical abstraction. At those sites, an empty field was not just an empty field; it was a place where men fought and died.

I also took great pleasure in hearing my relatives talk about their historical experiences, especially the wartime stories. One of my uncles was a medic in *Operation Overlord*, known to history as D-Day. After victory in Europe, he was positioned offshore from Japan and prepared for the impending invasion when the atomic bomb shocked the Japanese into surrender, thus ending World War 2. He credited this development with his survival. In 1952, the US Army drafted my Dad and sent him to the Korean War with very little training. It was a dangerous and unpleasant duty that doomed his first marriage, but he knew firsthand what an incoming artillery shell sounded like, and he could make that sound for me. The American Civil War, World War 2, and the Korean War were not abstract ideas unrelated to me or my life; they were stories of real people, some of whom I knew, doing courageous things without hesitation, because those were the times they found themselves in. I developed my love of history during this period.

Despite that early love, I never sought a professional education in history, though I was educated in many other subjects. The little historical education I received in public school was a boring compendium of dates and places. I'm interested in stories of real people. I enjoy learning how their stories fit into the larger story.

I designed this book to serve as a summary to help you, the individual citizen, consume American history faster and easier. I want to convey the broad sweep of the American narrative with facts that are not in dispute. This book is not meant to be comprehensive; it is more of a high level overview of the grand sweep of American history. There are thousands of books that delve into details of each historical period, and you can look deeper into those periods if you wish.

Note what was stated above about this book being a compendium of facts not in dispute. I've done my best to make that assertion a reality. I've deliberately including nothing about the recent Covid pandemic or anything about the presidency of Donald Trump because there are virtually no facts at this point that are not in dispute. Further, this book is also not meant to be a pro-American piece of historical propaganda. Every period of the conquest of the Americas by Europeans and each period of the history of the United States since then involves conflicts that often turned deadly and cost many men, women, and children their lives. American history is a tale of tragedy as well as triumph. Innocent people and whole cultures came to ruin to make way for the United States. The full story must include their story, and it is here.

But make no mistake: I love my country. My relatives left their European homeland hundreds of years ago and I have no connection to Europe any longer. As far as I'm concerned, I am an American and only an American. I am a native of this land like any other Native American. I love this country in the way people love many flawed, imperfect things and people. I love my country with full knowledge of the past.

A brief word is in order about terms. I have avoided whenever possible the term 'Indian' except as it relates to people in India. The people who inhabited the Americas before the arrival of Europeans are referred to as natives or Native Americans. This is easier to spell and remember than the term 'indigenous' and, at some point, anyone born in the Americas is indigenous. I have also avoided the color-coded categories of people like white, black, brown, red, and yellow as much as possible. I've used terms such as 'European-derived' or 'African-derived' or 'colonist' to describe people from other places who came to the Americas, and 'Anglo' to describe the English speaking European immigrant population when they needed to be distinguished from the Spanish speaking, or 'Latin' immigrant populations. Past a certain point, every citizen of the United States is simply referred to as Americans.

I hope that you will discover America's past in the pages of this book and then draw your own conclusions based on the facts of this country's incredible development. Consider this book your ticket to travel on a 500-year journey that made the United States of America.

SECTION 1: CONQUEST

The Landing of Columbus by Albert Bierstadt

"For I, with the force I have under me, which is not large, could march over all these islands without opposition. I have seen only three sailors land, without wishing to do harm, and a multitude of Indians fled before them. They have no arms, and are without warlike instincts; they all go naked, and are so timid that a thousand would not stand before three of our men." — From the logs of Christopher Columbus, 16 Dec. 1492

"A traitor is everyone who does not agree with me." — King George III

"I have no intention of sharing my authority." — King Louis XVI

A BOLD AND RESTLESS SPECIES

We humans are a restless species. We are forever in motion, forever seeking out new lands and opportunities. This restless nature is a universal rule that applies to all peoples everywhere on earth. Some species live their entire lives very close to where they were born, but that generally is not true for humans. The earth's continents as we know them today were already in place and empty before some restless band of humans walked up and claimed some piece of land.

For tens of thousands of years, all humans were tribal migrants forever in search of food and safety. The advent of agriculture made food more abundant and people less likely to move around. From that point forward, the history of every tribe and nation is a tale of people conquering new lands and subjugating the incumbent population, if there was one already established.

Agriculture created wealth and made the land a buy-and-hold proposition. The wealth and incentive to stay put allowed for cities, but stored wealth of any kind invites warfare and conquest. That is the way of *Homo sapiens*. It is what we do. It is in our nature.

European history is rife with continuous rivalry and subjugation. After centuries of warfare and conquest over each other, the people of Europe evolved into powerful nations led by religious authorities and rapacious monarchs. They possessed militaries, ocean-going ships, and in many cases, excess populations. They were bound to eventually seek out new opportunities beyond their borders. By 1492, European ships had already made it to the African coasts. It was only a matter of time and technology before they turned west. The moment of European breakout had long been incubating.

All peoples and cultures begin their human journey as tribesmen. The powerful Romans evolved from a tribal to a civilizational society. As the Roman Empire, they held territories around the Mediterranean. The Romans operated established institutions, such as a formal government and a standing military. They led an empire that extended far beyond traditional European borders.

After Rome fell, the tribal peoples the Romans had previously defeated (people such as the Gauls and the Celts) developed into their own civilizations. Gallic tribesman became nominal citizens. Celtic warriors became officers. Traders became merchants. Shamans and healers became priests and popes. Those formerly tribal countries on the Atlantic (mainly Spain, France, Portugal, and Britain) once subjugated by the powerful Romans were able to send explorers, adventurers, religious exiles, and militaries to the west. They crossed the oceans in technologically advanced ships and established a presence in the "New World' or the Western Hemisphere.

When the Europeans arrived in the Western Hemisphere, various native peoples already occupied North, Central, and South America. These Native Americans were descendants of those who had crossed the Bering Strait from modern Russia to modern Alaska deep in the past. Anthropologists believe this migration occurred in an ice age when sea levels around the world were lower. Once the waters rose again, those people lost touch with the bulk of humanity.

However they made it to the Western Hemisphere, they began to penetrate the land south and chose the best areas for hunting and later, cultivation. In the same way as it had happened in Europe, powerful civilizations emerged over the centuries, building cities and monuments and developing elaborate cultural expressions.

These cultures were inventive, but by the 15th century, they were behind the Europeans in many areas of development, including shipbuilding and weapons making. The people of Europe, the Middle East, Africa, and Asia had traded in goods but more importantly, they traded in ideas. And there was another problem: unbeknownst to them, they also traded in germs and viruses. The survivors developed essential immunities to certain pathogens. The Western Hemisphere's populations, cut off from many of humanity's most potent ideas, were also cut off from developing their personal defense systems. They had no immunity to the pathogens that arrived on their shores with the Europeans. Those viruses began to spread and kill on the first contact. This proved to be decisive in many ways in the coming centuries.

EMPIRES FALL AND RISE

At first, the Spanish dominated in this complex immigrant journey from Europe to the west. It was the Spanish who sent the Italian Christopher Columbus west to find an ocean path to the Indies, which included India and parts of East Asia. A perilous overland trading route known as the Silk Road connected East and West, but it was dangerous and uncertain. Columbus and many others thought a sea route to Asia was possible and would stake their lives sailing west to find it.

Queen Isabella of Spain financed the Columbus voyage. She told Columbus that he would achieve the rank of admiral and be the governor of whichever lands he could claim for Spain in his quest to reach Asia.

Sailing west with three ships in 1492, Columbus reached what is now the Bahamas, and later charted other lands in Central America. His reports to Queen Isabella set off a migratory pattern that changed the world forever.

Other Spaniards followed. Only twenty-eight years after Columbus, Hernán Cortéz conquered the Native American empire of what is now Mexico in 1519. Other Spanish explorers laid claim to thousands of square miles of territory, including portions of North America. With only 900 men, Cortéz prevailed over a densely populated Aztec Empire that could not fathom how to defeat the Europeans, though they had conquered all the Native Americans within their domain. Steel, explosive weapons, body armor, and huge horses proved to be effective against the larger Aztec armies. In a tale of treachery for the ages, a Spaniard named Francisco Pizzaro managed to conquer what is now the nation of Peru, an empire of millions, with even fewer men than Hernán Cortéz had at his command. The Spanish sent men of incredible will and daring to the New World, and that indomitable will paid off handsomely.

After the Spanish came the French explorers, and then the Dutch. Finally, in 1607, the English-speaking people from Britain landed in what is now Virginia and Massachusetts, and the British colonies were born. Demographic trends all over Europe meant there were plenty of immigrants willing to go to the new lands even though the prospects of survival were highly uncertain. Europe's burgeoning population in this period demonstrates a truism that drives all histories: *demographics is destiny.*

The people of Britain developed colonies in North America and expanded them over time. People from Holland, Sweden, Germany, and other parts of northern Europe followed, but the British absorbed those colonies either through war or treaty.

By the time British colonial independence arrived in 1776, thirteen legal entities ran along the Eastern seaboard of North America. Those colonies were legally based on Royal Charters, land grants, and often, religious ideology. The original 300 or so people who arrived in 1607 had grown to 2.5 million souls spread across New Hampshire, Massachusetts, Connecticut, Rhode Island, New York, New Jersey, Pennsylvania, Delaware, Maryland, Virginia, North Carolina, South Carolina, and Georgia. Those thirteen colonies and those 2.5 million people were the national starting point for what is now the United States of America.

To their west, the French laid claim to much of the central part of North America. To their south and further west to the Pacific, the mighty Spanish Empire was still growing. Back in Europe, revolutions were simmering below the surface and soon would burst out into the open. In this combustible period, the world was on fire with change.

MYTHS GIVE WAY TO DOCUMENTS

Unlike many nations, the United States has a thoroughly documented beginning. The people who wrote the foundational documents governing the nation are perfectly known. There is no mythic past concealed by legend and time. In England, no one knows for certain who built the massive stone structure called Stonehenge. In Mexico, there are abandoned stone cities the jungle has covered over. All over the world, there are relics, stories of origin, and often, abandoned structures, but in the relatively young United States, the founding people and documents that established the country are no mystery. Anyone can see the original Declaration of Independence, the US Constitution, and the Bill of Rights in the rotunda of the National Archives Building in Washington, D.C.

The colonies had unique characteristics as a result of being founded by the Anglo-Saxons. Unlike the Spanish, which sent primarily conquerors, militaries, and Catholic clergy to the New World, the British colonists that came to North America were true colonists; they brought families with the intent to stay and build societies similar to those from which they came. The British chartered and allowed this kind of system because the colonies had a high economic value and were a source of raw materials for the nascent British trading and industrial systems. The colonies were also a safety valve for restive excess populations.

Being a colonist was a very perilous life in the beginning. Crossing the ocean in a small sailing ship was only the beginning of the danger. The first English speaking colonists were often persecuted as religious minorities in the lands they left, and so they were willing to take high risks to practice their faith as they saw fit. Building a society in North America gave them religious freedom. This kind of liberty was a strong and persistent motivator for them to take the risk of coming to an unknown land with the intent to stay.

The rift in Christianity started by Martin Luther in 1517 jumped the ocean to the Americas, informing the New World Catholic and Protestant blocks. The differences were as significant in the New World as they were in the Old. This religious split, known as the Reformation, was to have a profound effect on Europe as well as the colonies and, as we shall see, the Catholics and Protestants varied greatly in their habits and goals once they crossed the great ocean.

In 1607, when the first English colonists arrived, the Protestant/Catholic wars in Europe were far from over. Many colonists were refugees from that blood-soaked and long term conflict. Massachusetts, for example, was a refuge for the Puritans who wished to purify the Church of England of all remnant Catholic habits. Maryland, named after Queen Henrietta Maria, known as Queen Mary, was a refuge for English Catholics.

A pattern in naming these colonies was developed; Spain referred to what is now Mexico as 'New Spain' but there were also New France, New Sweden, and of course, New England. In time, the names of the places often reverted to what the Native American inhabitants called them. The native people of New Spain were called the 'Mehicas,' for example, inspiring the naming of Mexico. Sometimes, the sovereign name stuck; Elizabeth I, known as the Virgin Queen, inspired the naming of Virginia.

In all the European colonies, Christianity was the driving force in human affairs. The Muslim Moors had been pushed out of Spain the same year that Columbus left for the New World, and the Spain that had driven out Islam was rigidly Catholic in 1492, so all Spanish colonies were, by extension, rigidly Catholic. This was not the case in the British colonies which were less uniform in their religious habits.

Jamestown, established in 1607 and named after King James, was the first successful English colonial town. The Jamestown colonists were led in part by an Anglican vicar named Robert Hunt, who conducted the first Protestant religious service in the Western Hemisphere. Most of those in the original party died after a few months of desperate struggle. Over time, new inhabitants replaced the old ones and the colony began to thrive. Jamestown established the English presence in North America.

In both the Catholic and Protestant domains, the societies they built were explicitly meant to support their faith. The Spanish colonies were direct extensions of the Spanish crown, which desired gold first and foremost, but they also promoted the Catholic faith and converted, often by force, the natives in their domains to their religious beliefs. The Catholic Church sent priests and friars to the New World who put a Catholic overlay on the religions practiced by the Aztec and Inca peoples, and in short order, the Spanish Conquest was complete.

The Protestants in North America took religious freedom very seriously and therefore, took far less interest in the spiritual beliefs of the natives they encountered. In the British colonies, there were Puritans, Quakers, and other Protestant Christian breakaway groups who had very specific ideas about the best religious practices, and they did not organize around converting the natives to their faith. They had no missionary class. The different motivations between the Catholic Spanish and the Protestant British played themselves out over centuries and differentiate the nations that evolved from those colonies to this day.

Colonial policy in the originating countries had other far-reaching, long-term implications beyond the domain of religion. The Spanish conquistadors, for example, were generally not allowed to bring their families to the colonial outposts, and the Catholic clergy were not to marry at all. This resulted in the Spanish and Portuguese men often coupling with the native women of the lands they subjugated, so their populations are far more ethnically mixed; the term 'mestizo' refers to a person of mixed ancestry, which is part of the current Mexican identity. Over time, the North American colonists brought whole communities with them and remained ethnically homogenous for several generations.

The British colonies had a far more tolerant immigration policy than the Spanish. They allowed in other Europeans including Dutch, Scandinavian, and German colonists, though these immigrants did not represent the interests of their countries' governments. The British military crushed any colony not loyal to the British crown.

The colonists also brought their European political systems with them. Since there were no democracies in Europe, all colonies were—to varying degrees—kingdoms with a Christian overlay. When the English colonies were established in 1607, England already had a parliament that was hundreds of years old, and the citizenry shared a bit of political power, but all remained answerable to the Royal sovereign, including the distant colonists. In Spain, there was no parliament and no sharing of power. The church and the crown were one entity. The legal separation of church and state was an American improvement that came later.

Both the Spanish and British colonies brought in African slaves to do the agricultural work. The Native Americans could not—and would not—become an enslaved workforce for the new European agri-business activities. This refusal opened the door to a captive labor force from Africa. Native American susceptibility to European pathogens was also part of the labor force problem. Again, pathogens drove significant historical events.

It was during this period that the so-called "iron triangle of trade" came into being. European goods were traded for slaves in Africa, those slaves were traded for raw materials in the Americas, and those raw materials were sold in Europe to be made into manufactured goods. The same ship would transport all three commodities: goods, slaves, raw materials.

The Spanish, French, and British transferred their cultures to the varying geographies of the New World and those cultural roots grew into the mighty trees of new nations over time. They were different from each other, as were the Native Americans they encountered. Those three factors—national origin (which included the two competing branches of Christianity), geography, and differing native populations—drove historical events over the following centuries, and shaped the nations that exist today.

A DISTANT AND DISENGAGED KING

In the English-speaking colonies, the leadership on both sides of the Atlantic developed diametrically opposed goals over time. The colonists wanted more trade freedom and representation in British politics. The political leadership in Britain wanted all trade with the colonies to be with the home country. In that sense, the standoff between colonial America and imperial Britain was no different than any other political conflict where people wanted the power and autonomy to choose their fate and pursue their fortune while their political masters opposed them.

Every revolution starts this way.

From the beginning to end of the American revolutionary period, King George III led the British and stubbornly refused to allow the colonies to have representation in the British parliament. The colonies paid taxes, but did not have any advocates in the British political system. The colonists referred to this situation as "taxation without representation."

George III (1738–1820) by Allan Ramsay

George III took the reins at age twenty-two and ruled for sixty critical years, from 1760 to 1820. Besides being rather young when he took power, George III was in a delicate dance at all times with the other major European powers. For all of George's reign, there was warfare with his European rivals. A recurring theme of American history up until the end of World War II is how the fate of the United States often gets wrapped around the axle of European history. The early days of George III's reign are a good example.

His ascendency in 1760 occurred in the middle of the Seven Years' War, which was an iteration of the global rivalries between the British, French, and Spanish. The French and Indian War in North America was a tributary in this larger river of conflict. It was there that another George—young George Washington—gained invaluable military experience.

George III resolved this bloody conflict temporarily via the first of many "Treaty of Paris" compacts in 1763, but at the price of his colonial ambitions in North America. Affairs in distant Prussia, Austria, Madrid, Portugal, London, and Paris all figured into the wars and treaties that were defining life for the colonial peoples who wished to push west. They knew this and did not like it one bit. George III had no plan to resolve this dilemma for his distant subjects, and he certainly would not meet any of them; he never traveled out of southern England throughout his entire life.

There is also a long-held belief that George III suffered from some form of mental illness that was the result of a genetic disorder. Whatever it was, it was his downfall; by 1810, George was still the king, but deemed unfit to rule. His son George IV was in power until George III died in 1820. We will never know how much his illness affected his judgment during the war with his colonial subjects.

King George had ministers who advised him on policy, but they underestimated the quality of the emerging population in the economically and educationally advancing colonies. While George III was possibly descending into madness, he was facing off against colonials such as George Washington, Thomas Jefferson, James Madison, Benjamin Franklin, and Samuel Adams. These men were native-born to the colonies and educated in the classics of western thought about rights and liberties. They were all students of the Age of Enlightenment, an intellectual trend towards logic, tolerance, and science. These men were no longer interested in opaque rule by distant kings and queens, whose arbitrary use of power conflicted with their own ideas of balance and order. In the royal courts of Europe, monarchal idiosyncratic behavior was still tolerated; it was the norm. In the more-practical colonies, the consequences of royal rule were keenly felt and the colonists grew increasingly unimpressed.

The leaders of the American revolutionary movement were serious men on their home turf. They were also keen strategists falling into conflict with a distant king who was continuously distracted by warfare, possibly mentally ill, and surrounded by politicians with their own European agendas. These men with differing abilities and agendas set the table for rupture and then warfare.

George III was still the king in power after the colonists won their War for Independence. He, or his Prime Minster, saw to it that there was a new and stable peace with the former subjects. This was a smart move for the British, since new wars with France were on the horizon. Prime Minister William Pitt aided King George III in this period. Pitt had considerable influence over the British political system after 1783, and he was instrumental in bringing the Americans back into the British fold.

Additionally, Pitt was a close friend to the abolitionist William Wilberforce. George III abolished the Atlantic slave trade in the British Empire in 1807. Pitt, Wilberforce, and George III shaped British policy on the Atlantic slave trade, which was then at its peak. Cutting the New World off from a fresh supply of African slaves drove up the value of the existing slaves, and this economic change was to make it more difficult for the United States to resolve the festering issue of slavery in the future.

When George III finally died, blind and isolated in 1820, the American Civil War was still forty-one years away. His son George IV ascended to the throne for ten years. When he died, another son, William IV took power for only seven years before he died. George III's granddaughter, Queen Victoria, took the throne for the rest of the 19th century. The long period of peace under Queen Victoria's reign helped the United States grow in power and size. It was not until her death and the outbreak of World War I that the British and American fates became intertwined yet again.

But by then, the United States would stand with the British not as colonies, but as equals.

REVOLUTIONS OF BODY AND MIND

The early United States was incredibly lucky in its timing. If the American Revolution had started earlier or later than it did, the outcome would have been very different. Also, unlike many revolutions of that period, the American Revolution was not a revenge plot against the previous rulers. The people who supported a break with the mother country did not seek the overthrow of George III, only his rule over their own territories. It was a revolution of ideas first and foremost. The ideals of the American Revolution had the greatest impact on the country and the world, long after the men who conceived them passed from the scene.

The American revolutionaries did not seek to subjugate and kill those that opposed independence. The Declaration of Independence explicitly states this in its opening: "When in the Course of human events, it becomes necessary for one people to dissolve the political bands which have connected them with another…" There was no call for the overthrow of the British government in this remarkable document. They wanted to "dissolve the political bands"" and that was all.

This sentiment stands in stark contrast to other European revolutions, particularly the French Revolution, which began in a similar timeframe. European revolutions during the late 18th century were blood-soaked affairs of mass violence. The French Revolution was horrible, even by European standards, and its brutal nature affected the United States in many ways.

A full-scale rebellion against the French monarchy began in May of 1789. In a pattern repeated the world over, the revolution quickly devolved into blood and public executions. The French King, Louie XVI, was publicly beheaded in 1793, just as the United States was implementing its new constitutional order. Unlike America's founding generation, who owned land and traveled continuously across their country, the French king knew virtually nothing of the French countryside or the people he ruled. The founding generation of American leaders was made up of wealthy, powerful men, but they were not isolated, pampered aristocrats. They knew the land they came from and its people. George Washington led his countrymen in battle; Louis XVI never led battles during his lifetime; he rarely even left Paris.

The blood lust of the French people was not slaked with the murder of the king, of course. His wife, Marie Antoinette, and thousands of other elites were beheaded and their heads displayed before the baying crowds in Paris. Nothing of the kind happened in colonial America.

The American Revolution did not devolve into public executions because it was about a revolutionary experiment in the philosophy of self-rule. The Declaration of Independence, the formal document authored by Thomas Jefferson, captured the American Revolutionary ideals nicely. It listed twenty-seven grievances against the royal government, all of which had to do with the unrestrained use of British power, including the murder of colonists by uncontrolled British military units. It is a remarkable document that describes a people fatigued by an unrestrained authority that wielded its power in an arbitrary, capricious manner. It describes a people who desired to live under a restrained government and recognizing the rights of individuals to live in peace and security.

As the Declaration of Independence describes, the British monarchy provided neither the peace nor the security the colonists wanted. The preamble to that document states: "We hold these truths to be self-evident, that all men are created equal, that they are endowed by their Creator with certain unalienable Rights, that among these are Life, Liberty and the pursuit of Happiness. That to secure these rights, Governments are instituted among Men, deriving their just powers from the consent of the governed…"

The entire American Revolutionary Period was about rejecting one form of government and creating another that limited its power and respected its people. The first words of the US Constitution are: "We the People…"

The rule it created was designed to bring a stable peace by restraining the use of government power. When power resides with moral and disciplined common people, they may live respectfully free. Britain, France, and Spain shared no such sentiment during the same period, nor were such sentiments recorded in any other part of the world at that time. Limiting government power in a Constitutional framework is a uniquely American philosophy and inheritance. It is rare even in the world today where unrestrained governmental power is the rule.

Portrait of King George in 1771 by Johann Zoffany

SECTION 2: CREATION

Washington Crossing the Delaware by Emanuel Leutze

"A free people ought not only to be armed but disciplined; to which end a uniform and well-digested plan is requisite; and their safety and interest require that they should promote such manufactories as tend to render them independent of others for essential, particularly military, supplies." — George Washington

"I have sworn upon the altar of God, eternal hostility against every form of tyranny over the mind of man." — Thomas Jefferson

"Freedom of speech is a principal pillar of a free government; when this support is taken away, the constitution of a free society is dissolved, and tyranny is erected on its ruins" — Benjamin Franklin

The timeless text of the Declaration of Independence states unequivocally what motivated the leadership in the American colonies to reject English rule and seek to stand as a free nation. It reads in part: "We hold these truths to be self-evident, that all men are created equal, that they are endowed by their Creator with certain unalienable Rights, that among these are Life, Liberty and the pursuit of Happiness.--That to secure these rights, Governments are instituted among Men, deriving their just powers from the consent of the governed, --That whenever any Form of Government becomes destructive of these ends, it is the Right of the People to alter or to abolish it, and to institute new Government, laying its foundation on such principles and organizing its powers in such form, as to them shall seem most likely to effect their Safety and Happiness. Prudence, indeed, will dictate that Governments long established should not be changed for light and transient causes; and accordingly all experience hath shewn, that mankind are more disposed to suffer, while evils are sufferable, than to right themselves by abolishing the forms to which they are accustomed. But when a long train of abuses and usurpations, pursuing invariably the same Object evinces a design to reduce them under absolute Despotism, it is their right, it is their duty, to throw off such Government, and to provide new Guards for their future security."

All of American history is driven by the ideas presented in this extraordinary document.

WAR BEGINS

It has long been noted that there is no History, only the historical record of the things people did and the consequences. Most of history is entirely accidental; it only seems foreordained after the fact. Often the events that set forces in motion are the inexplicable result of individuals making choices for reasons only they would know. The American Revolution falls into that category; it was not inevitable. It came about because of the choices individual people made.

The first actions of the American Revolutionary War occurred in the towns of Lexington and Concord in Massachusetts. Absolute independence and final victory began here.

The cold standoff suddenly turned hot between the increasingly dissatisfied colonial subjects and the British military (who were supposed to be there protecting the colonies) because the colonials had had their fill of the British military enforcing the unpopular edicts flowing from London and King George.

In December of 1773, a group known as the Sons of Liberty entered Boston Harbor dressed as the Mohawk, a native tribe. They threw several chests of tea into the water to protest the taxes they were required to pay to Britain under the Townshend Act. The British parliament passed these taxes without any colonial representatives present.

The harbor raid came to be known as the Boston Tea Party and the British government responded by ordering punitive changes to the charter government in Massachusetts. Afterwards, tensions between the British military in Boston and the colonial population escalated. The colonials responded to these changes by assembling more of the colonists into the militias that were initially designed to resist attacks from Native Americans. They now prepared for action against the British Army.

The assemblies and militias controlled all of Massachusetts outside of Boston. The King's government responded in February of 1775 by declaring the entire colony to be in open rebellion. The British military was ordered to seize and destroy the supplies of the colonial militia units, since they were now considered to be opposing British rule. This order was the spark that set the coming fire.

The Midnight Ride of Paul Revere by Edward Eggleston

British military movements were constantly observed by the citizens of Boston and reported to the countryside. When British Army troops assembled to march west and grab colonial military supplies, Paul Revere and other patriots rode the eighteen-mile route from Boston to Lexington and Concord issuing the warning, "The British are coming!" The militias and their Minutemen, so named for how fast they could be ready, assembled for action.

On the morning of April 19, 1775, a group of about eighty colonial militiamen led by John Parker exited Buckman Tavern in Lexington and assembled in Lexington Common, which was a public square. Parker thought the British military would march past his assembly, search for supplies down the road in Concord, and when they found none (knowing in advance that searches were coming, the militias had moved their supplies), march right back to Boston, as they had done before. He also knew that the approaching British forces were much larger than his own and he did not intend to confront them in open battle, but rather, show determination by assembling his men in ranks as the British marched past.

This moment became a turning point and the place where common individual choices turned the wheel of history. When the British arrived at Buckman Tavern, they did not march past it. Under the direction of a British Marine named Jesse Adair, they turned towards Lexington Common, where the colonial militia was standing in formation. The British troops began to fan out and surround the alarmed colonials and then a British officer ordered the militiamen to lay down their muskets. It is not known who fired the first shot, but the blast of musket fire filled Lexington Common.

Musket fire is deadly. Several colonial men were killed in the short fight that followed. The militiamen down the road in Concord could hear the booming musket shots, which served as a warning that the British were there to fight, not just search (or at least that is what they thought).

Shortly afterward, the British forces reached Concord and began a rough and fruitless search for supplies. Meanwhile, in the surrounding hills, the Minutemen were pouring forth and gathering in larger numbers. The danger to the British soldiers in Concord was growing by the minute. Without hesitation, farmers grabbed their weapons and headed out to face the fire.

With that many armed men in such a small space, more fighting was highly likely. Conflict came at North Bridge, a small wooden footbridge over the Concord River. A British military force gathered on one side as colonial militiamen approached on the other. Both sides fired furious musket volleys across the river at each other. The fight was on.

For the rest of that day, the British were on defense, trying to retreat back to Boston along roads where colonials gathered in ever larger numbers and fired at them. Only British reinforcements sent from Boston saved their fellow soldiers, who were exhausted and running out of ammunition. The retreat along the eighteen-mile path from Concord back to Boston was a running battle that cost the lives of several British soldiers. These actions would not go unanswered, as everyone knew.

The results for the day were a stunning victory for the Minutemen, both in military terms and in its value as propaganda. This inspired other colonists to join the fight and encouraged colonial leadership to believe that the British could, in fact, be defeated. George Washington was a former colonial militiaman who had fought for the British years earlier. He received news of events in Massachusetts and wrote to a friend that "the once-happy and peaceful plains of America are either to be drenched in blood or inhabited by slaves. Sad alternative! But can a virtuous Man hesitate in his choice?"

The American War of Independence was on.

INDISPENSABLE MEN: WASHINGTON AND JEFFERSON

There were many events and many people involved in the independence movement in the colonies. Twenty-five thousand soldiers lost their lives in the battles to follow, but it was a soldier named George Washington who was the indispensable figure in the period. Washington bridged the gaps and differences of opinion and strategy among the other colonial leaders. Just behind him, as ranked by influence on the revolution and the Revolutionary mindset, was Thomas Jefferson.

These men, along with others of the founding generation, promoted the ideas and ideals that radically advanced the rights, privileges, and prosperity enjoyed by human beings all over the world to this day. They were pioneers in the rights of people to direct their own fate. All of humanity owes a debt of gratitude to these brave and visionary men.

Further, these men advanced human rights at considerable peril to themselves; George Washington put his life on the line many times. Washington was the leading military commander of the Continental Army, as the American forces were known. This small army was arrayed against the formidable British military, which was, at that point, likely the most powerful on earth. There was nothing foreordained about Washington's victory when the fighting started. In fact the outlook was poor; a small, ragged army was to battle the formidable British lion. If Washington hadn't achieved victory, he would have surely been hung by the victors.

In the Battle of the Virginia Capes, the French fleet prevented the British
from entering Chesapeake Bay and relieving Major General Lord Cornwallis' army
at Yorktown, Virginia. Second Battle of Virginia Capes by V. Zveg

George Washington was born in Virginia in 1732 and died in 1799, so for his entire life, he was the product of 18th century America. His only trip outside of North America was to Barbados, where he contracted smallpox, which left several pockmark scars on his face. In 1752, Washington received a commission to join the Virginia militia representing British interests to the west. The French were trying to consolidate their North American claims at that time, and Washington was appointed by the British as a special envoy sent to the Ohio Valley to demand that the French forces leave. Washington completed his mission, but when the French refused to leave, he was made a commander of more Virginian forces and he led those men into battle in the French and Indian Wars.

Washington distinguished himself in this conflict with the French. He learned many valuable lessons about British and French military tactics. Later, in the War of Independence, Washington personally knew many of the generals the British appointed to put down the rebellion. When the revolution arrived, Washington became Commander and Chief of the Continental Army in 1775.

For the following eight years from 1775 to 1783, Washington led the American forces in many battles at Boston, Saratoga, on Long Island, and in many other colonial towns and cities. He stayed with his troops through several brutal winters in which thousands of Continental Army soldiers froze to death. The Revolutionary War was a long, ugly, brutal slog that lasted twice as long as World War II. The Continental Army was not a professional military and was woefully undersupplied. In every year of the conflict, the Continental forces were too small, had too little food, and were staffed by farmers with guns rather than professional soldiers. However, they were on their native soil and had the support of the surrounding populations.

Washington and his ragtag army had additional critical help. The French sided with the Americans in 1778, so Washington led troops from the nation he had formerly warred with against the nation he formerly represented. The French Navy aligned with the overmatched Americans against the British Navy. This was critical for bringing in supplies and additional troops from France. In fact, war debt from helping the Americans was a factor in the coming French Revolution.

The war came to an end when Washington and his combined American and French forces defeated the British at Yorktown in 1781. The French were indispensable in this effort and tipped the balance of power towards the Americans in the French monarchy's last decade of power. The British negotiated terms afterward and the independence of the colonies was secured with the signing of another Treaty of Paris in 1783.

The Surrender of Lord Cornwallis by John Trumbull

In recognition of his leadership, Washington became known as the "Father of the Country" and served as the first president under the new constitution. He died at age 67 of a throat infection, but he would always be remembered as the indispensable leader during the revolutionary period. The history of the colonies would have been far different without his presence.

Thomas Jefferson was another towering figure of the founding generation. His intellectual influence was primary in developing the early United States.

In his youth, Jefferson studied languages and the violin. He loved nature and the mysteries of the natural world. He declared that he could not live without books and developed his own library, which eventually housed more than two thousand volumes. Jefferson was the principal author of the Declaration of Independence and served as the third president of the Republic from 1801 to 1809.

Jefferson was a roving intellect with many interests and accomplished competencies. He brought the spirit of enlightenment to all meetings about independence and the follow-on meetings about securing the government. He faced many issues in the early days of the republic, from slavery to rampant piracy to diplomatic relationships with the European powers. He also founded the University of Virginia.

Given the importance of slavery in US history, it is worth noting that Jefferson's attitudes and actions on slavery fit the pattern of many from the founding generation. Like Washington, he owned slaves, up to six hundred, but he publicly and privately expressed his reservations about the institution of slavery. He is said to have treated his slaves well and he did support Virginia legislation making it easier for slaves to achieve freedom. Slavery was at the bottom of a continuum of rights and freedoms, and while Jefferson seemed to abhor this sliding scale of privileges, he did little to address slavery when he had the power to do so.

Further, Jefferson's wife died in 1782 and modern DNA analysis indicates Jefferson fathered six children with Sally Hemmings, a female slave who worked in his household. Hemmings was of mixed race and the half-sister of Jefferson's wife, Martha (neé Wayles) Jefferson. Sally and Martha had the same father.

Thomas Jefferson was born in 1743, and so was a decade younger than George Washington. He lived much longer than Washington, and influenced 18th and 19th century American developments. While Washington and Benjamin Franklin did not live to see the 19th century, Jefferson and many other founders lived for decades after independence and shepherded the ideas of the country into actual practices of governance. Jefferson died on July 4, 1826 from a brief illness which prevented him from attending the ceremonies marking the fiftieth anniversary of the signing of the Declaration of Independence, considered his most influential writing.

SELF RULE

With French help, the Americans decisively defeated the available British military units in North America at Yorktown in 1781. This put them in a position to negotiate the terms of their now-inevitable independence.

Most of the fighting had been between colonial militia and British Army units, but due to the complex and overlapping claims that the other European nations made on New World geographies, conflict settlement negotiations were held in Paris with French, Dutch and Spanish government representatives involved.

Benjamin Franklin, the future President John Adams, and other dignitaries represented the Americans at these negotiations. Benjamin Franklin was a fascinating figure—a well-respected intellectual with a strong interest in the sciences. Born in 1705, Franklin was the oldest of the founding fathers by far. He was twenty-eight years older than George Washington and thirty years older than John Adams, who was more of a legal scholar. Franklin was decades older than the average man in colonial America, yet he remained active in the independence movement.

Since the Spanish were looking to secure the return of Gibraltar, the negotiations for American independence that took place in Paris involved issues unrelated to North America. Unknown to the other European powers, the British began to conduct direct negotiations with the Americans on the idea that they could retain favorable trade with the soon-to-be-former colonies and forgo the cost of militarily defending them. The American delegation also thought a better deal was possible with the British if they held talks directly, so the locus of talks shifted from Paris to London. The basics of the subsequent agreement were hammered out at the home of the British Prime Minister Lord Shelburne.

The final treaty was very generous to the Americans and established in the first article the sovereignty of the former colonies. Other articles established the boundaries of the new country, which were to run from the boundaries of Spanish Florida in the south to various geographies in the north in the territory that is now Maine. The treaty allowed for the return of prisoners of war, recognized debts to be paid, and secured the rights of Loyalists still in the colonies.

The treaty settled the dispute, but it was flawed. The uncertainty regarding geographic features and maps meant the agreed-upon borders were poorly defined and this oversight assured fighting would resume between all sides over boundaries and claims eventually. Nevertheless, the treaty was signed by the American delegation and the British representatives on September 3, 1783. The final ratified and signed copies were exchanged in Paris in May of 1784, just five years before France devolved into its own revolution. As a new government and regime were being born in North America, an older and sickly one was entering its final days in the heart of Europe.

The American delegation returned to the newly formed United States, secure in their treaty with their former colonial masters, and began the work of setting up a new government.

STATECRAFT

The first governing framework adapted by the former British colonies was called the Articles of Confederation and it provided virtually no foundational federal government. As many had anticipated, the former colonies were now states and they began to function as their own nations with little coordination or cooperation between them.

The new federal government had no power to even defend the nation from attack. The United States Army had only 625 men in it, and they were not being paid on time. A few British military units were still on American soil, and the US Army could not remove them. At a convention in 1786, the many problems facing the thirteen states were discussed. At the convention, James Madison, one of the signers of the Declaration of Independence, openly questioned if the Articles were even sufficient to call the country a "United States" at all.

At a series of conventions over the following three years, Madison drove the debate over what new form of government was needed to organize the states into a unified country. The result of those conventions is what we have today—three branches of government with specific powers operating separately to arrive at a consensus. The three branches are the judicial, made up of judges; the executive, which is inhabited by the president; and the legislative, which is two-fold, consisting of the House of Representatives and the Senate.

The original design called for each branch to serve, through delicately crafted rules, as a check on the power of the other two. These checks and balances are a safety system ensuring no portion of the federal government rises to complete dominance.

Even with the checks and balances in place, the drafters of the rules were overwhelmingly concerned that there was still the potential for abuse of federal power. This prompted them to add rules known as the Bill of Rights. These are the rights of citizens beyond the federal government's grasp to restrict, no matter what. No congress, no set of judges, no majority of voters, and no president could take away these fundamental rights, which were covered in the first ten Amendments which are referred to collectively as the Bill of Rights.

The 1st Amendment captured many concerns. It states the absolute right of people to choose their religion and it forbids the creation of any official religion sanctioned by the government. The United States was not to wade into the Catholic/Protestant morass. This act alone spared the United States from further warring along religious lines, which had occurred in Europe and still occurs all over the world. The 1st Amendment also provides for the absolute power of people to speak openly about the issues they believe to be important, referred to as the freedom of speech. There was also the freedom of people or organizations to publish the news of the day which is referred to as freedom of the press. It was envisioned in the 2nd Amendment that the citizens would be able to own personal means of force, such as various weapons. Many of these amendments were meant to keep the US government from doing what the British had done—forcing citizens to feed and house soldiers. The US federal government is forbidden, according to the amendments, from arbitrarily searching through a citizen's possessions, and it must provide specific reasons for detaining a person, referred to as a "writ of habeas corpus" (which means 'show me the body' in Latin) and hold a trial in which a citizen is presumed to be innocent if any rights or freedoms are to be withheld.

The emergent document, now called the Constitution, made rules around slavery without actually using the word 'slave' or 'slavery' or forbidding it. In what was to be the first of many compromises on the issue of slavery, the Constitution declared the slaves were people worthy of being counted to define how many congressmen a state might have in the House of Representatives, but only at the rate of three-fifths of a non-slave.

The exact text of this passage reads: "Representatives and direct Taxes shall be apportioned among the several States which may be included within this Union, according to their respective Numbers, which shall be determined by adding to the whole Number of free Persons, including those bound to Service for a Term of Years, and excluding Indians not taxed, three fifths of all other Persons." The use of the term "free Persons" and "those bound to Service" when the words "slave" and "non-slave" were available, is illustrative. Clearly, the drafters did not wish to trigger a disagreement over slavery which was already a controversial topic. Regardless, the slaveholding states wanted the slaves counted at full value, and the non-slaveholding states did not want them counted at all. The three-fifths count was a compromise and it was needed to get the southern slave-holding states to agree to the rest of the Constitution.

The entire document was adapted in 1789, President George Washington was elected, and the first congress seated. The adoption and implementation of the Constitution was a triumph for James Madison. Like Jefferson, Madison served as president and lived well into the 19th century. He died in 1836, long after the colonies ceased to be wards of the British. Instead, the colonies were rising in power, size, scope, and influence under the rules Madison had written.

GOD-GIVEN RIGHTS

As a governing philosophy, the US Constitution captured a radical set of ideas for its time. Those ideas about common people having sovereignty over their own lives are still unique. The Constitution begins with the words "We the People" because the men who wrote it wished to create a self-governing structure that could be administered without divine authority. Kings and queens, and, of course, popes, were said to rule by divine right; God ordained them to have dominion. The founding generations set out to create a governing structure for people who were clearly not divine.

The newness of this idea cannot be overstated. The Roman Republic, the British Parliament, the Papal States, the ancient Jewish governments described in the Bible… none of these resembled the government outlined in the US Constitution. This was a new form of governing architecture, with a balancing of powers and the needed structure to form and remain stable. It was designed to secure the liberty of the ultimate unit of citizenship, which was the individual. It was meant to replace the rule by force of monarchs or powerful military cabals, or even well-meaning despots that saw the individual as a meaningless cog in the whole. It was to be the rule of agreed-upon law by the citizens who had to live under it. Equality under that law was sacrosanct.

One of its primary features is referred to as federalism, which is the practice of parity between two levels of government; state and federal. At the conventions in 1787 where the Constitution was being debated and written, much of the discussions centered on the powers of the would-be federal government and what powers would be reserved by the states. The idea was to reserve and distribute power to the lowest level possible so that rulers and ruled would be in closer proximity to each other.

However, the US Constitution had a near-fatal flaw in proposing a government of "We the People" without addressing the paradoxical issue of slavery. The new ideas of individual liberty acknowledged explicitly that slaves were people (and therefore had to be counted for representation) without trying to address the inherent conflict in the ancient institution of slavery, which also defined those people as property.

Slavery was ubiquitous in the world in the 18th century, even in places where the people were ethnically identical. In the Americas, slavery had taken on an ethnic complexity by operating as a system of buying and selling people primarily from Africa. It wasn't designed that way on purpose, but it emerged that way because of the pattern in which Europeans bought and transported slaves from the territories they were exploring in Africa at the same time as labor was needed in the New World.

There were plenty of Europeans and other non-Africans who were desperately poor in the early days of the United States and forced into what was called 'indentured servitude' but they weren't part of the legal regime of slavery. The indigenous peoples of the Americas had practiced many brutal forms of slavery, but when the US Constitution was ratified, slavery in the United States was a unique and legally defined European concept with African captives at the heart of it. It included the practice of chattel slavery, meaning slaves were deemed assignable property. They could be freed, but otherwise, they were property to be bought and sold. Worse yet, their children were also deemed property and so they were born with a price on their head. This economic component to the American slave system made it even harder to eradicate once it had become culturally unacceptable. Even the Native Americans, as disliked and distrusted as they were, were not held as slaves, which ironically precluded them from having any economic value and assured their doom.

If abolishing slavery had been added to the Constitution, the states that were more dependent on slave labor would never have signed on, and the United States as it came to exist would never have happened. And so, as a matter of practical necessity, the issue of slavery was postponed for future leaders to address.

The handwritten US Constitution is only four pages long, but it details a new governing structure such as the world had never seen. It is on display in Washington DC for all to see.

SECTION 3: COMING-OF-AGE

Boone's First View of Kentucky by William Ranney

"One man with courage makes a majority." — Andrew Jackson

"Men may not get all they pay for in this world; but they must certainly pay for all they get." — Frederick Douglass

"I was born upon the prairie, where the wind blew free and there was nothing to break the light of the sun. I was born where there are no enclosures and where everything drew a free breath. I want to die there and not within walls." — Para-Wa-Samen (Ten Bears)

It took 177 years from the founding of the first English colony in North America at Jamestown in 1607 until the Treaty of Paris was signed and the independence of the colonies was secured in 1784. During this period, three hundred colonists began a journey that resulted in a new country of 2.5 million souls being born on North America. This new nation faced several threats and opportunities from the very beginning.

The first threat was the possibility that some European power would insert itself by force of arms into the nation's affairs. In fact, a second war with the British was coming, but the early Americans kept friendly relations with the French, even as France descended into its own revolution and war. Spain was an empire fully engaged in its problems, and they had not conquered any portion of North America despite making claims upon it for three hundred years. The real threat out of Europe was still the British.

The second threat was the Native Americans. They remained present in the colonies and on the frontiers. When they banded into loose confederations, as they sometimes did, they were a formidable military force. Even as small bands, they were an effective guerilla fighting unit that never went away. The Native Americans lived their lives in a way that was simply incompatible with the European-derived manner of living, and further, they were fragmented into thousands of tribes whose only commonality was their inability to become American citizens and their shared disinterest in doing so. Only a halt to Western advancement would have settled the conflict but it was the unofficial consensus of the American people that they were headed west regardless of policy or cost. This was a civilizational conflict of the kind seen the world over, and such conflicts resist a negotiated settlement. No settlement was coming for the natives.

The third threat was the largest, but it was not quite so obvious in 1776 or 1784, or even when the United States bought a third of North America from the French in 1803. That threat was a fracture in the nation over the fate of the millions of humans held as slaves. This bit of unresolved Constitutional business took decades to reach its fully disastrous flowering. The seeds of the Civil War were planted as the United States finally began to expand west in earnest. From 1784 until the start of the Civil War in 1861 was seventy-seven years—one lifetime, really—and there were many players and unexpected turns of fate along the path. In a pattern that was to repeat itself for two centuries, the most defining event that drove the United States to civil war began back in Europe.

THE GIFTS OF NAPOLEON

The French Revolution began in 1789, the same year the Americans formally adopted the US Constitution. This event helped the United States in one key way: it was so blood-drenched and horrible that eventually, the French military stepped in and took control of the country. Their leading general was Napoleon Bonaparte. He compounded the French revolutionary disaster by launching a series of disastrous external wars, the kind so common in Europe at the time. Napoleon lived only to 51, but he was one of the most consequential European leaders ever and his legacy is still debated. Napoleon's rise ended the period of the French Revolution known as "the terror," so called because of all the murder, beheadings and chaos, but his rule began a period of brutal, endless warfare.

The Napoleonic Wars brought France into conflict with many countries, including Britain. Regardless of what George III and the British leadership wanted, war had arrived yet again and Britain had to fight the French, a sister people just across the English Channel. Under Napoleon, the French waged war in all directions; he was boundlessly ambitious and belligerent.

The French Revolution and the Napoleonic Wars created overwhelming debt for France. The new wars also engaged French forces all over Europe and took them away from the New World. Further complications in the Americas led Bonaparte to make a fateful decision in 1803. Under his leadership, the French sold all their claims in North America to the United States for fifteen million dollars.

This transaction is known as the Louisiana Purchase, and it was the single greatest real estate transfer in history. In one fell swoop, this purchase decision allowed the United States to double its territory without having to fight a European power for it. The Revolutionary War had cost 25,000 lives and lasted eight years, but now, the United States could buy a territory similar in size to the original thirteen colonies from a European power at a price the country could afford. The terms were so favorable that the US Ambassador to France, Robert Livingston, signed off on the deal before he could get authorization from President Thomas Jefferson back in America. He did not want a deal *this* good to go sour.

The purchase included New Orleans, which gave the United States full control of the Mississippi River and its outlet to the Gulf of Mexico. All by itself, this was a godsend for the US and its burgeoning Navy. The land included what was to become most of the state of Louisiana, plus what would later become the states of Arkansas, Oklahoma, Kansas, Iowa, Missouri, Nebraska, Colorado, Montana, Wyoming, plus North and South Dakota.

Shortly after the US concluded the deal, Jefferson commissioned a group led by Meriwether Lewis and William Clark to explore this new territory. A team started out from Pittsburgh, crossed the Mississippi River near St. Louis and traveled through Native American territory. They eventually made it all the way to the Pacific Coast. Their journey took three years. They documented observations on the people, geography, weather, botany and zoology of the territory now claimed by the United States. Their records are the first look at what the Americans would encounter over the rest of the 19th century.

The long Napoleonic Wars ended in 1815 when the British defeated the French at Waterloo, a small town in Belgium. In the end, Napoleon's reign was a disaster for Europe. He not only sold the French claims to North America, claims that went back hundreds of years, but he also deposed the Spanish monarchy, which brought Mexico into conflict with the United States. Those two events, the Louisiana Purchase and the Mexican-American War, were what gave the western two-thirds of North America to the United States. Both were the byproducts of Napoleonic rule. Both accelerated the expansion west, doomed the Native Americans, and drove the question of slavery to a deciding point.

In many ways, Napoleon was a more consequential European than even George III.

This painting, called 'Napoleon Crossing the Alps,' celebrated the hero General's early conquests before he was deposed and exiled. Napoleon's wartime decisions delivered the western two thirds of North America to the United States.

PARTING SHOTS

The long and destructive Napoleonic Wars had yet another side effect: it prompted the British to seize American citizens and force them into the British military. This was known as a "press-gang" or "impressment." By 1812, it was estimated that some fifteen thousand Americans had been impressed by the British and forced to serve in their military. This occurred in the tense aftermath of the Revolutionary War.

The cold peace between the United States and the British was bound to turn hot again. While the 1783 Treaty of Paris technically ended the hostilities between the British and their former colonies, the two nations had not yet formed the "special relationship" they would in the 20th century. The two English-speaking countries were continuously at odds with each other in the early decades of the United States as an independent nation, and conflict often turned hot along the border of Canada, which was still British sovereign territory.

Further, the British covertly sided with the Native Americans to the extent that they provided weapons to the natives to attack American settlements, which were already expanding west at a breakneck pace. A Native American leader named Tecumseh created a confederation of indigenous nations, Tecumseh's Confederacy, to fight the American westward expansion into the Great Lakes region. He received aid from the British, which the Americans eventually discovered.

As a result of British meddling, President James Madison asked for, and received, a declaration of war in 1812. The simmering conflict with the British came to a full boil when the Americans became intent on finishing the issues the Treaty of Paris did not resolve.

The first actions were entirely predictable. The powerful British Navy blockaded American ports, cutting off trade. The American land forces headed north into Canada. A series of battles followed between American and British forces in the Canadian theater: in Detroit, at Queenston Heights, and on the Thames River in Ontario, where the British had sided with Tecumseh's Confederacy. None of these battles had the power to swing the conflict one way or the other.

In August of 1814, British forces marched on Washington, now the federal capital, burning many buildings to the ground, including President Madison's residence (then called the Presidential Mansion, but later renamed The White House). President Madison had to flee the city before advancing British troops. The British stayed twenty-six hours in Washington and then retreated. The British also attacked Fort McHenry in Baltimore and its defense is what inspired an amateur poet, Francis Scott Key, to write the words for what would become "The Star-Spangled Banner." In the end, there was no effort by the British to reacquire the colonies.

There were many battles fought along the southern frontier where American claims, Spanish claims, and the British military met. The boundaries established under the Treaty of Paris were being renegotiated on the ground by soldiers in action.

After years of mostly fruitless warfare, the American and British ambassadors met in Belgium and negotiated the Treaty of Ghent. Both sides had gained something. The Americans claimed they had ended the forced pressing of their citizens into the British military. The British sealed the territorial sovereignty of Canada, which finally had an unmovable and well-defined border. The British had more pressing affairs with Napoleon to address and they viewed the entire conflict as yet another manifestation of the dreadful Napoleonic Wars. The Americans saw it as a coda to the Revolutionary War.

In an odd twist of fate, one of the most consequential battles of the entire conflict occurred after the war had officially ended. The Treaty of Ghent was signed *before* the costly Battle of New Orleans was fought in January of 1815 but neither the British nor American forces in New Orleans knew that the war had already ended. The American victory secured by General Andrew Jackson in that battle launched him into the national spotlight and his political ascendency was to change the course of American history in the years to come. The British suffered a very high casualty rate in that encounter and never fielded soldiers in the territorial United States again. The British departed the scene, but Andrew Jackson's time in the sun was just beginning.

MANIFEST DESTINY

The early days of the United States were uncertain. American leadership worried that European powers would strangle the country in its infancy to regain a foothold in North America. The British and Spanish empires were still active in the New World, even though the Spanish were already in steep decline and the French were mostly gone.

Still, the British were in Canada and technically, Mexico was still the property of Spain, and the western part of North America was not yet fully under American control. These uncertainties and realities led

American leaders to ponder aloud the idea of strategic security, which meant securing in American hands the continent to the Pacific and preventing another European settlement from ever taking root.

In early America, western expansion was still an open question. There was nothing inevitable about the spread west. Events could have gone many other ways. The North American continent could have ended up with several separate countries within it, each with long land borders. If that had occurred, North America would have been territorially like Europe with the same endless wars that occur when competing neighbors have no natural barriers between them. The Middle East is replete with this exact situation today. England, Wales, Scotland, and Ireland fought for centuries because no one was safe from predation. The founding generation of American leaders recognized the problem of competing sovereignties forced into a limited geographic space. Even though it was not written into the Constitution, their goal was to unite the continent under one nation. It was an unspoken policy and practice, but not a law.

Early on, it was impossible for the United States to simply seize the west because it was militarily weak, relative to Europe, and further, each state had wildly different economies, interests, and populations. They had different Christian sects and plenty of religious fundamentalists. They could have broken up in the earliest days as easily as they stayed together, but their leadership knew the end result of a fractured nation, and they wished to avoid that fate. They would face the many threats from Europe, the Native Americans, and possibly even from each other, so they hung together until events like the Louisiana Purchase slowly fell their way. In early American history, luck played an enormous role.

And so, since there was no official law about spreading west and no way to know in which manner this might be accomplished, Manifest Destiny was emphasized as a cultural theme. Manifest Destiny was the idea that the country would eventually extend across the continent and the idea came to fruition over the length of the 19th century. Cultural ideas are often far more powerful than actual laws or stated national objectives.

Manifest Destiny was predicated on the idea that the United States was special, virtuous, and *should* spread west. The people who promoted the idea wanted the western half of the North American continent to mirror the eastern half. Americans, it was said, were all tasked with fulfilling this duty.

The term Manifest Destiny is credited to journalist John O'Sullivan, who began using it in his reports about various American territorial conflicts in Texas and Oregon. He described Manifest Destiny as something that would occur naturally, not as a government mandate, but as part the special mission of the citizens of the United States who answered to a "higher law" and who had special moral obligations. He wrote in 1845: "And that claim is by the right of our manifest destiny to overspread and to possess the whole of the continent which Providence has given us for the development of the great experiment of liberty and federated self-government entrusted to us." Note the lack of any reference to the law, government policy, or a military invasion.

The idea was opposed by many who saw it as a glossy overlay to hardnosed ambitions of territorial conquest. Regardless, it became an underlying theme of both US policy and practice as the nation did go west. Manifest Destiny was relevant long after the boundaries of the United States reached the Pacific Ocean. The concept linked the United States to the idea of a perpetual frontier and the moral ideal of the frontiersmen. The Kennedy Administration was using the term New Frontier long after the United States had fulfilled the original idea of Manifest Destiny.

The United States cultural zeitgeist meant the nation had to seek a new Manifest Destiny to replace the prior ones. The surge west eventually led to surges in all directions, including up. Manifest Destiny placed an American on the moon over John O'Sullivan's head, and sent robotic explorers to far-flung planets. As a cultural theme, Manifest Destiny is still with us.

COMINGS AND GOINGS

Time eventually claimed all the founding cohort of American leaders. Benjamin Franklin was 70 years old when the Declaration of Independence was signed, and he and George Washington were men of the colonial world who did not see the arrival of the 19th century, but many others did. The first five US presidents were all part of the founding cohort of leaders and four of them lived well into the next era. The first five presidents and their terms in office were George Washington from 1789 to 1797, John Adams from 1797 to 1801, Thomas Jefferson from 1801 to 1809, James Madison from 1809 to 1817, and James Monroe from 1817 to 1825.

For the first thirty-six years, from 1789 to 1825, the presidency was occupied by men who had designed the foundational government of the United States. This was an incredible stroke of good fortune for the country. These were the men who wrote the US Constitution and they hung around long enough to see its design tested and adjusted. They made sure its concepts were embedded into the country's institutions. Each of these men lived an extraordinarily long time relative to the average age of the day. They left behind volumes of writings and ideas. It wasn't until John Quincy Adams, the son of founder and previous President

John Adams, became the president in 1825 that the founding generation of leaders finally faded away and the country was run by people who had only a distant memory of Colonial America.

Men like Andrew Jackson were the next wave of leaders whose entire life experiences were almost exclusively as citizens of the United States. This generation began the process of turning rebellious Englishmen and other European identified people into American-born and culturally identified Americans.

As the country started the spread west, distinctly American characters began to emerge that were native-born and they began adopting more primitive ways of living. These were the quintessential American Frontiersmen. They lived off the land and were hearty, fiercely independent types. They knew how to survive in the unsettled parts of the country and seemed to know and admire the indigenous peoples who had done the same things for generations. This generation, more than the one previous or the ones after, moved more easily in the Native American population and adapted to their ways.

One such man was Johnny Appleseed, who was a real person from Massachusetts born as John Chapman. He was an ascetic, devout Christian, and a nurseryman who planted seeds of apples in several counties across Massachusetts, Pennsylvania, and Ohio on the theory that when other settlers came along behind him, they would have apples growing already. He was a rare vegetarian in his time. Appleseed/Chapman had a love for animals and it is said he had high regard for the Native Americans, who also regarded him as one touched by the gods. His legacy was personifying the frontiersman, who regarded the American landscape as sacred.

Another frontiersman from this period was Davy Crockett. He became known as the King of the Wild Frontier in popular culture, but in his lifetime, he was a restless man who roamed the fringes of American civilization and ran for elected office in Tennessee, as had Andrew Jackson and Sam Houston. He served in Congress when Andrew Jackson, the heroic general of the Battle of New Orleans, was president. Crockett opposed Jackson's Indian Removal Act, which led to an electoral defeat. In anger, he headed off to the new boundaries of the frontier, which had extended to the Mexican-held territory of Texas. Here he would meet his fate in a few short years.

Crockett, Appleseed, Daniel Boone, and others were written about in the nascent press of the Eastern cities and as such, entered the national consciousness as frontiersmen and heroes who carried the country relentlessly west as per the imperative of Manifest Destiny. By the time westward expansion was a *fait accompli*, the frontiersman had become an archetype of the period and the subject of study and fiction. If the wise Founding Fathers were the first archetype, the wild Frontiersmen were the second. The frontier fused the wildness of the Native American spirit with the language and cultural habits of the English.

The author Mark Twain's characters in *Tom Sawyer* and *Huckleberry Finn* borrow heavily on the life of Johnny Appleseed and the frontiersman archetype. Huckleberry Finn was a fictional character in a book that was not published until 1884, but it captures the national character of second-generation Americans and is a classic of American literature. Twain's characters inhabited the frontier that was then positioned at the territory of Missouri and the Mississippi River. His stories muse upon the lives in post-Independence, pre-Civil War United States. In Huckleberry Finn, Huck flees his abusive father and teams up with Jim, a runaway slave. They go on a series of frontier adventures as close friends. In the end, Jim is freed and Huck heads west, modeling the actual history of the United States as seen through the lives of individuals.

From the end of the Revolutionary War until the beginning of the Civil War in 1861, the national character was being formed over the Appalachian Mountains, and in the wilderness zones that led up to the western jumping-off point at the Mississippi River. Ironically, as Mark Twain was writing about the frontier-type American in the 1880s, all around him were men pushing cows here and there. In due course, the cowboys out of Twain's window would replace the men in Twain's imagination as representatives of the quintessential American occupation and type. In a sense, the Founders represented the wise eastern colonial thinker, the Frontiersmen represented the wilderness dweller from the Appalachians to the Mississippi River, and then the Cowboy archetype seized the imagination all the way to the Pacific.

ANDREW JACKSON AND THE TRAIL OF TEARS

Andrew Jackson was a uniquely American character and the most influential person of the post-Independence frontier United States. He was an irascible, violent man of incredible will and ambition who earned his nickname "Old Hickory." He served as the seventh president from 1829 to 1837, which was a critical period of development. He had lifelong scars from the practice of dueling. In one particular encounter with a rival horse breeder, Jackson stood still and let the man shoot at him from a few feet away, as per the dueling rules of the day. The musket ball entered Jackson's chest but did not kill him. When it was Jackson's turn to fire, he shot the man dead. The bullet Jackson took stayed in his body for the rest of his life.

Jackson was only nine years old in 1776, so most of his long life he lived free of British influence, though he hated the British with a white-hot passion. Jackson was none too fond of the Spanish either, and leading a force of mostly volunteers from Tennessee, Jackson swept through many of the southern states and territories largely under his own direction and authority, fighting British and Spanish forces. He also led many military campaigns against the Native Americans, including the Creek under a leader called Red Sticks. The Native Americans would sometimes ally with the European forces, sometimes not, but Jackson fought them all under multiple circumstances. These many conflicts culminated in the Battle of New Orleans, which occurred after Jackson and his troops had vanquished all that dared oppose them. Later battles with the Spanish, and the Native Americans referred to as the Seminoles, secured Florida for the United States. The city of Jacksonville in north Florida is named in his honor.

Andrew Jackson by Ralph Eleaser Whiteside Earl

Based on his success and reputation for ruthless effectiveness, Jackson became president in 1829. This did not bode well for the thousands of native tribes still living in what was later the southern United States. In 1830, Jackson signed The Indian Removal Act, the heart of which was the idea that Native Americans needed to be forcibly moved out of areas flooded with white settlers and deposited in the lands to the west. This pattern repeated itself over and over, and was established as a legal, congressional act. The results were entirely predictable and disastrous for the natives.

After passage of the law, the next step was getting the tribes to move. Many did so after being offered a price for their land, but most refused. Some simply had one tribesman sell the land without consulting with the other dispersed members of the same tribal confederation. The loose bonds between tribal groups that were not rigidly enforced or written into law worked against the tribes over and over. Treaties devolved into confusing messes and competing claims, and appeals to the government to sort out the logistics.

When a territory that was covered by a treaty with the Native Americans became a state, the state governments would simply override the treaty provisions. Nothing was binding except the facts on the ground. Between 1830 and 1850, some 100,000 people from the "Five Tribes" (the Creek, Cherokee, Chickasaw, Muskogee, and Seminole tribes) were moved either voluntarily or via forced marches west to the land that became Oklahoma or the huge territory claimed by Mexico called Texas.

During this period, there were many battles, both physical and legal. The Native Americans resisted and often sought to use the legal system of the United States to hold land. They prevailed in limited circumstances. The Americans revered their legal system and would honor its decisions…for a time. Once land became commercially valuable, however, it was time for the Native Americans to vacate it, since they had no commercial instinct to develop land along the European pattern. Many Native Americans were marched west under military guard, some returned, some moved on. The period became known as the Trail of Tears, but it was not one trail or one march; it was more the slow and sometimes fast process of driving indigenous people from their historical land and from their historical way of living. They lost everything in the long run; the trail only went one way. The Native Americans who were already on the plains past the Mississippi River suddenly had their land flooded with the destitute Native American refugees from the south.

Under Andrew Jackson's driving, and easily offended, personality, both the European militaries and Native American populations were driven out of the southern territories. What resulted were new American states including Alabama, Mississippi, Louisiana, and Florida, where slavery was legal. Their leadership took over the land and began to thrive without any Native American presence. Under the Spanish system, the land was overtaken, and the Native Americans were reduced to the state of European peonage. Under the American system, the land was overtaken, the Native Americans were run out, and the labor force was imported slaves. As brutal as it was, it made economic sense and the new states began to economically thrive.

By the time Andrew Jackson left office in 1837, Texas had detached itself from Mexico but was not yet a state. Objections over slavery in Texas had yet to be resolved. Jackson, like his predecessor and his successor, did not resolve the issue of slavery which was building towards a cataclysm. Before that conflict emerged, the United States made another enormous territorial gain from the Spanish in acquiring Texas. Texan independence set the United States up for another big step in its unofficial goal of Manifest Destiny.

TEXAS

Napoleon Bonaparte offered more gifts to the United States by invading Spain in 1807 and starting the Peninsular Wars. France, Spain, Portugal, and Britain were all drawn into this giant, life-destroying bonfire on the Iberian Peninsula. This inferno triggered the series of events that resulting in yet another territorial gain for the United States. Frontier America just kept catching the breaks, aided by a huge demographic army of tough people who poured over the Appalachian Mountains. Behind them, steely-eyed leadership stuck to their plan of achieving strategic security in a North American fortress.

The Peninsular War fundamentally ended the Spanish monarchy, then lead by Queen Maria Luisa. Her monarchal end led to the eventual independence of Mexico. Maria Luisa was the niece of Louis XVI, the King who had been beheaded by French mobs two decades earlier. These same mobs mandated the rise of Napoleon, who invaded Spain, thus freeing Mexico by default. The Mexicans didn't reject their sovereign; they simply ceased receiving orders from the missing Spanish monarchy.

Naturally, a brutal civil war followed in Mexico. This ended up being a great boon to the United States, who never failed in those days to capitalize on a rival's misstep. Mexico and much of the rest of the Spanish Empire was set adrift by the loss of the Spanish monarchy, centuries of Spanish mismanagement, and the rapaciousness of the French under Napoleon.

Like France, Spain claimed parts of North America for its own, but the Spanish had never held and developed any territory north of San Antonio in Texas. After Napoleon inadvertently set Mexico free, Mexico had to hold its territory adjacent to the Louisiana Purchase from being seized by a surging, confident, and militarily powerful United States. If Napoleon never invaded Spain, the Spanish could have held and possibly developed Texas, but the chaos in Spain ended any coherent strategy to develop a Spanish North America.

After years of internal fighting, coups, and counter-coups, Mexico began to form its own independent identity. Mexico organized a government, declared a republic, and drafted a constitution in 1824. This constitution governed what had been called New Spain, including the territory in North America. The border for what the Mexicans considered their territory in the United States was the Sabine River, which separates Texas and Louisiana to this day.

The Spanish failed to tame their northern territorial claims, but not for lack of trying. They placed Catholic missions and towns in California, and those entities thrived. However, the Spanish were never able to establish and hold a town very far north in Texas. The Spanish claims in North America were 1,000 miles of desert away from the political power center in Mexico City and there wasn't a large pioneering class amongst the Mexicans that was willing to go north. Under Spanish rule, there was a European-based ruling class in Mexico and a subject indigenous peonage, and neither of those groups cared to face the extremely violent Comanche tribes in Texas. Even other Native American tribes viewed the Comanche as particularly aggressive and violent.

The Spanish gave the Texas settlement a half-hearted try, but many missions failed, usually with a great loss of life. The Comanche would let these settlements thrive for a short time, but eventually, they would overrun them as they did at San Saba. The Comanche raids were a problem, even for cities deep into Mexico. However, since the Comanche raiding territory was still far away from the center of power in Mexico City, neither Spain nor Mexico were willing to dedicate enough resources to defeating the Comanche and finally settling Texas.

Since the Comanche had proven too hard to handle, the Spanish came up with a plan to allow thousands of 'Anglo' settlers from the United States to enter Texas under the supervision of *impresarios* who would govern them. They were called Anglo, meaning they were European of English decent, as opposed to the Latins, which were Europeans of Spanish decent. The Mexicans thought these settlers would be able to hold the land so dear to the Comanche and for years, this plan was largely working. The Anglos were creating farms, ranches, tiny towns, and markets in Spanish Texas. Many of these settlers died at the hand of the Comanche, but they organized ways to fight back.

The success of the Anglos was its own problem, however, since Mexican authorities were deeply suspicious of the settlers. They viewed Anglos as possible unstated agents of the hostile United States. Buried into this suspicion was the larger Hispanic view of the barbarians of northern Europe, as the Roman Catholic Spanish saw them. Like the Romans before them, the Latin mind saw the Anglos as industrious, but without culture or warmth. Anglo success was beginning to pique Hispanic pride, and this conflict was brewing as the Anglo hordes kept coming and the Comanche depredations meant these people would be hardened and well-armed.

One of the original impresarios was Moses Austin, but he died, so the Mexican concession to allow Anglos into Texas was passed to his son, Stephen. Stephen Austin recruited Anglo settlers to Texas with promises of free land in an agriculturally promising location far from Spanish meddling. For virtually free, farm families could acquire 4,400 acres of good land in mostly East Texas, as long as they dedicated their time and money to develop that land. Originally, three hundred families moved into Texas under Austin's supervision.

After Mexico declared independence, these Texas settlers were, in theory, living under Mexican, as opposed to Spanish, rule and subject to the Mexican Constitution of 1824. This constitution was very much like the one in the United States and so the Anglo settlers of Texas accepted it and pledged their loyalty, for what it was worth, to the government in distant Mexico City.

There was always a bit of theater to the agreement the Mexicans had with the Texans because the Anglos of Texas were also supposed to be Catholic, which they weren't, and all of their leadership had been born in the United States. The Texans received no help from Mexico to fight the dreaded Comanche, so they had developed their own fighting forces, called the Texas Rangers, by 1824. The Texans were mostly independent in a land barely governed by distant authorities, and they knew it. In the end, this theatrical play couldn't go on forever and it ended when the Mexican leadership decided to push the Anglos out.

Mexican leader Antonio Lopez de Santa Anna dissolved the Mexican Congress and replaced the constitution with a governing form more to his liking in 1834. Under the new constitution, his office became the single source of law in the country. In response, the Anglo Texans went into open revolt. A group of men seized the only defendable fort in the entire territory; the massive stone-walled citadel in San Antonio called The Alamo. The Texans had been raised under the American concept of liberty and they found Santa Anna's betrayal of the original agreement of 1824 to be deeply offensive.

It was here that the Latin-Spanish-Catholic and Anglo-British-Protestant worldviews came into direct military conflict in the New World. They had much in common; both the Mexicans and the Texans did not want further interference in their affairs to come from Europe. Both groups had native-born New World leadership; Santa Anna was from Veracruz, not Spain. However, the Anglos believed they had not surrendered their inalienable rights when they crossed the Sabine River into Texas. The Spanish Mexicans believed all subjects should abide by whatever they are told by the central authorities. Centralization of authority was a defining difference between the two peoples. The Spanish monarchy and the Catholic Church demanded and received absolute fealty to their authorities. The Americans were both mostly Protestant and the products of a political system with an emphasis on the dispersal of power. These opposing worldviews were bound to clash.

Stephen Austin traveled to Mexico City seeking to secure some kind of compromise before war started, but he was thrown into prison for eighteen months without ever being charged with a crime. When he returned to Texas, his health was ruined. What he found on his return was the Texans ready for a fight. Forces had been set in motion that he could not stop.

A new chapter in the story American territorial growth was about to be written.

Antonio Lopez de Santa Anna

THE ALAMO

The Anglos of Texas would not accept a distant Mexican caudillo as their unrestrained ruler. Also, Santa Anna would not recognize any special arrangement with the "guests" living in Mexican territory. A war between the Texans and the Mexican government was the only way to settle the issue.

In late 1835 into 1836, the Alamo began to fill with characters from Texas and the frontiers of the United States based on the letters sent forth declaring Texas as the next New World battle for freedom. Men assembled with weapons and prepared the presidio for the coming siege, which would begin when uniformed troops arrived from distant Mexico. The men who came to fight included Davy Crockett who had served in the Tennessee legislature, James Bowie, for whom the Bowie knife is named, and a soon-to-be-famous William Travis.

These men did not have to wait long for the Mexicans to arrive; on February 23, 1836, Santa Anna reached San Antonio de Bexar with 1,500 Mexican troops with the intention to take the sealed citadel by force. He left Mexico City with his army months earlier promising publicly to either expel or exterminate the Anglos in Texas who were in open rebellion and a threat to Mexican sovereignty. Mexican independence was newly gained from Spain and after centuries of Spanish dominance and decades of chaos in the country after independence, a nascent Mexican national identity was being formed. Santa Anna was prepared to defend it. This threat from the Texans was so serious that Santa Anna himself, dressed in absurd finery, decided to lead his troops into battle. This decision would prove to be a costly unforced error.

When Santa Anna's forces arrived in San Antonio, he ordered that a long red pennant be raised over the only other high building in the town which was the Cathedral of San Fernando. The pennant indicated to all that no quarter would be given and everyone inside the Alamo would die. In response, Bowie and Travis, the co-commanders of the garrison, ordered that a cannon be fired. Both sides had acknowledged that the battle between the newly free Mexicans and these English-speaking agents of the United States who had been allowed into Mexican territory would be a fight to the death.

Inside the Alamo, William Travis was writing letters and dispatches that were being snuck outside the walls and past the Mexican troops. Travis was born in Alabama, but like the rest of the settlers, moved to Texas in search of land and opportunity. When the Texas rebellion against Santa Anna's new form of government broke out, he flocked to the Alamo to defend his new homeland from what he and the other Anglos defined as tyranny. From the Alamo, he wrote letters inviting more to come to join in the fight. His impassioned missives are considered to be rousing patriotic declarations in support of individual liberty. His letter, titled "To the People of Texas and All Americans in the World," reads: "The enemy has demanded surrender at discretion otherwise, the garrison is to be put to the sword, if the fort is taken. I have answered the demand with a cannon shot, and our flag still waves proudly from the walls. I shall never surrender or retreat."

Fall of the Alamo by Robert Jenkins Onderdonk

Travis sent the letter in an envelope marked "Victory or Death," and it was one of the last messages before the Mexicans breached the Alamo on March 6. As promised by Santa Anna's red pennant, no prisoners were taken and all inside were killed. The battle was brutal, with Mexican soldiers falling under heavy fire as they tried to rest ladders against the stone walls. The frontiersmen inside were expert marksmen who had been firing rifles and hunting game all of their lives. But there were only 150 of them, and eventually, the Mexicans fought their way in. In the final desperate hours, the fighting involved hand-to-hand combat with swords and knives and muskets fired at close quarters. It was a slaughter.

Travis, Bowie, Crockett, and the rest died at the Alamo, but the letters written by Travis inspired others to join the fight. Their messages turned the defeat at the Alamo into a rousing patriotic victory. The Texas Revolution, as the war came to be known, showed that the Anglo Americans would were not prepared to accept a dictator from Europe or a native-born one either. The Mexicans set this conflict in motion when they rejected their own constitution from 1824 and allowed their governance to slide in to dictatorship. What Santa Anna and the other Spanish Mexicans had viewed as an affront to Latin pride was to the Anglos an unacceptable affront to their basic rights.

Santa Anna had little time or reason to celebrate. Breaching the Alamo didn't quell Anglo Texas; in fact, it was a pyrrhic victory for the Mexican army who lost so many men taking the Alamo— up to a third of their fighting force—that when he faced another Texan, Sam Houston, just a few weeks later, their depleted forces would not prevail. And further, by joining the campaign himself and putting so many resources into the Alamo, Santa Anna sealed his defeat, which was now only a few weeks away.

SAM HOUSTON AND TEXAS STATEHOOD

There is no one like Sam Houston in American history. He was born in Virginia but moved with his family to Tennessee when he was a teen. He ran away from home and lived three years with the Cherokee Indians, where he earned the nickname "Raven." He fought alongside Andrew Jackson in the War of 1812 against the British, served in the US House of Representatives, and was the Governor of Tennessee all *before* he moved to Texas. He arrived in Texas just in time for the Texas rebellion against the Mexican government and Santa Anna. Houston led his men in the final battle of that conflict at San Jacinto, which is now within the area of the city of Houston.

In April of 1836, just a month after the siege at the Alamo, Sam Houston led a large force of Texas militiamen east. They were being chased by Santa Anna's huge army which he brought up from Mexico. Near the tiny town of San Jacinto, Houston retreated with his men until his forces had their back to the waters and swamps of Buffalo Bayou. On April 21, they stopped retreating; his men would fight or die; they knew what had happened to the other Texans at Goliad. There, Mexican troops had killed over four hundred Texas prisoners via firing squad. They also knew the fate of everyone at the Alamo.

When Santa Anna's depleted forces (depleted from the siege at the Alamo) took a rest in the middle of the day, Houston ordered his men to charge and attack across the thousand yards of grassland that separated the two armies. The Texans took the resting Mexican forces by surprise and routed them in eighteen minutes with barely any casualties on their part. It was an overwhelming victory for Houston and his men.

The following day, the Texans captured Santa Anna himself who had removed his plumage as a general and was dressed as a private. The Texans figured out it was Santa Anna by the way the other prisoners addressed him. Now not only had the Mexican military been defeated, but the Mexican President himself was in the hands of the Texans.

As Houston lay on the ground under an oak tree nursing a wound from the previous day's fighting, he forced Santa Anna to sign a hastily made treaty conveying Texas to the Texans. That surrender legally ended the short Texas Revolution in victory for the Texans. Santa Anna was sent to Washington where he met with President Andrew Jackson, and then he was sent back to Mexico.

Texas statehood, however, was not automatic. Even though Texas broke with Mexico in 1836, the Texas Republic didn't become a state until nine years later in 1845. A majority of Texans wanted to be annexed by the United States, but politicians in the US didn't want to stumble into war with Mexico. Despite Santa Anna's signature, Mexican authorities subsequently made it clear that they did not accept Texas independence, so the territory wasn't available to become a state of the larger United States. In spite of his disastrous performance in Texas, Santa Anna was able to become the Mexican President again in this period and he was not going to concede the territory.

And there was an additional problem; Texas allowed slavery and the ascendant abolitionists in the northern free states didn't want two more pro-slavery senators from Texas to enter the Congress. These objections were eventually overcome, in part because there were plenty of people in Texas who opposed annexation, and in the years of independence, the Texas state government had begun acting as its own nation. When the Texas Republic began speaking directly with the British government about exchanging ambassadors and Texas opened an embassy in London, sentiment in the US began to change. The leadership in the United States didn't want the British to regain a foothold in North America by forming a relationship with the independent-minded Texans, and the territory was critical to the whole unstated goal of Manifest Destiny.

In light of all of this, Texas became the 28th state in December of 1845. As feared, war with Mexico began just a few months later. Sam Houston was the first governor of the independent nation of Texas, but he also helped secure Texas as a state in the United States. He died in 1863 while Texas was fighting as part of yet another nation, called the Confederacy.

THE MEXICAN-AMERICAN WAR

The Mexican-American War started just after the United States annexed Texas in December of 1845. This was the second of three wars with the Spanish and their colonial descendants. First was the Texas Revolution, then there was the Mexican-American War, and finally, in 1898, there was the Spanish-American War. All three had the effect of peeling away lightly occupied and weakly defended portions of the once gigantic Spanish Empire and handing them to the ascendant United States.

The government in Mexico City was not prepared to accept Texas becoming a state in the larger United States. The sitting Mexican president by that time, Mariano Paredes, refused to acknowledge the treaty that Santa Anna had signed under an oak tree and under duress in 1836. Santa Anna had since been exiled to Cuba. President Paredes declared that Mexico intended to enforce its claims to Texas to the Sabine River at the Texas-Louisiana border. When the US Army entered Texas as part of sovereign US territory (as far as the US government was concerned), the conflicting claims meant war was imminent. By December of 1845, many US Army soldiers were in the area of Brownsville, right on the Rio Grande River, and just across the river from the Mexican forces in Matamoros.

The United States sent a delegation to Mexico City to negotiate. Offers were made to Mexican authorities to buy not only Texas but virtually all Mexican territory north of the Rio Grande; those offers were not accepted. Offering to pay for the territory only aggravated the Mexicans, who had no intention of selling the land. President Paredes ordered his troops to cross the Rio Grande at Brownsville and there was a short engagement between a scouting party of eighty US Army soldiers and a much larger Mexican force, which resulted in a defeat for the Americans. This short battle prompted President James Polk to go to Congress and ask for a declaration of war. He got it.

Once the war started, the American forces quickly moved south past the Rio Grande. The US Army also went west past the Texas borders and into the territory of what is now New Mexico, Arizona, and California—a region the Mexicans called Alta California. From there, they turned south and entered Mexico.

The US Navy blockaded most Mexican ports and so Mexico was cut off from any outside help. One person who got through the naval blockade was the exiled General Santa Anna. He offered to help Mexico fight the Americans, but he also was secretly negotiating with the Americans to represent the sale of Mexican territory. This is how he was allowed through the blockade. What his actual agenda was can't be known. He did lead the Mexican military into battle upon his return, although he did so with his previously established level of effectiveness.

As the US Army pressed south, they engaged in several heavy battles including the Battle of Monterey. Many Mexican cities were built of heavy stone and adobe construction materials and the Mexican forces retreated to them where they were safe from US bombardment. When the US soldiers walked into the city on the open streets, they were cut down by the Mexican forces hidden in the sturdy buildings. This fight marks the first time, but not the last, that American soldiers were required to fight an urban warfare campaign in a foreign country with limited knowledge of the terrain or tactics. The soldiers from Texas who had fought the Mexicans in the Texas Revolution taught their fellow soldiers to "mouse hole" through the walls between buildings and fight close in, often hand to hand. The Mexican forces were driven out of Monterrey once the US soldiers employed this fighting style.

General Santa Anna returned to fighting the Americans, and the Texans among them, at the Battle of Buena Vista. He marched yet another Mexican force north that was many times larger than what he had led at the Alamo. They met a much smaller US force in the mountain passes near Saltillo in Northeastern Mexico. In a way, it was the Alamo all over again, except this time Santa Anna left the job undone. The Mexican forces pressed hard on the American soldiers, and causalities were high on both sides, but the US forces were never completely overrun, in part because of the Mississippi Riflemen led by the future president of the Confederacy, Jefferson Davis. Santa Anna decided to cut off the fighting and withdraw before the battle was completely won. The Mexican general had snatched defeat from the jaws of victory yet again.

Hernán Cortéz was the Spanish conquistador who secured Mexico for Spain in 1519, 326 years before the Americans arrived. He landed at the tiny village he called Vera Cruz (which means True Cross) and eventually marched from Veracruz on Mexico City. President Polk decided not to rely on the army led by Zachary Taylor, who had fought at Monterrey and the Battle of Buena Vista. Instead, he backed an army led by Winfield Scott, who landed 12,000 soldiers at Veracruz, right where Cortéz had started his march on the Aztec city of Tenochtitlán. This was the first large-scale, amphibious landing in American military history, and a preview of what would happen on the beaches of Normandy in about a hundred years. Among those 12,000 men were Robert E. Lee and Ulysses S. Grant, who would meet again at Appomattox in Virginia to end the US Civil War.

General Scott took the same path Cortéz had taken to Mexico City, but this time, it was a Spaniard, Santa Anna, rather than an Aztec like Moctezuma, who tried to forestall a foreign force from reaching the great capital city. Santa Anna was not successful. In September 1847, the US Army entered Mexico City under the direction of General Scott. This final defeat marked the end of Santa Anna's long and ignominious career.

After three years of fighting, and mostly American lopsided victories, including the occupation of its capital, the beleaguered Mexican government relented. The Treaty of Guadalupe Hidalgo was signed in 1848. It was welcomed on the American side as well, since the war had gone on for far longer than President Polk had anticipated. The presence of American troops in the Mexican capital had begun to raise the prospect of a US incorporation of the entire country of Mexico. This idea brought the US for the first time, but not the last, to debate if the nation was to remain a republic, or to become an empire in its own right. In the end, the idea of the country as a republic with a southern border on the Rio Grande was accepted on both sides and the treaty was signed.

As part of the treaty, the US paid Mexico fifteen million dollars for Texas, what would become New Mexico, Arizona, California, Nevada, and Utah, parts of Kansas, Oklahoma, and Wyoming. It was the same price the Americans had paid Napoleon for the Louisiana Purchase. The Spanish presence on the North American continent was now completely wiped out after three centuries of unenforced claims.

The Mexican-American War set the pattern for the relationship of the United States to Mexico, which was cold and tense, and unlike the relationship the US developed with Canada and eventually the United Kingdom, it never developed into any kind of trusted partnership. To this day, the United States does not have the same relationship with Mexico, a fellow New World, and formerly colonial, nation that had to throw off a European monarchy, as it has with the United Kingdom, its former colonial masters.

Mexico struggled throughout the 19th century to find stability in part due to continuous European meddling. Many governments and presidents came and went, usually through violence and assassination. The European powers tried on many occasions to regain control of Mexico, and the French invaded the beleaguered, demoralized country. They even sent the Mexicans an Austrian Hapsburg Emperor, Maximillian, to rule over them with royal prestige and authority. He was eventually cornered and killed by native-born Mexicans. Maximillian's death marked the true point of no return for the Mexicans, who finally showed that they would not be ruled from abroad by any nation.

Nevertheless, there would always be a long, troublesome border with the United States. One of the longest-serving of the many 19th century Mexican presidents was Porfirio Diaz, who served thirty-one years, from 1884 to 1911. Diaz is credited with this summary of the Mexican relationship to its giant northern neighbor:

"Poor Mexico," he said, *"so far from God and so close to the United States."*

A TICKING CLOCK FOR THE SLAVES
AND THE NATIVE AMERICANS

The entire history of the United States is the story of people struggling to make true the maxim that "All men are created equal" and deliver on that maxim with good government. It is slow, painful, and often counter-productive work, in part because the forces that put the lie to that maxim are as old as humanity. By the mid-19th century, the ideals of the United States, as articulated in its governing documents, were coming into direct military conflict with ancient human ideas of work, freedom, culture, conquest, and law. A compromise was no longer available and blood would be shed. In this warfare, the fate of the Native Americans and the fate of the slaves would widely diverge.

Family of slaves in Georgia, circa 1850

Slavery was ubiquitous in both the ancient and modern world. Slavery has been recorded as an economic arrangement in every society on earth. There are still economic relationships all over the world that are akin to slavery today. Abraham Lincoln defined the relationship as "someone works and someone else eats." Slavery in the early United States was not unusual as an institution on earth, and further, there was never any legal conception of slaves in the colonies, or later the United States, that recorded them as anything less than fully human. They were the humans with the lowest economic status; their economic status was so low, they were fundamentally property. They were human tools; humans, but humans whose worth was attached to their labor status. It was a miserable arrangement, but it was not anti-human.

In most societies, slavery was not associated with race or ethnicity. In the United States, it was linked to race, and as previously noted, primarily reserved for people of African origin. This added element proved to be a particularly difficult problem in eradicating slavery and its downstream consequences. The poor of other ethnicities also had very limited prospects and could easily die of starvation or predation or sickness, as many did, but legally, they were not considered to be slaves. They could pursue a more promising future as they saw fit; the slaves could not.

The African slaves had limited legal rights, but not a complete absence of rights. The US Constitution allowed slaves to be counted for the purposes of taxation and representation, though they were counted at 3/5th of the value of a non-slave. This figure was a compromise but gets to the point of slaves being deemed as people rather than strictly property. Slaves were *always* recognized as people and they too had certain "inalienable rights," just like non-slaves, so the law was always meant to apply to them. The Constitution does not mention race as it related to slavery; those laws were later crafted by the individual states.

The language of the US Constitution implies that it already contemplated that the country might exist one day without slavery as an institution. What they didn't contemplate was the vicious war it would take to make the US slavery-free. The long march from the development and adoption of the US Constitution in 1789 to the fracture of the country at the beginning of the Civil War in 1861 involved a witch's brew of competing philosophies and events that made peaceful resolution of the slavery issue less and less likely.

British Christians and later, many American Christians, forcefully opposed slavery. They believed it was a scourge on all humanity. At the same time, the warmer southern US states were providing raw materials, such as cotton, to the rapidly industrializing British economy. Those raw materials were produced through slave labor. African slaves were the machinery of the southern agricultural economies. In a pre-industrial economy, there were few obvious alternatives to slave labor, even though anti-slavery laws were being passed by the British Parliament and in the American states that did not require slave labor to thrive. From an economic standpoint, slavery served a vital function. From a cultural standpoint, it was intolerable to a growing portion of Western society.

Throughout the United States, evolving philosophies and divergent economics were becoming more and more at odds with each other. Each compromise avoiding the final settlement of the issue merely raised the stakes a little higher, setting the bar for the next conflict.

The massive Louisiana Purchase in 1803 opened the path for millions of US citizens to flood over the Appalachian Mountains. As people flocked to the various territories, the government believed some of those places would eventually gain enough people to become new US states. This happened in Louisiana in 1815. The creation of new states was built into the design of the Constitution.

Many newcomers settled into what became known as the Missouri Territories. When their population passed a certain mark, the territory was qualified to become a state. Missouri statehood set off the first struggle over slavery, and the conditions under which new states would be admitted to the Union. The debate about Missouri being a slave or free state spilled onto the floor of Congress as larger issues regarding the future of the country were debated. In 1820, the giant territory of Maine, which was a part of Massachusetts, was carved out as a separate free state, and Missouri was allowed into the Union as a slave state. This arrangement was called the Missouri Compromise and it kept the Congressional balance of power equal for a time. It allowed for slavery in the Louisiana Purchase lands below a certain geographical line that divided north and south, and it mandated free states above it.

The Missouri Compromise only settled the slavery issue for a few decades. The next big slavery impasse inevitably arrived, resulting in the Compromise of 1850. By the mid-Century, there were even more territories to fight over, since so much land were acquired as a result of the Texas Revolution and the Mexican-American War. The 1850 Compromise was a series of new bills that passed Congress settling the Texas borders, allowing California into the union as a free state, and setting boundaries on more of the territories acquired in the Louisiana Purchase and the war with Mexico. However, the big new compromise did little to reach a final settlement to the burning issue of slavery and it ignored the fact that the territories in question were still occupied by an unknown number of Native Americans who were living as they had been for centuries. It placed boundaries on the map but did little to settle the issues on the ground.

TWILIGHT OF THE PLAINS TRIBES

By 1850, the mid-point of the 19th century, the country was primed for the war that would free the slaves, and the following wars that would doom the Native Americans. Nothing in the Congressional acts regarding slavery tried to forestall what was coming for the Native Americans in the subsequent decades since the Natives weren't a part of the Constitutional order.

The indigenous population's situation was a slow-motion disaster that took centuries to play out. The sustained arrival of Europeans after 1492 released pathogens to which the Europeans had developed immunity, having lived for centuries in dense population centers, but the isolated native peoples hadn't developed a similar immunity. There had been larger Native American cities in North America in the distant past, but those cultures disappeared for reasons not fully known.

In the centuries after 1492, some portion of the indigenous population died of sicknesses driven by Old World pathogens. Even the native population deep in the interior of North America who had never seen a European, eventually came in to contact with the viruses. Their populations began to fall. Historians estimate at least half of their populations perished in these pandemics.

Even if the pathogens hadn't decimated the Native American population, compromise would have been unlikely with the people of the western plains and mountains. The dominant issue, aside from ethnic differences, was lifestyle and worldview. The settlers who arrived in an endless trickle were firmly European in their goals, lifestyle, methods of agriculture, preferred types of housing, personal relationships, the relationship of man to the environment, and religious ideas about the nature of the divine. The Native Americans differed in all of these issues and many others. The Europeans believed land should be improved by clearing portions of the forest, planting crops, and erecting buildings for living in, conducting business or worshipping the Christian God. The Native Americans' idea of life was nomadic; there would be no fixed structures, no large-scale agriculture, no commercial economy, and no fixed schedules outside of that dictated by nature. To live as they did, the Native Americans needed a lot of habitats, and settlers were cordoning off more and more of their territory.

The result of these enormous lifestyle clashes was conflict without compromise. This conflict was settled by warfare. The Native Americans certainly knew war since they had warred with each other for centuries. Further, the Native Americans of the open plains were transformed when the Spanish brought horses to North

America and the horse was transferred to the Native Americans. At certain points in the mid- to late-19th century, the Comanche and other tribes were the continent's preeminent armed light cavalry and the Anglo wave that was sweeping west was—for a moment—stopped, at least in Texas.

Over time, the Americans had the demographic numbers to grab and occupy the entire West. The American Army had unmatched technology that the Natives could not develop, mainly artillery and cannon fire. The government lacked the desire to enforce any treaty or obligation that required law enforcement to police the settler population. The American Army was never tasked with rooting out settlers and driving them back east. Because the Native Americans were militarily weak, they resorted to the tactics that weaker military forces use all over the world. Whole towns of settlers were slaughtered by native tribes in attacks noted for their bloody viciousness. There were instances of torture, kidnappings, rapes, and the murder of children. There were Native American depredations across the frontier. Even when one band of people was desperate for peace, another might attack a settlement and bring the US Army down on them all. US Army attacks were sometimes equal in viciousness. The various treaties that were signed designating Native American territory were equivalent to the compromises over slavery, but the Native Americans couldn't, and the US military wouldn't, enforce the treaties, so they failed to settle the issue.

By 1850, the clock was ticking for the slaves and the Native Americans. Their fate would be driven by two competing cultural movements. For the slaves, the religious and social movement referred to as abolition was working in their favor. For the native population, the American belief in Manifest Destiny had already sealed their fate. For the slaves, freedom was just around the corner. For the Native Americans, existential disaster loomed.

THE ABOLITIONISTS

In the 1850s, slavery was already boiling over into violence between the abolitionists, those opposed to slavery, and its supporters. The abolitionists were angry and politically ascendant. The slavery supporters were not ready to give up on the institution they associated with their economic security and cultural order.

Into this as-yet-ignited maelstrom stepped John Brown.

Brown was a fire-and-brimstone abolitionist who was willing to use violence to end slavery and did so. He led attacks on slavery supporters in Kansas as the debate over the entry of new territories as slave or free states boiled over yet again. This time, compromise was not forthcoming.

The proximate cause of John Brown's rise and the crisis he became involved in was the passage of the Kansas-Nebraska Act in 1854. By this time, the Louisiana Purchase was fifty-one years old and yet most of the territory it covered was still not organized into states. The Kansas–Nebraska Act was meant to add two more states, but it ended up being another, and the most important, weigh station on the way to war over slavery. The act organized these territories and prepared them for statehood, but it also repealed the Missouri Compromise from years earlier. The new law proposed that the new states' positions on slavery would be decided by popular vote, rather than geographic location.

Since the issue of slavery would be decided by vote, both pro- and anti-slavery forces flooded into the region of Kansas and Nebraska. But of course, these territories were occupied by untold thousands of Native Americans. Battles began as these invading forces collided. In the standard pattern, the Native Americans suffered greatly. White farmers moved in and the military refused to dislodge them, even though they had landed in what was clearly set aside as Native American enclaves from the Trail of Tears Era. Political concern over slavery overshadowed any concern for the fate of the Native Americans.

Events on the ground were particularly bloody in Kansas. Pro-slavery forces in neighboring Missouri entered the area while the Free State supporters flooded in from the north. Conflict was likely and firebrand abolitionists like John Brown made sure it occurred. In May of 1856, Brown and his sons attacked pro-slavery farmers at Potawatomie. Six men were hacked to death with knives and swords.

Brown also led attacks at Harper's Ferry in Virginia that was meant to start a slave liberation movement. Brown tried to get the black leadership of the anti-slavery movement to participate, but they thought his plan was suicidal and did not rise. At his follow-on trial, Brown was evasive about his role in the massacre at Potawatomie, but he was found guilty of treason, not murder, for his role in the raid on Harper's Ferry. Seven people were killed in this attack and Brown was captured by a contingent of US Marines led by future Confederate General Robert E. Lee.

John Brown was publicly hanged in December 1859, and he was unrepentant to the end. His trial was covered extensively in the press and his many statements were inflammatory and uncompromising. Tensions and disagreements over Brown's actions and execution accelerated the march to Civil War, which was now less than two years away. His execution was witnessed by John Wilkes Booth, who, in a few more years, would assassinate the US president.

The debate over the Kansas-Nebraska Act elevated the public profile of a previously little-known former representative from Illinois, Abraham Lincoln, who spoke out forcefully against slavery. This catalyzed the formation of the Republican Party, which was organized in the North as an anti-slavery political entity. By creating an exclusively abolitionist party, the path to war locked in ever tighter.

Political parties in the United States changed from the Revolutionary period up until the Civil War, but by and large, they have not changed since. The original parties were the Federalists and the Democrat-Republicans. They debated over the power of the federal v. state governments. After the Federalists fell out of favor, the Democrat-Republicans broke into the Democrats, led by Andrew Jackson, and the Whig Party, which was opposed to Jackson and his positions on slavery, among other issues. After the Nebraska-Kansas Act became law and the issue of slavery boiled over, the Northern Whigs moved to the abolitionist Republican Party which was able to elect President Abraham Lincoln in 1860.

The Civil War started weeks later.

SECTION 4: CATACLYSM

Abraham Lincoln in 1863, photo by Alexander Gartner

"If destruction be our lot, we must ourselves be its author and finisher. As a nation of freemen, we must live through all time, or die by suicide." — Abraham Lincoln

"I am tired and sick of war. Its glory is all moonshine."
— Gen. William Tecumseh Sherman

"I prayed all night long for my master. Till the first of March; and all the time he was bringing people to look at me, and trying to sell me. I changed my prayer. First of March I began to pray, 'Oh Lord, if you ain't never going to change that man's heart, kill him, Lord, and take him out of the way.'" — *Harriet Tubman*

Cultural ideas proliferate in a way that no one can predict. An idea will percolate for years, sometimes hundreds of years, and suddenly find resonance and became the dominant idea and finally, the law. Like scientific breakthroughs and many aspects of economics, the timing is nearly impossible to predict. When an idea goes viral, its power is impossible to ignore or deny. Ideas and cultural trends always prevail over actual laws and policies.

By 1860, slavery was an idea in the Anglo world that had become culturally unacceptable. It has been a ubiquitous institution since the dawn of economics, and there are economic situations today that many equate with slavery, like sex trafficking. By the late 18th century, the impulse to outlaw slavery was finding its way into legislation in Britain and the United States. The cultural imperative to end it had reached the highest levels of power. Both societies were very religious and their revulsion to slavery had a strong whiff of Protestant Christianity to it.

In Pennsylvania, where the Quakers were prevalent, the process of outlawing slavery began in 1780 via gradual emancipation. By 1804, all of the Northern states had statutes on their registries restricting or abolishing slavery. The British passed laws against the international trade in slaves in 1807 and abolished it in all of the British Empire except India in 1833. The French colony of Saint-Domingue, later Haiti, declared independence from France in 1804 and was the first nation to ban slavery outright.

By 1860, the states in the southern United States were running against a tide that had been turning for at least eighty years. Their economies and cultures did not create any corresponding impulse to abolish slavery. The violence of the abolitionists had hardened the southern position, but there were also the sheer numbers of slaves to consider. In many communities, black slaves made up at least one-third of the population. No colony in the British Empire or state in the United States had ever tried to mix ethnicities of these proportions under the ideas enumerated in the Constitution. Ideas of inalienable rights and individual liberty had been conceived within a European framework for people of European culture. If slavery ended and those many African-originated slaves were free, a grand experiment in passing the European ideas to non-Europeans would begin and the southern states did not wish to be a part of this experiment. They were trapped between an old world that was passing away and a new world that did not look promising, seemingly promoted by people that did not face the same demographic reality. Consequently, the people of the southern states dug into their position as war moved ever closer. The war to come would leave more dead than the Revolutionary War, the War of 1812 and the Mexican-American War combined.

THE LAST FOUNDING FATHER

The proximate cause for the start of the Civil War was the election of Abraham Lincoln in 1860. The southern states gave up on the United States when Lincoln was elected.

Abraham Lincoln was born in 1809 and so was in no way a part of the founding generation. He was born during the final days of the presidency of Thomas Jefferson, but he was also born in obscurity and would have never met the powerful and well-connected men that made up the founders, though many were still alive in Lincoln's early life. Yet Lincoln is a critical figure in the history of the country. In many ways, he is considered to be a 'founder' that drove the country to fulfill its founding idea of all men being created equal, and all citizens being treated equally under the law.

Abraham was the second child of Thomas and Nancy Lincoln, named after Captain Abraham Lincoln, who commanded troops in the Revolutionary War. Captain Lincoln moved to Kentucky to land that was still disputed by the Native Americans in the area and he was shot and killed by a Native American in full sight of his son Thomas. Surely Thomas Lincoln relayed the story of his father's death to his son Abraham in later years.

When he was nine years old, Abraham's mother died from "milk sickness," and his eleven-year-old sister Sarah took over the household duties. When she died ten years later in childbirth, Abraham was devastated. His father remarried a woman who had three children of her own and Abraham eagerly took to his new family. When he reached adulthood, Abraham married a woman in Springfield, Illinois in 1842. Over the course of their union, they had four sons but tragedy stalked Abraham's life even as an adult; only two of his sons lived to adulthood and the youngest, Tad, died when he was 18, just six years after his father's death. Only the oldest, Robert Todd Lincoln, lived a full adult life. Abraham's life was bound up in sudden death, and that includes his own sudden demise in 1865.

Abraham spent many formative years in Indiana before moving to Illinois. All of his youth passed by in the country, on farms, and in the woods, and so he was very much of the frontiersman generation. The young Lincoln was a tall, reserved, and stoic figure who both wrestled and read many books, so one could say he was both a very vigorous physical and intellectual person. His stepmother later noted how much he disliked farm work, but how much he loved to read.

As a young adult in Illinois, he struggled. For a short time, he was part owner of a retail store, but he sold his share. He ran for office in the Illinois General Assembly and lost. For a short time, he was a Captain like his namesake and his militia fought in another Native American conflict called Black Hawk's War, but his unit was not involved in combat. Early in his life, he showed no natural leadership skills or talents.

After many early struggles, he decided to become a lawyer and taught himself the law with various books and commentaries. In 1834, he ran again for the state assembly, and this time, he won. He served four terms in the Illinois State House of Representatives where he championed various economic development projects and suffrage (voting rights) for all white males. He practiced law in this same period and became known as a skilled courtroom tactician. His opposition to slavery was well known and he wrote about it extensively.

In 1846 during the Mexican-American War, Lincoln won his election to the House of Representatives from Illinois's 7th district. He opposed the war in general, thinking it was President Polk's campaign for glory, but he supported the Wilmot Proviso that was meant to ban slavery from any territorial gain resulting from that war. This did not endear him to the southern representatives, and they had long memories. He pledged upon election to serve only one term, so in 1848, he returned to private life in Springfield.

For the next sixteen years, Lincoln served dutifully as a country lawyer, handling hundreds of cases across a variety of areas of the law, including criminal law. He appeared before the Illinois Supreme Court many times and represented men charged with murder, which elevated his public profile. He was an effective attorney who earned the moniker "Honest Abe." During this period emerged the personality he was famous for later in life.

The Kansas-Nebraska Act drew him back into politics. The Act was meant to allow popular sovereignty, or voting, to decide if slavery would be legal in newly admitted states. The Democratic senator from Illinois, Stephen Douglas, supported this idea. Lincoln did not. He did not think that slavery should be put to the vote, but rather, should be abolished outright as an affront to nature, as well as the Constitution.

Lincoln had been a member of the Whig party. At that time, the two dominant parties were the Democrats, founded by pro-slavery Andrew Jackson, and the Whigs. Slavery split the Whig party into pro-slavery and anti-slavery factions. When Douglas was up for reelection in 1858, he secured yet again the pro-slavery Democrat nomination, while Lincoln secured the nomination of the newly formed and explicitly anti-slavery party known as the Republicans. It was the Republicans and the issue of slavery that doomed the Whigs.

As part of the election, Lincoln and Douglas agreed to several debates. These intellectual contests were raw, impassioned discussions about slavery and the meaning and purpose of the United States founding ideas. In the same way that William Travis was able to rally and inspire people around the nation with his letters from the Alamo, Abraham Lincoln used the debates with Douglas as a platform to articulate why slavery was a monstrous evil that had to be eradicated from the American landscape.

In one of those debates, Lincoln made his "House Divided" speech where he mixed quotes from the Christian Bible with the founding ideals of the nation. It is the most famous speech from his pre-presidency and is worth quoting at length because it states explicitly what the nation faced at the time. He began with a quote from the New Testament Bible in the book of Matthew where the text reads "… a house divided against itself shall not stand." Lincoln continued:

> *"I believe this government cannot endure, permanently half slave and half free. I do not expect the Union to be dissolved—I do not expect the house to fall—but I do expect it will cease to be divided. It will become all one thing or all the other. Either the opponents of slavery, will arrest the further spread of it, and place it where the public mind shall rest in the belief that it is in course of ultimate extinction; or its advocates will push it forward, till it shall become alike lawful in all the states, old as well as new—North as well as South. Have we no tendency to the latter condition? Let anyone who doubts, carefully contemplate that now almost complete legal combination— a piece of machinery so to speak—compounded of the Nebraska doctrine, and the Dred Scott decision."*

The Dred Scott decision Lincoln refers to was a ruling by the Supreme Court against a slave by that name who had sued for freedom when his owners took him from Missouri to Illinois. The court ruled that Scott had no inherent right to freedom and that the Missouri laws regarding slavery still applied. Scott was, in the eyes of the law as interpreted by the court, permanently a slave.

Lincoln lost the race for the Senate seat to Douglas, but the race honed Lincoln's skills and elevated his public persona. He took the text of his debate speeches and put them into a book which was subsequently published and widely read. In 1860, he secured the presidential nomination from the Republicans and prevailed in a four-way race to become the 16th US president.

The Southern states understood his election to mean that the North had no place for slavery in the future of the United States, so they began to secede from the Union before Lincoln took office in March of 1861. Lincoln walked into the greatest national disaster to fall upon the country, and spent every month of his Presidency fighting to preserve the nation as a single entity. As the Southern states began to drop out of the Union, they argued that the union of states was voluntary and they could leave if they wanted to. South Carolina was first in December of 1860. Mississippi followed on Jan 9, 1861, and Florida the following day. In the end, eleven states dropped out and formed the Confederate States of America.

There were many efforts in the final days to stop secession and find a way forward that would halt the break-up of the country, but those efforts failed. Secessionists thought that the rights of states to define their laws and nullify the laws that the federal government passed were part of their constitutional package, but behind it all was the burning issue of slavery and whether it would still be legally allowed. One-third of the nine million people in the Confederacy were black people held as chattel slaves, and so the status of these people was not an abstraction or moral debating point; Southerners felt as if their economy and entire way of life was threatened.

With Lincoln's election, the South believed there was no point in further talk. Lincoln was sworn in on March 4, 1861, and on April 12, Confederate forces in South Carolina began to bombard Fort Sumter, the federal fort situated on an island at the entrance to Charleston Harbor. As far as the people of the Confederacy were concerned, South Carolina was part of another nation and the federal fort in Charleston Harbor was housing a foreign force, and so they bombed it.

After decades of debate, the time for talk had ended. The Civil War was on.

THE CIVIL WAR

As war descended on the United States, the militaries of both sides prepared for the battles to come. Militias were formed all over the Confederacy to face the US Army that had a substantial head start in organization. The US military, however, in a pattern to be repeated again and again, had been allowed to atrophy to a small force. It was led by Winfield Scott, the hero of the Mexican-American War. By this date, Scott, who was born in 1786, was 75 years old.

The United States had a superior Navy that imposed a blockade on the entire southern US coastline preventing the Confederate forces from receiving any foreign help or resupply. This strategy had worked on the Mexicans, and now it was applied to the Confederacy.

The northern states were far ahead in industrial power, had a larger population, had access to open ports, and had a military head start. The South had skilled military leadership, soldiers fighting on their own turf, and—they thought—time. They thought that in time, the North would accept the partitioning and the war would end.

The leadership of the Confederacy, however, badly underestimated Lincoln. In Abraham Lincoln, the Union forces had a man fiercely committed to bringing the southern states back into the country, even at the incredibly high cost of the war, without giving any ground on the issue of slavery. Lincoln would not negotiate preserving the Union or ending slavery.

In the beginning, no one knew or understood just how high that cost would be in terms of lives lost. It was only in 1865, with hundreds of thousands of citizens dead, and the South nearly defeated, that Lincoln met with Confederate representatives to try negotiating a peace. That conference failed, and the war continued until its final victory and defeat in April of 1865.

By the end of the war, the estimated dead were 650,000 across the two militaries, representing two percent of the entire American population. Many thousands of civilian casualties were driven by disease and food shortages. There was an average of 449 military deaths per day for four years, and most of those rotted where they fell because there were simply too many dead bodies to bury them all. The militaries fought, and disengaged, and moved on, leaving the dead and dying behind.

For five winters and four summers, this went on. No war in all of American history was as deadly. If one considers only the population of white men in the South, every one out of five died in the conflict. There were hundreds of deadly interactions between Federal and Confederate forces throughout the war, and the casualty rate was extremely high in many of these engagements. There were engagements in Tennessee at Shiloh, in Mississippi at Vicksburg, and in Georgia at Atlanta. Many battles were fought in Virginia at

Fredericksburg and in Charlottesville. The deadliest day in American military history was at Antietam in Maryland where 23,000 men died in a 12 hour fight. Once the war started, neither side was willing to back down, so the war carried on until its bitter deadly end.

Battle of Antietam by Bror Thure Thulstrup

THE HIGH-WATER MARK OF THE CONFEDERACY

In the spring of 1863, Confederate general and leader of the Army of Northern Virginia, Robert E. Lee, decided to head north a second time and drive his forces into the heart of Union territory. Lee had been in the US Army for decades. He had been in command at West Point, had conducted surveys across the North, and in his capacity as an Army engineer, had extensive combat experience. He knew how to command men and conduct strategy. The irony was, Lee disliked slavery, yet he was the leader of the largest battle force in the Confederacy. He thought slavery was even worse for the slaveholder than the slave because it was corrupting to the individual. Like many in his station and geography, he did not wish to see the issue of slavery decided via government. He thought the end of slavery would be ordered by "a wise, Merciful Providence."

Lee reasoned that once he crossed the Potomac River and marched his troops north up the Shenandoah Valley he could threaten several northern cities, including Washington, D.C., and influence the course of the war. His correspondence from this period demonstrates that he thought his army could defeat all before it and that the northern population was war-weary and their representatives ready to negotiate. Further, he knew that 1864 was an election year and Lincoln had to face the voters. Lee believed the Republicans under Lincoln would face a tougher reelection battle if their territory was occupied by a large and invincible Confederate Army.

In June of 1863, his massive, 75,000-member Army of Northern Virginia crossed the Potomac, headed up the Shenandoah Valley, and marched into Pennsylvania. Lee threatened the capital city of Harrisburg before he came to know via a spy in the Union Army that the equally large Army of the Potomac was nearby and shadowing him.

That army, incidentally, included newly promoted Brevet General George Armstrong Custer, who would survive the coming battle to fight another day.

As a defensive measure, Lee consolidated his troops near the town of Gettysburg. A small contingent of soldiers was sent to Gettysburg to search for supplies, including, it was reported, badly needed shoes. They saw Union Calvary there and reported the sighting to their superiors, who didn't believe these riders were part of a larger force. They believed them to be a local militia and so on July 1, a detachment of Confederates moved to town to engage these forces. This maneuver marked the beginning of the largest battle of the war, which started before Lee could get his army aggregated into defensive positions or know the complete size, location, and strength of his adversary.

The first day of the fighting on July 1 found the Union forces dug in on the low hills near the city as they waited for the larger Union forces to reach them. Confederate forces moved into their positions from the west and engaged the Union forces on the ridges for hours. In many instances, the Confederate forces prevailed, but at a high price in dead and wounded. The Union forces also suffered greatly. Several of their generals were killed or captured. Even though only about one-third of the two armies rushing to the location were engaged on that first day, it was still a bloody and tough fight, yet just a prelude to the fighting to come over the next forty-eight hours.

On July 2, the rest of the Union and Confederate forces arrived. A minimum of 160,000 men had assembled to do battle on the doorstep of a tiny town of 2,400 in Pennsylvania. The Union forces were arrayed on the high ground in an arc. The Confederates were split into lines across from the Union forces. July 2 was a full day of furious fighting at places named Devil's Den and Little Round Top. Many survived to fight another day, but thousands of others either did not survive, or they had arms and legs blown off by artillery bombardments or musket shot or saber strike. As additional men arrived, day two passed into history and the third day, July 3, broke over the smoky land.

Robert E. Lee was determined to attack the Union forces directly and overwhelm them at a place called, appropriately, Cemetery Ridge. The morning of July 3, Lee spoke to his leading general, James Longstreet, and ordered that, after a sustained artillery bombardment, Longstreet was to direct his men to cross a long uneven field and breach the Union lines. In a sense, the conversation between these two men on that morning determined the outcome of the war. Longstreet wrote extensively about the discussions that morning after the war. He claimed that he advised Lee against a charge because they didn't have enough men, the Union soldiers would expect it, and the distance they had to cross was a mile of grass and it would occur under heavy fire. Further, Longstreet noted that Union muskets had a very long range and would reach the Confederate soldiers long before the Confederates could reach the defensive line. Undeterred, Lee estimated the distance his soldiers had to cross was less than a mile and was ready to order the charge in spite of Longstreet's objections. Lee and Longstreet discussed how many men were available to launch this assault and they concluded that the total was around 15,000 soldiers. Longstreet again argued that they did not have enough battle-ready men to accomplish the task at hand, but he later stated that Lee was impatient, determined to order the charge, and, after a time, no longer listening, so he had no choice but to carry out the order and initiate the charge.

Longstreet then spoke to General Edward Pickett and told him to prepare his men. Pickett and Longstreet knew each other well; they had both served in the Battle of Chapultepec in Mexico under Winfield Scott. In that battle, deep in Mexico and far away from Pennsylvania, Longstreet was holding the brigade colors, but he was wounded and could not go forward. He handed the colors to Pickett, who subsequently jumped a wall, fought his way to the palace they faced and unfurled the brigade flag on the roof for all to see. Under Longstreet's orders, Pickett and his men were about to jump another wall so to speak, but this one was a mile long and they would do this under heavy fire from far more modern weapons than had existed during the Mexican-American War. Those weapons were being brought to bear by the same army Longstreet and Pickett had once been a part of. Pickett did not object to the orders he received from Longstreet and began to prepare.

At 1:00 p.m., the Confederates began an artillery bombardment of the Union lines. In due course, the Union forces responded. This went on for nearly two hours and was likely the largest artillery bombardment of the war.

At 3:00 p.m., Pickett's men and several other Confederate divisions stepped out of the woods and began the long march towards what Lee thought was a defect in the Union lines at Cemetery Hill. Single file, 12,500 men made the walk that day, and the line they made was a mile long. As they advanced closer, Union artillery began to cut them down in large numbers. When the line of men came into range, the musket fire began. The thin lines thinned further. The Confederates did reach the Union lines at several places, but when it appeared they might break through, Union reserves would step into the breaches and fight back hand-to-hand.

After a brutal and deadly hour, the Confederates began to file back individually or in groups across the long field, now strewn with their dead or dying fellow soldiers. The charge had failed, and at tremendous cost. Of the 12,500 men who started on the journey, 6,555 were killed, badly wounded, or captured. A shaken Lee took responsibility for the action, but he was concerned about a Union counterattack. When he came across an exhausted Pickett, he told the General to rally his division for defense, but Pickett could only respond, *"General, I have no division."*

Pickett's charge on the afternoon of July 3, 1863, is considered to be the high-water mark of the Confederacy. While there were many more deadly days to come, the war was lost for the South. At Gettysburg, the Union forces repelled the Confederates at a high cost and Lee's Army of Northern Virginia retreated, never to step foot on Northern territory again. A quarter of the Union's Army of the Potomac was killed or wounded and a full third of Lee's army was killed, wounded, or captured.

In November, four months after the battle, President Lincoln traveled by train to the battle site to dedicate a cemetery to the thousands of fallen men buried there. At the ceremony Lincoln delivered the Gettysburg Address, considered to be the most famous and influential 271 words ever spoken by a US President:

"Four score and seven years ago, our fathers brought forth upon this continent a new nation, conceived in Liberty, and dedicated to the proposition that all men are created equal. Now we are engaged in a great civil war, testing whether that nation or any nation so conceived and so dedicated, can long endure. We are met on a great battlefield of that war. We have come to dedicate a portion of that field as a final resting place for those who here gave their lives that that nation might live. It is altogether fitting and proper that we should do this. But, in a larger sense, we cannot dedicate, we cannot consecrate, we cannot hallow, this ground. The brave men, living and dead, who struggled here, have consecrated it far above our poor power to add or detract. The world will little note, nor long remember what we say here, but it can never forget what they did here. It is for us the living, rather, to be dedicated to the unfinished work which they who fought here have thus far so nobly advanced. It is rather for us to be here dedicated to the great task remaining before us; that from these honored dead we take increased devotion to that cause for which they gave the last full measure of devotion, that we here highly resolve that these dead shall not have died in vain, that this nation, under God, shall have a new birth of freedom and that government of the people, by the people, for the people, shall not perish from the earth."

Lincoln did not describe the battle as a great tale of one side vanquishing another. It was not a victory speech. His language describes a great moral struggle on both sides. In eighteen months, the war would end and Lincoln himself would be added to the list of casualties.

An unidentified, and very young, Confederate soldier.

DEATH AND FREEDOM

The legal end of slavery was codified into the US Constitution by the 13th, 14th, and 15th Amendments, but the Amendments were preceded by an Executive Order issued by President Lincoln in September of 1862. Called the Emancipation Proclamation, it reads: "That on the first day of January in the year of our Lord, one thousand eight hundred and sixty-three, all persons held as slaves within any State, or designated part of a State, the people whereof shall then be in rebellion against the United States shall be then, thenceforward, and forever free; and the executive government of the United States, including the military and naval authority thereof, will recognize and maintain the freedom of such persons, and will do no act or acts to repress such persons, or any of them, in any efforts they may make for their actual freedom."

The Proclamation and the Amendments to follow delivered freedom to 3.5 million slaves, but they dropped them off penniless and without a role in a broken country where they were surrounded by a hostile majority. They were free in letter, but the road ahead for the first generations of free people was going to be a difficult one.

To enforce this proclamation, however, the armed forces of the Confederacy had to be either convinced to surrender, or be utterly destroyed.

By late March of 1865, Lee's Army of Northern Virginia was under siege in the area around the Confederate capital city of Richmond. Union forces under the command of Ulysses Grant had broken the Confederate lines and Richmond was poised to fall. Through the first days of April, there was heavy fighting around Richmond, Petersburg, and other locations in Virginia, including a small town called Appomattox. The Confederate forces were depleted, beleaguered, outrun, outflanked, and outnumbered by the Union forces all around them. When General George Custer captured and destroyed a trainload of supplies at Appomattox Station, supplies that were meant for Lee's troops, Lee began to receive messages from his Generals that they could not go on. He decided it was time to respond to the letters that he was getting from General Grant that surrender talks were in order and that terms would be generous. Grant had written to Lee that his forces were to stack their arms and munitions but that they would receive leeway to go home and take care of themselves: "The arms, artillery and public property to be parked and stacked, and turned over to the officer appointed by me to receive them. This will not embrace the side-arms of the officers, nor their private horses or baggage. This done, each officer and man will be allowed to return to their homes…" In other words, his men would not be tried for treason, and Lee knew that better terms would not be forthcoming if he fought on to a final and inevitable defeat.

A truce was arranged after a short exchange of messages, one of which was carried to Lee by General Custer. A meeting was agreed upon at a nearby home. Lee arrived first, dressed in his finest ceremonial uniform. Grant arrived a bit later in a mud-splattered coat that only had tattered shoulder straps to show his rank. This was the first time Lee had seen Grant in eighteen years; they had been acquaintances when they served together in Winfield Scott's army during the march on Mexico City. The men entered the home and sat, briefly engaged in small talk and then Lee brought up the purpose of the meeting. Grant had the terms offered in his letters to Lee drafted into an agreed surrender document. Lee signed the surrender agreement, stood, and left. Grant forbade his men from cheering the news as Lee rode away.

In the coming weeks, the remaining Confederate armies surrendered, and the war was over. There was much talk of the two armies being countrymen again, but that talk could not change the facts on the ground, which was that a brutal civil war had left hundreds of thousands dead, many more injured, and slavery ended not by agreement, but by force of arms. The resolution had come at an extremely high price.

THE ASSASSIN

Many people in the southern states could not accept the surrender, including an actor named John Wilkes Booth. Booth was born into a theatrical family where his father and brother were well-regarded theater actors. He was a well-known actor in the Eastern United States, and his brother Edwin was even more renowned. John Wilkes Booth was something of a celebrity, and Lincoln was familiar with his work.

Booth attended Lincoln's second inaugural address in 1864 and had made casual threats on Lincoln's life previously, all motivated by the war and Lincoln's position on slavery. He hinted to friends before the assassination that he wanted to kidnap Abraham Lincoln.

Around noon on Friday, April 14, 1865, Booth stopped by the Ford Theater in Washington to pick up his mail. He had performed there many times and was well known by the staff. It was there he learned that Lincoln would be attending a play at the theater that evening with General Grant. Booth surmised that this was his chance to strike a blow for the recently defeated South by killing both the president and the North's leading general. The opportunity was just too great for him to let it pass by. It was Good Friday, but he spent the rest of the day preparing for a murder.

At 8:45 p.m., Booth met with three friends and told them what he intended. The four men proceeded to concoct a plan in which Booth would kill Grant and Lincoln, and the other three would kill the Vice President and Secretary of State. They were going to decapitate the US government in a bid to save the Confederacy.

In the end, only Booth followed through with success. He had no trouble accessing the Ford Theater and moving around inside. He entered the theater at 10:00 pm and by 10:15 had made his way to the door that led to the viewing box where Lincoln, his wife, General Henry Rathbone (Grant had declined to attend and Rathbone had taken his place) and Rathbone's fiancé were focused on the play, "My American Cousin." Booth entered the viewing box, approached Lincoln from behind, drew out his .41-caliber Derringer, and shot the president once in the back of the head. After shooting Lincoln, Booth jumped from Lincoln's viewing box to the stage below and is reported to have yelled *"Sic Semper Tyrannis!"* to the stunned audience.

Bleeding and unconscious, Lincoln was taken across the street to a house where he lingered through the night and died the next day.

For twelve days, Booth was on the run, subject to the largest manhunt in US history at the time. He fled Washington with his co-conspirators and was helped by others as he fled, but many were questioned, and eventually, Union forces discovered Booth's location on Garrett's Farm in Virginia.

On the night of April 25, Booth was cornered in Garrett's tobacco barn. He yelled out to the soldiers surrounding the barn and tried to negotiate the terms of his surrender, but eventually, the barn was set on fire and a US Army soldier shot him through a crack in the wall of the burning building. Booth died at the scene. His co-conspirators were hung after a massive trial just a few weeks later.

Lincoln was buried in Springfield, Illinois. His plans for reconciling the war-torn nation, whatever they were, were buried with him.

Booth's older brother Edwin was a Union supporter, and he was shocked at the actions of his younger brother. For weeks he did not leave his house, but eventually, he went back to work and spent many years acting in the theaters of New York City. The Booth Theater in midtown Manhattan is named in his honor. Edwin Booth was somewhat comforted when he later learned of a chance incident that had happened in early 1865, just a few weeks before his brother John shot Abraham Lincoln. Lincoln's son, Robert Todd Lincoln, the only one that survived through adulthood, had been on a rail platform in New Jersey when he slipped and his leg fell between a train and the platform. Before he could be dragged under, a man grabbed him by his coat and pulled him to safety. Robert Todd Lincoln recognized the man; it was the famous actor Edwin Booth. Lincoln thanked Booth and Booth departed, not knowing, of course, that the man he had just saved was the son of the president who, in weeks, would be assassinated by his younger brother.

Dead Confederate soldiers after the Battle of Antietam. Photo by Alexander Gartner

SECTION 5: COLOSSUS

Torch and part of the arm of the Statue of Liberty at the 1876 Centennial Exhibition in Philadelphia.

"I do not think that there is any other quality so essential to success of any kind as the quality of perseverance. It overcomes almost everything, even nature."
— John D. Rockefeller

We are poor… but we are free. No white man controls our footsteps. If we must die… we die defending our rights." — Sitting Bull

Give me your tired, your poor, your huddled masses yearning to breathe free, the wretched refuse of your teeming shore. — from 'The New Colossus' by Emma Lazarus

The Civil War in the United States settled the issue of slavery once and for all, and resolved whether it would be allowed in the western states. It did so at tremendous cost in blood and treasure, a cost that was borne particularly in the former Confederate states where so many men had been killed and their economic systems had been disrupted. The American South lagged behind the rest of the nation economically for at least the next hundred years. In many ways big and small, the consequences of that conflict are still with us.

But the end of the war also ushered in an era of breakneck economic growth as the country surged west and made Manifest Destiny a manifest reality. From the end of the war in 1865 until 1890 is a period of only twenty-five years, but the 1890 census revealed that there was no detectable frontier anymore. The entire west had masses of American citizens in it. It was during this brief period that the quintessential occupation that would come to define the period, the venerated cowboy, had his entire career. The proud and warlike western native tribes were subdued and in the process, functionally destroyed. It was in this period that telegraph lines linked the east and west electronically, while train lines were linking the east to the west physically.

America's economic growth, and the burst of freedom it engendered, represented opportunity to the rest of the world. This created a strong pull for immigrants to move to the United States. Aspiration-minded Irish, Italian, Eastern European, Chinese, and other Asian citizens were attracted to the chaos of the United States, and the United States took them in. The descendants of the Nordic and British peoples of the early colonial days were now joined by millions of people with slightly to radically different cultures and traditions.

The enormous promise of the United States was now being realized.

RECONSTRUCTION AND DESTRUCTION

The turbulent period after the US Civil War is referred to as "Reconstruction." This went on from the war's end in 1865 until 1877 when the last federal troops left the former Confederate states. The Emancipation Proclamation ended slavery, but to make the idea stick past Lincoln's executive order, the 13th, 14th, and 15th Amendments were added to the US Constitution during this period. The 13th Amendment outlawed slavery, the 14th granted citizenship to the formerly enslaved, and the 15th granted them the right to vote. The issue of slavery was finally and permanently settled.

The Reconstruction period was guided in the early phase by Lincoln's vice president, who had assumed the Presidency upon Lincoln's death. President Andrew Johnson was a Democrat and former slave owner himself. His guiding principle was to reconcile the warring states as quickly and leniently as possible, which was consistent with Lincoln's vision of national reconciliation.

But these plans were not to be. Bitter politics took over the legislature after the war ended and Johnson became the first president to be impeached. He survived being removed from office by a single vote in the Senate, which was mostly comprised of victorious Republicans. The alleged offense prompting Johnson's impeachment trial was said to be a "violation of the Tenure of Office Act," but much of the political wrestling was around his appointment of people, mostly military officers, who were designated to administer the former states of the Confederacy. Johnson's defense in his Senate trial was that he had the right to make appointments as part of his powers as the president. So, in that sense, the affair was yet another contest of powers between the executive and legislative branches of government. In the background, however, it was really war politics at its most venal, and it would not be the last time that bitterness over the war would consume the federal government.

After Johnson left office, Ulysses Grant, the former Union General, was elected and took office. He was one of five former Union soldiers elected to the presidency. Only the founding generation had so dominated the executive branch of government previously. The leadership of the former Confederacy was legally barred from holding any elective office. The Republican hold on federal power in the decade after the Civil War was directly related to the politics of both the Democrat and Republican divide, and the relative position of power between the representatives of the southern versus the northern states.

By 1874, however, the Democrats from the South achieved a majority in Congress for the first time since before the war and the period of Reconstruction and federal occupation began to close. A disputed election between the Republican Rutherford Hayes and Democrat Samuel Tilden in 1876 resulted in a compromise to settle the issue in 1877, but for accepting the Republican victory, the Democrats in Congress demanded that the last of the Federal troops of occupation be withdrawn from the southern states, and they were. American troops were still present in the southern states, but they were on military bases and were part of the broader defense of the nation and no longer victorious troops of occupation. In a sense, this marked the true end of military hostilities related to the southern rebellion.

The now unfettered southern legislatures, released from any federal oversight and unconcerned about the presence of Union militaries, went to work setting the stage for the next phase of American ethnic conflict. They began to pass laws that functionally segregated the white and black populations and put the former slaves in disadvantaged positions whenever possible. These were the Jim Crow Laws that would become the subject of more federal conflict in the 20th Century (Jim Crow was a fictional black character performed by white actors in minstrel shows).

While the horrific war, death and disunion had settled slavery, the issue of race was in no way dead; it was just pushed deeper into the law at a different level of power and made largely subterranean. Slavery was not allowed, but to the southern lawmakers, segregation was the next best thing.

RISE OF THE SLAVES

The first generation of former slaves was cast adrift in the Deep South and often punished and isolated by the people who had formerly enslaved them. The newly freed immediately sought ways to thrive despite the opposition they faced. They organized into associations and cooperative arrangements, focusing on ways to elevate themselves from the position of powerlessness. They were aided in this process by Christian churches, both black and white. Many were successful, and some were spectacularly successful. Two such men were Booker T. Washington and a man well known to him, George Washington Carver.

Booker T. Washington was born into slavery in Virginia in 1856. He retained a memory of it throughout his life. His mother Jane was a slave, and his father was said to be a white man from a neighboring plantation, whom Booker never knew. His life was tough and he recalled in his many later autobiographies the indignities of slave life.

After Emancipation, his mother married a man named Washington and they moved to West Virginia, where Booker painstakingly learned to read and took his stepfather's name (He was simply known as

"Booker" before that). He worked in the coal mines for years to earn money and then took advantage of the educational institutes that were being set up for "Freedmen" around the country. He attended the Hampton Institute in Hampton, Virginia, and later the Wayland Seminary in Washington, D.C. The seminary, the church, and sympathetic Christians impacted the emancipation and rise of the former slaves.

When he was 25, Washington was invited to move to Alabama and lead the new Tuskegee Normal and Industrial Institute, which was meeting in one room donated by a local church. Eventually, he was able to purchase a former plantation, and the Tuskegee Institute, now Tuskegee University, was born.

Over his lifetime, Washington was a tireless promoter of black education as a way for black people to rise in a white majority society. He traveled for speaking engagements and met with several presidents and industry leaders. He was also a tireless fundraiser and adamant advocate for black self-reliance.

Many of his speeches and ideas came under criticism by other newly emerging black leaders for being too accommodating towards segregation. This rift in black leadership, between those who were more careful and those who were more confrontational, was to play itself out many times in the decades after the end of slavery and well into the era of Civil Rights. Washington did not see the Civil Rights era, however. He died in 1915 of kidney disease and was buried at Tuskegee University.

George Washington Carver was only a one-year-old when slavery ended, but he was also born to it in Missouri. During the war, at just one week old, he and his family were kidnapped from the farm where they worked, taken to Kentucky and sold. His white master, Moses Carver, hired a detective to find the family, but only George could be located and returned.

Moses Carver and his wife Susan raised George as their own child and saw that he was educated, though he had to go to school miles from home. He would introduce himself as "Carver's George," meaning the George that was the possession of the Carver's until the woman at the boarding house where he lived when he was in school told him that going forward, his name was to be George Carver. Like Booker T. Washington, he had only a first name until well along in life. Carver added Washington to his name later.

After a year of schooling in Missouri, he moved to Fort Scott, Kansas. There he witnessed a lynching, which in the context of American history is the public execution of a black person by a white mob (lynching in its purest definition means "judgment without a trial"). Carver left that town and was able to finally graduate from high school in Minneapolis, Kansas.

After high school, Carver moved to Iowa but was unable to get into college initially. He worked as a farmer like so many other former slaves, and took odd jobs as a cook and a ranch hand. Others noted his interest and ability with plants. Eventually he was able to get into Iowa State University, where he was the school's first black student. He earned his master's degree in agriculture there and became the university's first black faculty member.

Booker T. Washington at Carnegie Hall in 1906. Mark Twain is seated just behind him

At that point, he came to the attention of Booker T. Washington, who recruited Carver to move to Alabama and work at the Tuskegee Institute, where Carver rose to prominence. Carver began researching methods for increasing crop yields in the areas that had formerly grown the cotton picked by slaves. His methods instructed black farmers to rotate crops and perform other necessary functions that would make their farms more self-sufficient. He advised that fields be alternated between cotton and various legumes, including the peanut, because that would return nitrogen to the soil, provide an additional cash crop, and improve the nutrition of the local population.

While the two men had similar backgrounds, Carver and Booker T. Washington clashed frequently, but Washington praised Carver as "one of the most thoroughly scientific men of the Negro race with whom I am acquainted."

Carver's work promoting the many uses of the peanut eventually gained him public prominence, and he consulted with three presidents and many other industry figures. He advocated for tariffs on imported peanuts and spoke before many conferences, including the US Congress, on various agricultural matters. As successful as he was as an academic, his various business ventures with peanut products were not successful. He stayed in Alabama for the rest of his career. He never married and died in 1943 after falling down a flight of stairs at the Tuskegee Institute where he had lived most of his life.

Carver was recognized and awarded many times in his lifetime and even more times after his death. A ballistic missile submarine, the USS George Washington Carver, was named after him in 1965, as well as countless high schools and research laboratories. Like so many of the first-generation black Americans post-slavery, he made his mark with tenacity, smarts, and fearlessness, primarily because there was no other way.

TWILIGHT VICTORY BEFORE DEFEAT

With the settlement of slavery as a national issue, the full occupation of the territories gained in the Louisiana Purchase and the Mexican-American War could finally get underway in earnest. Former soldiers, and in many cases, former slaves, flooded into the regions that were still occupied by untold thousands of Native Americans. The conflict was inevitable and did not take long to culminate into battle. These twenty five years of conflict are known as the Indian Wars.

The entire period of warfare with the Native Americans is complex because of the sheer number of parties involved. The Native Americans fought with each other and would use the US Army as allies when circumstances allowed. They would also ally with each other against the US forces if advantageous. In the hundreds of years since the Europeans arrived until the time that the Native Americans had dwindled to a tiny remnant, they simply could not form the kinds of large-scale alliances that would have allowed coordinated actions against the wave of settlers, ranchers, and militaries that were washing over them. They often had difficulty coordinating a single battle plan.

By the late 19th century, many tribes had been forced to live on reservations and were dependent on US provisions, while others kept to their traditional way of life as hunter/gatherers. This divided the Native Americans into what were called "Agency Indians" and the ones still living their traditional lives. White settlers crept into the regions where the Native Americans lived, sometimes under military protection and sometimes against the rules established by treaties. These were immigrants who had, illegally in many cases, crossed boundaries to be where they were, but the government policy tended to remove the Native Americans in those instances, and not the settlers. The settlers often had commercial interests, as was the case with miners, who wanted to build roads through the territory still occupied by the natives, and the US Army always sided with the business interests.

This period was marked by continuous military confrontations between the US Army and the Native Americans, but it was mostly a low-level conflict that foreshadowed the guerilla warfare in the coming 20th Century. The Native Americans lacked sufficient numbers to mount direct assaults, and they lacked the advanced weapons needed to win such engagements. They had rifles, for example, but not cannons.

There were a few set-piece battles. One such battle was at Little Big Horn. The Civil War veteran, General George Armstrong Custer, led the 7th Cavalry, which was made up of hundreds of Civil War veterans like him, many of whom had just completed duties patrolling the defeated South. Custer was skilled and experienced, but he made a terrible error at the end of a long career that would place him in the historical record as an epic bumbler.

History last recorded Custer delivering a message from General Grant to General Lee at Appomattox in April of 1865. But eleven years later, in June of 1876, he was in command of the 7th Cavalry and fighting in the Great Sioux War. This was a conflict between the allied Sioux and Cheyenne tribes against the US government over the possession of an area that spans from South Dakota to Wyoming known as the Black Hills. Gold had been discovered in the hills and prospectors were moving in. In a conflict that had played out over and over, the Native Americans were being asked to give way to American interests. The Native Americans refused to move, so the US Army began the campaign to clear them by force.

There were several battles between the loosely organized Sioux and Cheyenne Native Americans in the summer of 1876. The US Army forces aggregated at the newly formed Fort Abraham Lincoln and deployed into the hills and valleys to the west. Several divisions began to encounter large numbers of armed Native Americans and the fighting grew in intensity.

In early June, several of the Plains tribes gathered on Rosebud Creek in Montana for the annual Sun Dance. This was a religious rite of renewal. It was here that a Native American leader named Sitting Bull had a vision of US soldiers "falling like grasshoppers from the sky." At about the same time, US military forces were leaving camp and heading towards the Native Americans to disperse them.

On June 17th, US Army soldiers came in contact with what they knew to be an unusually large number of Native Americans. There was a short battle along the Rosebud Creek that resulted in no definitive conclusion, but did result in many US Army casualties. Custer and his cavalry were nearby, and his scouts reported seeing large pony herds assembled. The Native Americans, it appeared, were cooperating and aggregating in a way they normally did not. Custer believed he was facing 800 or so "hostiles" in the area, but what he was actually arrayed against was 1,500 to 2,500 warriors who had arrived for the Sun Dance and the annual buffalo hunt. Bad intelligence led Custer to make a fatal mistake.

Photographers often traveled with General Custer and he would gladly pose for them.
Here, he is seen with a bear he was said to have killed. To his right is Bloody Knife,
a Sioux scout who died with him at Little Big Horn two years later.

On June 25, Custer attacked a village at the Little Big Horn River that he estimated was only lightly defended. The ensuing battle cost Custer the lives of 268 of his 700 men, including his own. Masses of warriors attacked the 7th Cavalry, and there were running battles for the rest of that day and into the next. Warriors on horseback shot and attacked the panicked and overwhelmed soldiers. Others, including the women, walked the battlefield with heavy mallets bludgeoning the wounded to death. The survivors fled and made it to a small steamship that transported the wounded away from the battlefield. With them, the news of the defeat spread far and wide. When other units of US Army soldiers made it to the location days later, the Native Americans were gone but the scalped and mutilated bodies of the dead 7th cavalrymen, including Custer, lay where they fell. All were buried in mass graves at the site.

Over the years that followed, many Native Americans claimed to have been the one that personally killed Custer, but it is likely none knew that the forces they were fighting were led by Custer, or even what he looked like. Still, Custer was well known in military circles and an accomplished soldier promoted to General at the age of 23. He served with distinction at the Battle of Gettysburg and several other Civil War battles. His death was sensational news, but the direction of the war against the Native Americans was not changed by his defeat and inglorious death. His legend was burnished by the continuous efforts of his widow, who was a prolific writer and speaker. She never remarried; promoting the legacy of her dead husband became her job. Slowly, Custer's place in history grew, while tribe by tribe and skirmish by skirmish, the Native Americans of the western part of North America suffered the same fate as the tribes of the eastern part of the continent. They were moved to reservations where they remained dependent on the US government for food, were absorbed into the now-dominant culture, were killed, or just died.

Custer's legend in defeat lived on while the tribesmen who defeated him did not.

INDUSTRIALIZATION

The period after the Civil War is marked by the rapid advance of several industrial projects and products that began altering the nature of the previously agrarian United States. Patterns of employment began to change in ways that would fundamentally alter American social relationships and later, restructure portions of the government. At the hundred-year mark, the country was rapidly moving from a primarily agricultural and pastoral society to an industrial one. Previous generations of wealthy Americans held their wealth in land and, in the South, much of their wealth was held in slaves, but the new wealthy were "industrialists" whose wealth was based in control of industry and manufacturing.

From the end of the Civil War in 1865 until the breakup of Standard Oil in 1911, American industry grew rapidly, with very little regulation or oversight. For some, this provided a level of wealth undreamt of in pastoral America. The era is sometimes referred to as belonging to the great "Robber Barons." Charter members of this informal club included John D. Rockefeller in oil, Cornelius Vanderbilt in transportation, Henry Ford in automobiles, Andrew Carnegie in steel, and J.P. Morgan in finance. These men and others amassed fortunes that European royalty could not fathom. The daughters of these men, the Gilded-Age heiresses, often married European nobility, gaining a title in exchange for the American industrialist wealth to repair and run the European husband's costly estates. It became such a trend that Edith Wharton was prompted to make it the subject of her novel *The Buccaneers*.

There were many landmarks along the way to mass industrialization. The first transcontinental railroad track was finished in 1869 when Leland Stanford (later the founder of Stanford University) nailed in the last spike at the meeting point of the east and west tracks in Utah. Linking the east and west with a contiguous rail line triggered the intersection of government, culture, and industry.

A short time later, telegraph lines ran parallel to the railroad tracks and were seen in other parts of the country as electronic communication became more common. There would be no more situations such as had occurred in the Battle of New Orleans where a conflict continued after the war's end had been decided.

In 1876, American inventor Alexander Graham Bell invented the telephone, which allowed people to speak at a distance. This was the first time in history face-to-face communication was being replaced by a device and the human voice could be carried along a wire.

All of these revolutions in transportation and communication had the effect of accelerating many cultural and business processes already in place. They created jobs that had never existed and created wealth in new places where it had not been present. Someone had to be a telegraph operator, a shipping coordinator, and a station master. While the war-ravaged South languished, the west coast boomed with new people and supplies. Many southerners moved west. Raw materials from the west coast poured east to factories and customers. America as a legal entity and defendable geography was being molded into America as an economic and cultural statement on how to live.

THE COMMODORE

Cornelius Vanderbilt was an early example of the new industrial elite. He was born on Staten Island in 1794 during the administration of President George Washington, and was the descendent of Dutch immigrants who had arrived in the colonies as indentured servants. His early life was as poor as any other and he was not connected to any wealth or elite circles of influence.

Instead, Vanderbilt started his business life operating a small ferry boat (he picked up the moniker "The Commodore" here) taking passengers and cargo from Staten Island to Manhattan in New York. He did not attend school past age 11.

In his early years, he worked for others, but then he began to buy his own boats. For years, he plied the ferry routes around New York and accumulated the business acumen he would need to rise. And rise he did; he came to understand both steamships and the legal intricacies of building a monopoly in a particular service. He pioneered the use of the legal entity of the corporation to strategic advantage.

Vanderbilt entered the railroad business early, before the Civil War, and was well-positioned to thrive in the business boom that followed. He had accumulated many ships and was successful in the shipping business, but he sold them all to focus exclusively on the railroads which were spreading west and consolidating the American hold on the continent.

The Commodore died in 1877 and left his wealth to a favorite son. He was buried in New York near where he was born and he embodied the first wave of American commerce and industry that was just getting started.

ROCKEFELLER AND THE TRUST BUST

Succeeding waves of industrial pioneers followed Vanderbilt's generation, and few embodied the early Industrial Age more than oil tycoon John D. Rockefeller. Like Vanderbilt, Rockefeller was born in New York but his family moved to Cleveland, Ohio when he was still young.

Even as a young man, Rockefeller was methodical, studious, and quiet. He took his first job as a bookkeeper when he was 16. At that time, firelight was the only way to see after dark and people used various methods to keep a fire burning in the home for light and heat. One way was to use whale oil in a lamp, but whale oil was growing more expensive as whales were hunted to near extinction, and in Pennsylvania, oil that came up out of the ground had been discovered. This oil had to be refined but from it, kerosene could be made, and it was a perfect substitute for whale oil.

And so Rockefeller entered the kerosene business. He also had an instinct for turning waste products into new business lines. With a few partners, Rockefeller developed Standard Oil into the largest and most profitable business in the world. Then, just as the electric light bulb was replacing kerosene to light up the night, the combustion engine was spreading around the world. The utility and fuel needs of these engines boosted the value of Standard Oil's product beyond imagination. His company moved from providing light to powering the trains that were headed west and the warships of powerful navies who had converted their engine rooms from sail and steam to diesel-powered motors with the fuel produced by Standard Oil.

In the coming decades, the number of uses for oil proliferated wildly and Rockefeller had an iron grip on providing it. He was ruthless and aggressive, but his practices kept the price of oil low enough to see that it was adapted in many places, but high enough to make the boom-and-bust cycle of oil a profitable and reliable industry. He served the industry well as both supply and demand grew steadily. American industry of all kinds came to rely on the wide availability and low price of oil. Standard Oil was one of the first and most prominent vertically integrated industries, meaning it controlled all aspects of its business from extracting oil to getting it to the customers.

Eventually, Rockefeller became the victim of his own wild success. The rapidly expanding oil industry boosted the growing military power to the United States, but it made many other industries and organizations hostage to Standard Oil. Rockefeller was not shy about crushing competitors and it was the success of the company that eventually caught the eye of journalists, unions, and finally the government. Standard Oil was forcibly broken up by the US federal government in 1911 to end its monopoly grip on the oil business.

The thirty-four different entities that resulted from the break-up grew separately, increasing Rockefeller's wealth further and making him part-owner of the post-break-up companies. In retirement, he turned his attention to philanthropy and further defined ways to give away money in the same way he had defined making it.

"John D.," as he was known, was a serious, religious, hard-working, and reserved man who set the pattern for a new kind of American: the business tycoon. He died in 1937 at the age of 97and is buried in Ohio.

THE COWBOY

Not all of the new businesses and industries made people rich, but they still could capture the public imagination. No job so defined the Western ethos and appeal more than the lowly cowboy.

By 1876, one hundred years after the signing and publication of the Declaration of Independence, the United States was a growing colossus, and the anchors on both coasts were driving the middle of the country to fill with people and business activity. One of those businesses was cattle.

Europeans brought both large cows and many kinds of horses to the Americas. Those animals were bred prolifically. The Spanish brought both animals up from Mexico, so in Texas, parts of the Midwest, and later in California, huge herds of cattle roamed the land foraging on the grasses available. Cattle were raised for local consumption, but with industrialized meatpacking in cities, the booming city populations, and the extension of rail lines into the interior of the United States, the cows that made up the huge cattle herds became more valuable. Cattle work was performed by cowboys and in this period, moving cows around became an actual specialized form of labor. This lowly profession came to emblemize a new type of American; rugged, stoic, and driven by a separate unwritten code of manly conduct. Cowboy work became the pastoral alternative to the industry-driven technical jobs like telegraph operators or newly emergent professional jobs like accountancy.

Cowboy work was dangerous. It meant branding cows so the ranchers could tell them apart when they were out grazing, and rounding them up when it was time to drive them to market. All of this occurred in open spaces over hundreds of square miles, and the cowboys rode this territory performing their job day and night.

Cattle drives were transportation events; the cowherds had to be walked to the railheads so they could be transported to the meatpacking plants in the cities. On a long cattle drive, injuries or attacks were often fatal. A cowboy had to master a horse, the cows, the elements, the Native Americans, the angry farmers, the calendar, and a host of other factors. It was not high paid or glamorous work. One out of four cowboys was black, often former slaves or their children.

Eventually, the railheads spread out from the margins and led right into the cattle grazing areas. Cattle drives became shorter and less frequent, until they were no longer needed. The invention and proliferation of barbed wire in the 1880s meant that it was cheap and easy to fence off massive portions of land and raise heavier, meatier breeds of cow locally.

The extension of the rail lines and the invention of barbed wire made the roundup and the cattle drive a thing of the past. The lone cowboy era came to an end after only about forty years, from 1850 to 1890. But the cowboy image was just getting started, and the cowboy as the embodiment of the American spirit was part of the new way in which a burgeoning America saw itself. The resourceful frontiersman evolved into the rugged rough-and-ready cowboy.

William Frederick Cody was a former Union soldier and hunter who came to be known as "Buffalo Bill" Cody in a traveling show that glorified cowboy themes. His shows traveled all over North America and Europe. In them, he and others would stage cowboy practices and act out battles with the Native Americans. Cody and "Wild Bill" Hickok became famous cowboys while the real cowboys labored in anonymity.

Cowboy work eventually morphed into a sport and event known as rodeo. Rodeo is the official sport of several states and the emblem of a cowboy riding a bucking horse is Wyoming's trademarked logo. When the cowboy entered the movies years later, he became, even for city dwellers, the Cowboy, the emblem of American resolve.

THE STATUE AND IMMIGRATION

At 151 feet tall, the Statue of Liberty is a massive work of art and monument that was gifted to the United States by France and dedicated in October of 1886. It stands on the Liberty Island pedestal in New York Harbor.

It was a French ardent abolitionist named Édouard René de Laboulaye who conceived of this large sculpture honoring the Union victory during the Civil War and the subsequent abolition of slavery. Laboulaye spoke to a French sculptor named Frederic Bartholdi about his idea. Bartholdi traveled to the United States and laid eyes on Bedloe's Island, a tiny piece of land that all shipping entering New York Harbor had to pass. This was where he wanted the statue to stand.

Back in France, Bartholdi began to draw conceptual sketches of the project. Both men began talks and correspondence to raise funds for the monument. The designs were focused on the best way to express the American idea of liberty. Designs gravitated towards the idea of a female figure derived from Libertas, the female goddess of freedom, worshipped in ancient Rome by emancipated slaves. A large torch-holding statue of a female captured several themes all at once and eventually the design basics were settled. The torch represented enlightenment, while in her other hand she holds a tablet inscribed with the Roman numerals for 1776.

Construction on the Statute of Liberty began in France in 1877

In 1877, work began in France and the famous head was exhibited at the 1878 World's Fair in Paris. The designers enlisted George Eiffel, engineer of the massive Eiffel Tower in Paris, to build the internal iron scaffolding of the statue's torso.

As the statue progressed in France, fundraising for the giant pedestal it would stand upon was carrying on in the United States. A few wealthy Americans made large contributions to the fund. As part of the money-raising efforts, the American poet Emma Lazarus was asked to write a poem about the statue. She eventually wrote the sonnet called "The New Colossus," which quickly became associated with the statue and the emerging status of the United States as a place where the immigrants of war-torn foreign lands could find refuge. Her poem transformed the statue from a monument to abolition to a monument about the US immigration policy in just a few carefully crafted lines.

The text of her poem reads in part "Keep, ancient lands, your storied pomp cries she with silent lips. Give me your tired, your poor, your huddled masses yearning to breathe free, the wretched refuse of your teeming shore. Send these, the homeless, tempest-tost to me; I lift my lamp beside the golden door!"

The first wave of immigrants to the colonies had been primarily English and Scottish, with a smattering of Danes, Germans, Scandinavians, and African slaves. In the frontier period through to the Civil War, events in Europe pushed millions of Irish immigrants to the United States. As the western states, particularly California, were economically developing, Asians—primarily the Chinese—began to immigrate to the United States, and the federal government was drawn deeper and deeper into the debate about who should be let in, and in what numbers.

In 1882, the Chinese Exclusion Act was passed. It put a specific limitation on the number of Chinese who should be let into the US. In 1892, the immigration center at Ellis Island in New York Harbor opened and ships entering the harbor filled with immigrants had to sail right past the Statue of Liberty, just as Bartholdi had envisioned. In the 62 years that Ellis Island was open, 12 million immigrants entered the United States there, including more Irish, but also European people from further east who were, in fact, fleeing from war and persecution in Russia, Poland, the Balkans, and anywhere Jews lived. Poverty in Italy drove millions of Italians to move to the United States. In each of these instances, these millions would find an unoccupied space or town and begin to work and rise, often creating tiny versions of their home culture in isolation. They retained their language and religion and food traditions, but in time, the follow-on generations would inevitably begin to gravitate to a cultural mean, which meant dropping their original language and adopting English.

There were many ugly cultural conflicts in this period, between both the native born and the immigrants and between immigrant groups whose foreign hatreds would sometimes carry over to America. But it was in this period that the United States and its unique culture came to be known as the "melting pot," where specific cultural differences from around the world would be melted down and blended into a unique American culture with pieces of the immigrant cultures woven in.

From the beginning, immigrants from non-English speaking cultures sometimes changed their names to something less foreign-sounding, and their original family names were lost, but this was a small sacrifice to make in the many instances where they realized the freedom and prosperity they sought. In time, the steel towns in Pennsylvania and Ohio were populated by first generation Slavic people. Places like Little Italy in New York carried on Italian traditions in tiny shops and bars. In various Chinatowns all over the United States, the non-Chinese came to eat Chinese food in Chinese restaurants. The older immigrant waves adapted their native cultures to define uniquely American cultural forms. Scottish and Irish folk music became the country music of the United States. The original non-European immigrants, the African slaves, contributed mightily to American culture in many ways, but especially in music. Blues, jazz, and eventually rock and roll came from black communities and the black experience.

The strategic security envisioned by the founders and summarized in Manifest Destiny worked for the many new immigrants. The United States was isolated from the dysfunction in other parts of the world, so many immigrated who *were* "tempest-tost," and the US *did* raise a lamp for them at the golden door. In a single generation, millions of poor from around the world came to the United States and rose to the level of the middle class, and some became incredibly wealthy.

THE END OF THE FRONTIER AT WOUNDED KNEE

The US Constitution requires that a census be taken every ten years. This count decides the number of representatives each state will send to the US House of Representatives. In 1890, the 11th census was taken and the census superintendent announced that there was no longer a detectable frontier line across the western United States. There was no longer a line that marked the furthest point where settlers had pushed. The defining American characterization as a perpetual frontier ceased to exist and Manifest Destiny was finally realized.

By 1890, there were still people pouring west, and territories yet to be organized into states, but all areas had boundaries and all territories had a predictable pattern of settlement. By 1912, the deed was done and every territory was organized into a state. The millions of square miles of land gained by the United States via the Louisiana Purchase 109 years previously and the Mexican-American War 67 years prior had filled with enough people to warrant a state government and representation in the federal government. Only in isolated pockets did the ragged remnant of the former tribal nations still exist. Their light was about to be extinguished forever.

The fate of the last Native American tribes was not uniform, but it was never good. The Native Americans had been invited by treaties and were often coerced by military force into moving to 'reservations' which were meant to set them aside and out of the way. The constantly surging and roving interests of the American population meant that the agreed-upon native territories were often invaded and nothing was done to correct these violations of the treaties. Tribal leaders would complain, and often there was violence, but this rarely worked out in the favor of the Native Americans, who were killed or pushed on to smaller and smaller plots of the least desirable lands. Such is the fate of displaced people, especially people who can't integrate and adapt. There had been Native American populations in the eastern half of North America who were more agricultural. In limited instances, they adapted to the European methods, but even they had been run off of the land if they couldn't functionally disappear. The dry, hostile conditions of the western half of North American meant that virtually none of those Native Americans were agriculturists with any possibility of integration. These were hunter/gatherer peoples who lived off the now-disappearing buffalo herds. With the decline of the herds, so went their pattern of living. They did not take to farm work, even where it was possible to farm. They wanted to live as hunters and said so. When buffalo hides became valuable to the industrial centers in the east, men with automatic weapons came to kill the buffalo in large numbers and take only the hides; the meat rotted in place. Eventually, nearly all game had disappeared from the mountains and woods of the west and the natives had nothing to eat.

The Native Americans were restless and dynamic like people everywhere. Many of the people that the US Army and settlers encountered had not lived on the disputed land for thousands of years; in many instances, the Native Americans had only recently taken the land from other tribes.

Further, Native American culture was not static, eternal, and unchanging; it had radically altered since Europeans arrived. Horses altered Native American organizations and mobilized them, making some of them even more war-like. Modern weapons made some tribes even more dominant over other tribes. What they never mastered was large-scale organization and advanced weapons, and horses and rifles were not enough to allow them to compete with the American military.

Many of the tribes that formed the final battlefront had migrated south after the arrival of Europeans in 1492, and they fought with each other for dominance. Intertribal warfare was a problem until they collectively faced the Americans and then it was too late. The Americans, as different as they were to each other with their competing European identities, were unified enough to continuously form a common front with any of the wildly differentiated tribes they encountered. The Irish and the English fought for centuries back in Britain, but were part of a unified front in the United States. The Native Americans, however, with their very specific way of life, could not unify unless they were forced into battle or onto reservations with old rivals, where they finally made peace with each other before dying off.

Kiowa natives captured by Custer's 7th Cavalry after the Battle of Washita

Many tribal chieftains had been invited to go east and meet various American political figures, including many presidents. Lincoln met with several Native American leaders. They would meet with "Indian Affairs" officers who pledged help and safety. These chiefs would return to their tribes with the disturbing stories about how many millions of Americans there were behind the few hundred soldiers and settlers the other tribesmen had seen. They saw the buildings and railroads and commerce that were behind the settler waves and so they knew beyond all doubt that they could not possibly win a war with the Americans. These men would advocate making peace, but when a peace treaty was broken, the men who advocated making peace were discredited. The young men especially had no interest in a long life on a reservation being fed the cast off leftovers provided by the US government. These young men would go on raids and kill settlers, which aggravated the situation with the military.

The Native Americans came to realize that they had only three terrible choices: submit, fight and die, or just keep running.

Many fought, many died, many kept running, and whoever was left was sent to reservations that still exist on US soil. The 2020 census recorded that there are around 6,000,000 Native Americans in the United States presently, which is less than two percent of the population. Whichever conflict marked the end of the Indian Wars was not recorded, since there was never an all-encompassing settlement, but the end might as well have been at Wounded Knee.

In the late 19th century, the remaining Native Americans across the West began to practice something known as the Ghost Dance, which was a slow, solemn ceremony that they believed would revive their lost ancestors and allow them to return to their traditional way of life. The Ghost Dance is credited with creating the will amongst the Lakota people to resist further encroachment on their territory. The Lakota were a division of the larger Sioux Nation and defeating them was part of the US Army's goal in the long-running Great Sioux War. What happened to the Lakota in December of 1890 was an extension of Custer's last stand at Little Big Horn in June of 1876.

The Lakota had been sent to the Pine Ridge Reservation in South Dakota, but on December 29, 1890, a detachment of the US Army's 7th Cavalry, Custer's old unit, was sent to the camp to disarm the Native Americans whom they believed to be dangerous and preparing for more warfare. Reports of the Ghost Dance inspiring the Native Americans to war were repeated in many quarters and the Army was prompted to act. The Lakota were camped near the Wounded Knee Creek, which is a tributary of White River, and it was widely believed then and now that the Lakota war leader Crazy Horse was buried in the vicinity after he was killed by the US Army in 1877.

As in so many other Native American-European confrontations, the cultural gap between the two people baked in the potential for armed conflict. The Sioux, the 7th Cavalry, and another Native American dance were a combustible mix that was likely to explode and at Wounded Knee, it did.

When the 7th Calvary entered the camp under the immediate command of Colonel James Forsyth, a misunderstanding was likely and conflict had been expected. Reports from the scene indicate that Army soldiers collected many weapons from the resentful Lakota, and were trying to disarm a Lakota named Black Coyote who was deaf, did not know any English, and did not understand why he was being asked to surrender his weapon for which he had paid so much. The Ghost Dance was being performed simultaneously nearby and tensions were high due to the shooting death of Sitting Bull a few days earlier. Sitting Bull had been at Little Big Horn, he was a hero to the Sioux and a villain to the Cavalry. His death at the hands of the tribal police electrified both sides of the conflict. When two soldiers tried to wrestle the rifle from Black Coyote, his rifle discharged and the shooting was on.

Native Americans grabbed the weapons that had been taken from them and started to shoot at the soldiers. The 7th Calvary returned fire. At some point, the soldiers turned a sort of early machine gun, called a Hotchkiss Gun, on the Native Americans, including the area where tents filled with women and children stood. Reports vary on what exactly happened next, but they do not vary on the outcome. Black Coyote, and up to three hundred other Lakota men, women, and children were killed, some more than two miles from where the deadly encounter began. Army officers either willfully or negligently lost control of their men and the killing went on unabated for some time.

A blizzard came through afterward, and in the days that followed, the Army hired civilians to bury the dead. Those grave diggers found humps of snow under which lay many dead Lakota and a few surviving infants. Colonel Forsyth was investigated and relieved of his command but never received a court martial.

Wounded Knee wasn't the only well-recorded massacre of the Native Americans and Forsyth wasn't the only US officer who escaped any repercussion for losing control of his men, but there were no more massacres because there were not many Native Americans left to kill.

The events in December of 1890 became known as the Battle of Wounded Knee, and it was one of the final battles in the Indian Wars. Without a mutually agreed upon and enforceable two-party arrangement to govern these two competing peoples, when one side gained total victory the war was won. The other side simply ceased to exist in any meaningful form.

The cultural mandate of Manifest Destiny was done, North America was conquered, and now the United States could turn its attention outward.

Sioux leader Sitting Bull in 1883

SECTION 6: CREST

The Wright Brothers conduct the first powered flight in the Kill Devil Hills in December 1903

"It is not the critic who counts; not the man who points out how the strong man stumbles, or where the doer of deeds could have done them better. The credit belongs to the man who is actually in the arena, whose face is marred by dust and sweat and blood..." — Theodore Roosevelt

"This is a war to end all wars." — President Woodrow Wilson

"No man is good enough to govern any woman without her consent" — Susan B. Anthony

The census in 1790 showed that the United States, under its new constitutional form of government, had 3.96 million citizens. The 1890 census showed a whopping 62.9 million people lived in the United States and they were distributed across the country, mostly in the east. So much was about to change as the United States surged onto the stage of the world. Equally significant, the world's power centers in Europe launched into a series of suicidal wars. The United States that entered the 19th century was wildly remade by the end of the 19th century. The same process of transformation was about to repeat itself with far greater velocity and far wider implications in the next century. The 20th century arrived in the United States full of promise in a world full of peril.

THE END OF THE VICTORIAN AGE

Napoleon Bonaparte played a critical role in the development of the United States by facilitating the two largest territorial gains in US history which provided the nation with a path to fulfilling Manifest Destiny. When Napoleon was defeated at the Battle of Waterloo in 1815, the Napoleonic Wars ended, and shortly thereafter, what is known as the Victorian Age began.

The period is named after Queen Victoria who ascended to the British throne and stayed there for a very long time. She was born in 1819 and died in 1901, so she was a dominating figure of the 19th century. Her reign as Queen lasted from when she was 18 and ascended to the throne in 1837 until her death in January 1901, for a total of sixty-three years.

The period is marked by many features, but it is known primarily for a long period of relative peace in Europe, and the expansion and settlement of many of the empires of the various houses of the European monarchies, many of which were blood relatives to Queen Victoria.

It was an age of technological and business innovation in Britain as well. Charles Darwin embodied the Victorian age in many ways, and his voyages around the world in 1839 and his book, *On the Origin of Species*, typified the boldness of the period and the transition from a pastoral viewpoint to a more scientific and industrial imperative around the Western world.

Queen Victoria's era was marked by the return of standards of personal morality, which was motivated in part by what the various monarchies in Europe witnessed in France. The British royals did not want a baying mob outside their castle, or their heads removed, which was the fate of the French monarchs across the English Channel. The Victorians would be hardworking and modest in habit and appearance.

When Queen Victoria died, the 20th century was just being born and no one could have foreseen that the long period of peace in Europe was just thirteen years away from ending and the horrors of the many religious wars and the intra-European Napoleonic Wars were about to return, but with modern weapons which would bring new and unprecedented bloodletting.

By 1900, little had changed throughout Europe for a long time. In Russia, Czar Nicholas II was firmly in control. In Germany, Victoria's grandson Wilhelm II was carrying on the Hohenzollern dynasty with no end in sight. In Austria, the ancient and sprawling Habsburg Empire, which was the successor to the Holy Roman Empire and had been in place for over nine hundred years, was perfectly intact. The Ottoman Empire, which began in 1299 and controlled most of the territory of the Muslim world, all of the holy lands in the Middle East, and parts of Southeast Europe, was secure in its place in the world. While the Spanish Empire had mostly met its end, and the French Empire had been remade, the British under Victoria and the many other empires to the East were thriving and the rules under which millions of their subjects lived seemed secure and cemented firmly in place. India was the crown jewel in this network of countries and disparate places controlled by the British.

These empires were held together by many varying brittle alliances and competing interests and they had accumulated many allies, formal and informal. They had also developed enemies, incubated many hatreds, and the many peoples and languages within them had multiple unspoken rivalries. These empire configurations often didn't make any sense in how they were put together; they had been formed haphazardly as the result of wars of conquest or royal unions or just accidents of geography.

The United States, with an entire continent under control and only two land borders to the north and south, had avoided many of these exact kinds of complicating factors even though as a country, the US was about to wade into the thick of world affairs.

A series of mostly uneventful presidencies occurred in the late 19th century, which encompassed President James Garfield, President Chester Arthur, President Grover Cleveland, and President Benjamin Harrison. The United States was building national muscle that would be evident to the world very soon, and briefly showed itself in the Spanish-American War, but nothing redefining had yet happened.

Queen Victoria died in 1901 with her son and successor Edward VII, and her eldest grandson Wilhelm at her side. Her funeral was the largest collection of European royalty ever assembled in one place, and would be the largest ever because many of them would no longer be royalty soon and the nations they ruled would no longer exist. Wilhelm, the Kaiser of Germany, was at her funeral, and yet, in a few more years, he would lead the Germans in war with his British cousins that would end his reign. The coming war would also critically wound the British Empire, doom the Hapsburgs, release the Middle East from the grip of the Ottomans, create a way for an Austrian landscape painter named Adolf Hitler to rise to power in Germany, and bring about a malevolent empire in Russia. The emergent Russian state would not be led by Victoria's blood relative, Czar Nicholas, who would be murdered with the rest of his family, but by the Soviets.

Europe's 400-year hold on the Western Hemisphere was about to reverse itself and the colonists were about to take the reins from Europe's dying grip on power.

20TH CENTURY INNOVATION ARRIVES

As the tumultuous 19th century was drawing to a close, a period of incredible technological innovation began to dawn. There was innovation coming from the scientists of Europe, and there were various innovations in the arts and letters from around the world, but the technological breakthroughs in the United States set the pattern for 20th century industry and radically changed the world, and how people live in it.

The Constitution set the stage for this explosion by encouraging businesses to invent via an exclusive period of commercial exploitation. The exact text reads: "To promote the Progress of Science and useful Arts, by securing for limited Times to Authors and Inventors the exclusive Right to their respective Writings and Discoveries." In other words, if you invented it, you have a short, protected window in which to commercially exploit it.

Many American inventors took this opportunity to heart, but none more than Thomas Edison. Edison was born in 1847, and, though he was a man of the 19th century, his 1,093 patented devices and processes defined the disruptive technological changes of the 20th. He established a research laboratory in New Jersey where the first electric light bulb was pioneered. No more would the night be illuminated by the smoking fire of burning wood or oil.

Lights needed electrical power and so Edison and company mastered mass power generation and the way to wire a city for power distribution, so in that sense, Edison invented the electric power utility company. He invented the battery to store electrical power which made electricity portable.

Edison invented the phonograph which meant that, when combined with photography, both images and sounds could be captured for people not present at the scene to experience what happened later. Only words and drawings had been able to accomplish that previously.

In the realm of photography, Edison pioneered the moving picture, where cascading chains of single images were projected quickly onto a screen and that process created the illusion of motion. The "movies" which grew out of this breakthrough wildly expanded the human imagination and interpretation of stories. Literature required reading and was thus unavailable to the illiterate, but the movies were for everyone.

Edison was part of the long process of inventing the x-ray, called fluoroscopy, which allowed doctors to peer inside the human body without cutting it open. When surgery was required, they knew what to expect.

There were many other inventions in the realm of chemistry and communications, and in many instances, Edison worked with other pioneers, men like Henry Ford, to drive mass manufacturing of the devices he was inventing.

Henry Ford was born during the Civil War, and he lived to see World War II, and in that period, his vision of the assembly line production of machinery came to pass. He founded the Ford Motor Company in 1903, and by 1908 began to manufacture the Model T automobile. Ford didn't invent the automobile, but his Model T popularized it and standardized its operations, and lowered the costs so that many more people could afford one. The era of personal transportation not driven by human feet or animals was upon the world. Ford's process allowed the United States to churn out machinery for World War I in a way none had seen before.

Thomas Alva Edison in 1922

Also in 1903, two brothers from Ohio, Orville and Wilber Wright, took their flying machine with a motor installed to the windy beaches of Kitty Hawk, North Carolina. There in the Kill Devil Hills, they managed to fly under motor power for the first time. The human longing to be released from the ground and fly like a bird was suddenly realized. The hot air balloon had taken humans into the skies, but the powered airplane put people in charge of their destiny in the air.

This was a period of unprecedented technological change which was invented and deployed with incredible speed. A child born the year the Wright Brothers flew their first flight would easily live to see space flight. In only 66 years, American men would take these early experiments in flight, expand upon the concepts, and deliver humans to the surface of the moon. No other period of invention in history compares to the American embrace of flight.

There were many other inventions in the period, and some were relatively trivial, like the candy apple, and many others were extensions of the big breakthroughs like electrical power generation. No one could have foreseen what changes they would unleash. Patterns of living, both big and small, suddenly changed.

The concept of the assembly line was transferred to food production, which meant that a new kind of retailer, called grocers, could bring an amount of food to people such as they had never seen. This drove changes to the human body. Connecting farms to machines and industrial chemicals radically increased food production. The preparation of food and the cleaning of clothes began to be transferred to "labor-saving devices" and this had a dramatic effect on the lives of women around the world. Suddenly they had time for other things such as higher education.

Electric lights drove changes in human sleeping patterns and changed the way homes and buildings were constructed. Wooden homes with fires for heat and light often caught on fire and killed everyone inside. Fire-related deaths suddenly began to fall.

Recordings on the phonograph meant that music could be stored and let loose at will, in the home, based on the taste of the listener. Tastes changed as people began to explore and find the music they liked and find people who liked the same kind of music.

The rapid proliferation of cars meant roads had to change, and young people could create some distance between themselves and the adults in their lives. The "teenager" was fundamentally born here. Piles of manure in the street, which was a public health menace, disappeared along with the horse-drawn carriage.

Young people could also get away from the older authority in a new space called a movie theater which was a building dedicated to the screening of images on film. Edison Studios made many of these short films, one of which was called The Kiss. It was only eighteen seconds long, but it transfixed audiences. The image was huge and it moved. These early short clips began to be strung together so the movie-going event was longer, and at that point, it was a short jump to many clips strung together to tell a central story.

One of the earliest celebrated films was made in 1915 entitled *Birth of a Nation*. It was directed by D. W. Griffiths, the son of a Confederate Army colonel, and it was based on a book called "The Klansman." *Birth of a Nation* shows in a positive light the development of the Ku Klux Klan as a needed defense of white people in the Reconstruction era southern states. It depicts black Americans in a very negative light, but it was the most complex film ever made to date, and it covered many parts of the American Civil War, and even reenacted Lincoln's death at the hands of John Wilkes Booth. It had a cast of hundreds of "extras" and many characters with overlapping storylines, and it used close-up shots, the earliest fade-out techniques and it had a musical score that was to be played live with the film. In short, it was a technological innovation in storytelling in a new medium, and it was a massive commercial success. *Birth of a Nation* played for 44 weeks in a theater in New York City and it was the first American film ever screened at the White House for a president. President Wilson was reported later to have said of the film "It's like writing history with lightning."

Wilson may have not said that, manufacturing fake quotes was another innovation from the movie business, but it hardly matters because it is true of motion pictures which went on to color the history of every country with filmed and highly stylized national characters. The movies began to influence memory and how history was remembered. None pioneered the movie star quite like the Americans. Movies, and not books, quickly took command of defining the American character and archetype, and it was movies more than any other medium that invented the Cowboy.

All the inventions of the period were world-changing and the world as we know it grew from the inventions of that era. Human habits were built around these inventions and in that sense, human existence was redefined. It wouldn't be until the invention of the computer and the Internet that such a radical transformation in the human relationship to technology and each other would occur.

THE SPANISH-AMERICAN WAR

The United States entered a war in every generation throughout the 19th century. There was the War of 1812, the Mexican-American War, the Civil War, and the long twilight war with the native tribes. Nevertheless, the long Victorian peace in Europe had benefitted the United States. For the most part, the European powers did not meddle with the United States or threaten American interests, and so the undefeated American fighting forces were able to apply industrial technology to military practices and radically increase effectiveness.

By 1898, 406 years had passed since Christopher Columbus crossed the Atlantic under the direction of the Spanish monarchy. Napoleon's invasion of Spain had cost the Spanish Empire not just Mexico but all of the rest of its South American colonial possessions, each of which drifted away in the period from 1810 to 1826. And yet in 1898, Cuba, Puerto Rico, and the Philippines, named for the long-dead Hapsburg Prince Phillip, were still part of the shriveled Spanish Empire.

At the same time, the surging United States had full control of formerly Spanish Florida, just 90 miles across the Florida straits from the northern shore of Cuba, and American business interests were firmly entrenched in Cuba. Since weakness is provocative, Spanish weakness and the proximity of Spanish possessions to the United States were making a conflict more and more inevitable. A strong United States and a weak Spain were likely to come in contact.

At one point, business interests in the pre-Civil War southern states had tried to convince the federal government to purchase Cuba from Spain in order to convert it into a slave-holding agricultural state. While that plan never came to fruition, various rebellions grew in Cuba opposed to further Spanish rule. Cuba entered a revolutionary phase centuries after the Spanish conquest, and long after Mexico had achieved independence. Those revolutionary forces received support from the United States, and the Cuban independence movement was supported by many US newspapers.

The Spanish government in Madrid issued statements declaring their unwillingness to surrender any ground in Cuba, which they considered to be an extension of Spanish territory rather than a colonial possession, and they forswore negotiations over their other island territory, the Philippine Islands in the western Pacific. As the Mexicans had done with Texas, Spain refused to acknowledge that a far greater power had made silent claims to territory and in doing so, invited a war which was not short in coming.

American warships moved into position in both Cuba and the Philippines as the likelihood of American action against the weakened Spanish increased. There were talks and negotiations regarding American interests in Cuba and the Philippines, but those talks came to nothing.

Finally, in January of 1898, the American battleship the *USS Maine* moved into Havana Harbor as a show of force, and on February 15, it exploded and sank, killing 251 of its 355-member crew. Spanish sabotage was blamed for the blast, and this locked in the course for war.

By April, the US Congress passed decrees demanding that Spain withdraw forces from Cuba so that the Cubans could create a free nation, and the US Navy began a blockade of Cuban ports. Based on the blockade, Spain declared war on the United States and the United States responded in kind. A pattern was repeating itself yet again; in the 18th, 19th, and 20th centuries the English-speaking mostly Protestant Americans had waged war with a Spanish-speaking and primarily Catholic country.

This war was short, lasting only sixteen weeks, and was marked by one American victory after another both on land and at sea. There were short battles in the Philippines at Manila, where the Spanish had ruled for over 300 years. In Puerto Rico, the Americans won battles decisively both on land and at sea. There was heavy action in Cuba, where Cuban and American forces attacked many Spanish fighting positions.

The American forces were led, in part, by future President Theodore Roosevelt, who supported war with the Spanish based on the nearly hundred-year-old Monroe Doctrine, which dictated non-interference in New World affairs by Old World powers. Battles at San Juan, El Caney, and Santiago de Cuba were mostly victories for the United States, and the few naval battles around Cuba were equally as disastrous for the outmatched, outgunned, and outnumbered Spanish squadrons.

Defeat in both the Philippines and Cuba meant the Spanish had no choice but to sue for peace and after short negotiations, yet another Treaty of Paris was signed in December of 1898 to assign formal control over Cuba, Puerto Rico, and the Philippines to the newly powerful United States.

This loss of territory meant the end, for all practical purposes, of the Spanish Empire, begun so many centuries earlier. An old power fell permanently as a new power, the United States, grew brighter in the emerging dawn of the 20th century. No one knew what new challenges, opportunities, and horrors the 20th century would bring, but whatever was to come, the United States would play an enormous part. Spain, exhausted after 400 years of outward expansion and activity, would not. The Spain that had conquered so much territory around the world was finally a spent force. The bold spirit of the conquistadores that had sent a few hundred men to conquer millions in Mexico and Peru was gone forever.

Theodore Roosevelt gained much attention for his exploits in Cuba and rode that fame to a position as the vice president on the ticket of William McKinley. When McKinley was assassinated in 1901 (he was the third president to die from an assassin's bullet, following Abraham Lincoln in 1865 and James Garfield in 1881), Roosevelt was elevated to the presidency.

The conclusion of the Spanish-American War presented yet another chance for the United States to become an empire like the Spanish or the British. The Mexican-American War offered the United States the opportunity to seize all of Mexico, and the Spanish-American War offered the chance to claim much of what the Mexican-American War had left out, and yet, the United States did not pursue these opportunities and did not at the end of World War I, or World War II either. Both Cuba and the Philippines were eventually reinstituted as new nations, and the United States did not go beyond the bounds of its original goal of Manifest Destiny to completely dominate North America and little else.

ROTTEN TO THE CORE

In 1914, the century of European peace following the Napoleonic Wars came to an end. Christian Europe, which dated back to the year 313 when the Roman Emperor Constantine legalized Christianity, could also be said to have died in the same disastrous war that began with the 1914 assassination of a Hapsburg Archduke in Sarajevo.

Archduke Franz Ferdinand, the heir to the ancient throne of Austria-Hungary, was on a visit to the capital of the province of Bosnia and Herzegovina when a young assassin shot and killed both him and his wife. His killer, nineteen-year-old Gavrilo Princip, was a member of a Serbian protest group called The Black Hand which had planned to shoot the Archduke along a parade route earlier in the day. However, those plans went poorly and the Archduke survived. In the confusion that followed the assassination attempt the driver of the Archduke's car became lost and eventually the car stopped in traffic right where Princip stood, and so Princip simply stepped forward and fatally shot Ferdinand and his wife at close range.

Princip was too young to receive the death penalty, so he lived to see what he could not have known he would set into motion by murdering the Archduke. Franz Ferdinand led an Empire that was at the crossroads of many ancient peoples and hatreds, which included the Slavic people, much of the Balkans where Muslims and Christians met and fought for centuries, and part of the Empire was linked to Germany via the German-speaking Austrian people. Of all the people to kill in this tinder box of creaking European monarchies, rivalries, and religious hatreds, the Archduke was not the guy. But there he was, dead at the hands of a Serbian nationalist.

What happened next was a domino effect where the Austria-Hungarians declared war on Serbia, since Princip was Serbian and acting as part of a Serbian cause. The Serbians were then backed by their fellow Slavs in Russia, which was backed by a longstanding relationship with France, which was allied with the British. The Germans allied with their linguistic cousins, the Austrians, and enlisted the Ottoman Turks to their aid. There were a few other alignments, and the entire witches' brew of competing militaries began fighting in at the end of the summer.

A bloodletting of unprecedented ferocity followed, as military tactics from the 19th century met military weapons from the 20th century. Soldiers standing shoulder to shoulder in a 19th century manner faced belt-fed machine guns made in Henry Ford's 20th century assembly-line factories. The war bogged down in the Western front as the Allied powers, primarily Britain and France, faced the German army in the relative safety of mud-filled trenches from which they would not escape for all four years of fighting. It was thought that the war would be short, but instead, it descended into a nightmare where a generation of young men would be lost. The wasteful slaughter of Pickett's charge at Gettysburg was made exponentially worse at places like the Marne, at Verdun, and Gallipoli, where men rushed at rattling mechanical machines of mass death. Casualties were counted not in tens of thousands, but in hundreds of thousands. Over 1 million men died in the first year of fighting alone.

The American people across the Atlantic in Fortress North America wanted no part of this widely reported slaughter. George Washington's admonition to avoid foreign entanglements, made in a speech at the end of his presidential term, had never seemed wiser.

President Woodrow Wilson based his 1916 reelection campaign around staying out of the war in Europe. To the degree that most Americans had chosen sides, there was a strong affiliation for the English-speaking British and lingering resentment of the Germans that went back to the revolutionary period, alongside widely circulated reports in the press about German atrocities against civilians in Belgium. Americans knew about the sinking of the British civilian cruise liner *RMS Lusitania* by German submarines. 1,198 passengers and crew died in the incident, including 128 Americans. These and other events meant that if the United States were to enter the war, the country would surely side with the British and French. All that was required to make this happen was a series of provocative moves by the Germans.

The first provocation was the deployment of German U-boats, or submarines, on transatlantic shipping routes. American industry had been providing both financial and material support to the British since the war started. The Germans intended to disrupt this supply chain by sinking ships that they knew would be American flagged vessels. They began this attack in January of 1917. By March, five US vessels went to the bottom of the Atlantic. By April, President Wilson asked for and received a public declaration of war.

The second provocation was the Zimmermann telegraph, which was a cable sent to Mexico and intercepted by the British. The message contained a German offer to help Mexico recover land lost in the Mexican-American War in exchange for help in the coming conflict with the Americans. The contents of the telegram were released to the public on March 1, just before the American ships started to fall prey to German submarine attacks. Mexican authorities refused this offer, knowing that the territories lost in 1845 would never come back, and Mexico stayed neutral for the rest of the war.

The American entry into the fighting had a galvanizing effect on the United States and was a definitive factor in ending the slaughter just a year and a half later. American industry ramped up production of US war vehicles. American navy vessels steamed to the places they could provide the most impact. And, most strategically significant, the US Selective Service drafted four million men into service, of which two million had arrived in France by the summer of 1918. At least half of those saw front-line combat.

By November, when the war ended, American forces were arriving at the rate of 10,000 per day, but the German lines were completely depleted and had no reserves of fighting men to spare. From August of 1918 until the end of the war in November, American forces committed to the 100 Days Offensive, which reversed gains the Germans had made in the spring of 1918 and boosted the morale of the British and French forces.

The war was a complex affair, but US forces clearly tipped the balance, and the war came to an end with a shattering German defeat. The Germans accepted a punishing and humiliating Armistice in November of 1918. In a German military hospital, a corporal named Adolf Hitler took the news of defeat hard; he would be heard from again.

The Americans had tipped the balance of power in the war. The American military had set foot in Europe just as several older European empires faded. In the same way that Napoleon had inadvertently boosted the United States due to events in France, the assassination of Archduke Ferdinand had opened the door to American military involvement, not within North America, but in France and Germany, with the British as allies and not adversaries. The United States entered the world stage confident, youthful, and brash. The 20th century was clearly to be one in which the Americans would play the leading role.

THE END OF EMPIRES

The First World War was called the Great War until the Second World War came along. It was great in the sense that it remade many parts of the world and set the stage for events that would shape the United States in the 20th century and well into the next.

The First World War produced many poisonous fruits, but few were more toxic than the creation of the Soviet Union. The Russian empire had been ruled by a series of Kings, called Czars, but in the aftermath of Russia's disastrous performance in World War I, the final Czar, Nicholas II, abdicated, and the Russians entered a violent revolutionary period that lasted until the Bolshevik forces prevailed in 1923. The new Soviet leaders executed the Czar and his wife and children at close range with pistols and bayonets.

Like the French revolution 120 years before, the Russian revolution featured mass violence from the start. Vladimir Lenin was the first leader of the massive new country, but upon his death, Joseph Stalin became the unelected and undisputed leader until he died in 1953. Under Stalin, the mostly rural country was forcibly industrialized at the cost of millions of lives due to preventable famines, forced labor camps, and outright execution. The idea of all communist countries in this period was to wrestle power away from monarchies and place it in the hands of "the people" in the same way the colonists did in what was to become the United States. Power to the people was the theory, but in practice, communist countries came to be led by a different kind of monarchy of brutal men who ruled with guns, force, intimidation, and all forms of terror. Few mastered this process on a greater scale than the Soviets, and in due time, the United States would have to face down this monster.

World War I also brought to an end to the Ottoman Empire which ruled much of the Eastern Mediterranean and all the Middle East. The Ottomans were Muslims who wrestled control of their territory from the crumbling eastern part of the Roman Empire in 1299 and they ruled with an iron fist. When the Ottoman Empire disintegrated after the First World War, many new countries were formed from their territory. Most of these new countries were constructed by the British who folded the territory into their still functioning but sickly empire. The borders of Saudi Arabia, Syria, Iraq, and eventually Israel, grew from the wreckage of the Ottomans and all of those nations would soon depend on the abilities and ambitions of the United States and draw the American military into several later wars.

The ancient Hapsburg dynasty that formed the Austria-Hungarian Empire was dissolved on November 12, 1918, the day after the Armistice was declared. The different nationalities that existed within its borders became their own nations in time and this trend was encouraged by President Woodrow Wilson. The Americans in this period began to impose their values and views of governance on a world that had known monarchal tyranny for millennia.

The discussion about ruling values was a new development. World War I had ended, but the contest of values between the United States and the rest of the world was just beginning. Governing concepts birthed and nurtured by the people of North America were about to be exported. The United States had denied itself the opportunity to become an empire in the classical sense on many occasions, but the country would become an empire of ideas about how people should live and govern themselves. The proliferation of those ideas would sweep across the world and alter the relationship of citizens to their government and each other. When those ideas reached the dead empires of World War I, they fell under the heading of 'national self-determination' which, in practice, meant the creation of many new smaller nations. Those new nations often formed beside other new countries full of bitter rivals, and they were not led by men like George Washington and Thomas Jefferson. National self-determination was a lofty goal, but in reality, its implementation set the groundwork for many smaller wars from which new despots and tyrants would rise.

President Woodrow Wilson participated with the surviving European powers to create a world governmental organization called the League of Nations, which was charged with replacing the diplomatic arm of national governments as the only way in which nations could manage relationships short of war. The League of Nations was suffused with Wilson's values and musings, and Wilson was awarded a Nobel Peace prize in 1919 for his efforts, but the US Congress refused to ratify entry into the League and so the United States never joined. Most Americans still viewed North America as a shelter from grubby old-world problems such as grinding poverty and endemic corruption.

The view of North America as a safe haven was bolstered by yet another wave of tragedy in 1918 when a pandemic swept the world. The Spanish Flu killed millions of people from 1918 to 1920 and its origins are still not known. It is possible that the pandemic reached the United States via returning soldiers, and the death and misery it brought was considered another good reason to seal the country off from the rest of the world.

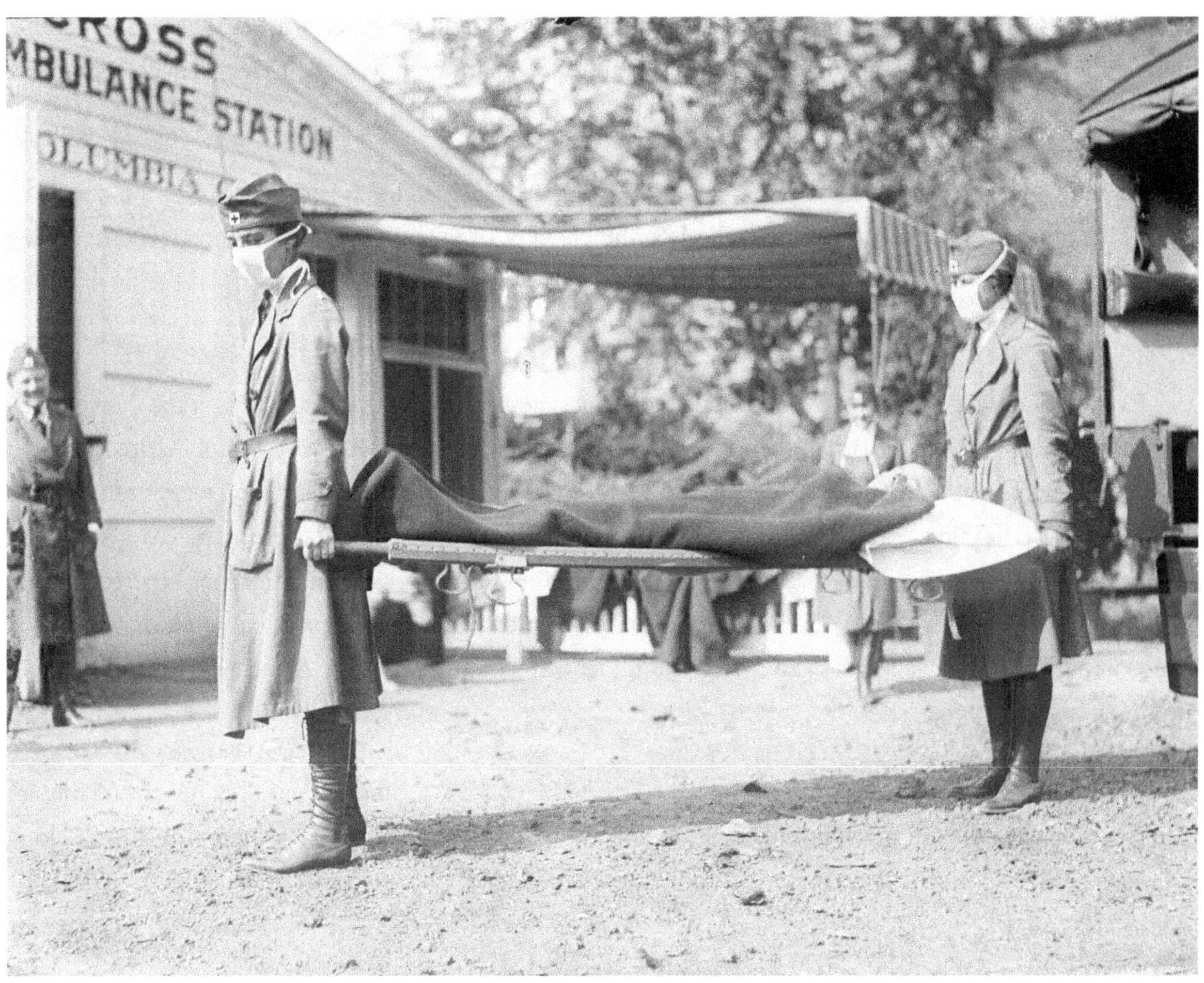

The Spanish flu ravages America

SUFFRAGE AND THE FRONTIER OF RIGHTS

The Bill of Rights and the Constitutional Amendments exist to define those rights that are lifted above politics. Taxes rise and fall and wars are won and lost, but the Bill of Rights and the various Amendments sets aside US citizens' civil liberties that are meant to be fixed and immutable. For example, the Civil War was a conflict over the rights of those held in slavery (as well as states' rights), and the 13th, 14th, and 15th Amendments to the Constitution enshrined in law their rights to the benefits of citizenship that could not be voted or legislated away.

As the United States developed and began to export its ideals to the rest of the world, the notion of rights came under closer scrutiny and in the US, the concept of extending rights to those who had been implicitly or explicitly excluded was explored. Slavery had been abolished, and many of the people who had advocated for its end also fought to expand the legal rights of women.

Every signer of the Declaration of Independence was a man, as was every member of the conventions that drafted the Constitution. But in the same way that the United States was not a wholly British or even European concoction, the United States was not an all-male enterprise. European men were never even a majority in colonial times, since there were women and children present and there were always African slaves performing the building projects and staffing the agricultural works. White European men drove the framework of the country, but in every other instance, women often did the physical work. Much less is known about the wives, daughters and loves that influenced the men who receive the credit for so much of American history.

Martha Washington was a widow when she married George Washington and they never had kids of their own, but he adopted her four children. She campaigned with General Washington during the long years of the Revolutionary War, going tent to tent to visit the sick, freezing, and dying soldiers. Where he went, she followed.

We will never know what love, if any, existed between Thomas Jefferson and Sally Hemmings, a mixed-race slave with whom he had multiple children. Jefferson took her and her family members to Paris with him when he was the American ambassador to France but he left no notes in any of his writings about her. She was clearly an important person in his life and while she left no written record of her thoughts about Jefferson, one of their sons, Eston Hemmings, claimed that Sally had negotiated with Jefferson and gained his promise that if she returned to slavery in the US after being a free person in France, he would free their children upon his death, which he did. Their children married white mates and in time passed in to white society. She was the mother of his many children and clearly more to him than a captive concubine.

Andrew Jackson was fanatically devoted to his first wife, Rachel Jackson. After he married her, it was discovered that her divorce from her first husband had never been finalized. Both were accused of bigamy and so their marriage had to be invalidated. She then had to clear up her first marriage, so she could marry him again. That scandalous story spread via the press during the election of 1828 and Jackson blamed the stress and embarrassment of the gossip for her death, which occurred just a few days before his inauguration.

Wives and women were critical foundations for the lives of the men and foundational in their own right. In every quarter of American society, women were working and achieving, even though their efforts were not often recorded. Still, a few are very well known, and their stories are as valuable as they are interesting.

Harriett Tubman was born a slave in Maryland in 1822, and she was abused in her childhood by various masters. She eventually escaped to Philadelphia, and later returned to Maryland to rescue her family. In the following years, she rescued hundreds of slaves through a network of trails and safe houses called the Underground Railroad, which led them to freedom in the North. She served as a scout and spy for the Union Army during the Civil War and led a force into battle against the Confederates in South Carolina. She was also involved in the suffrage movement, seeking the vote for women before she died in 1913.

Clara Barton was another American woman who stepped forward to participate in the life of the nation. When she was a child, she nursed her injured brother David back to health after others had given up on his recovery. She worked as a schoolteacher, and later went to Washington to work at the US Patent Office. She was still at the Patent Office when the Civil War began, and wounded men began to flood into the capital. At first, she simply showed up at a railway station littered with wounded Union soldiers and began helping wherever she could, but this service grew to become her passion. She was absorbed into the Army as a field nurse and was put in charge. She became known as the Angel of the Battlefield for her aid to the wounded on both sides of the war. After the war, Barton participated in the long and grueling process of finding hundreds of thousands of missing soldiers, and burying the ones that could be located.

Exhausted by her service in the Civil War, she traveled to Europe where she connected with members of the Red Cross, a new organization dedicated to improving the treatment of wounded soldiers on the battlefield. Signatories to the Red Cross conventions agreed to no longer treat wounded soldiers as combatants and recognize their medical providers as neutral third parties. Clara Barton brought these ideas back to the United States and saw them implemented. The American Red Cross evolved to be an organization that responds to natural disasters like floods, earthquakes, and storms as well as wars. Clara Barton's service made possible the help it provides today.

Harriett Tubman in 1868

The obvious and impressive performance of women in all fields of American life set the stage for the Women's Suffrage movement. Suffrage itself is a generic term for the right, or franchise, to vote, and everywhere voting exists, it has been withheld from somebody for something. It was withheld in the early United States based on race and gender, but it was also withheld based on land ownership, tax status, literacy, religion, criminal history, and a whole host of other categories.

Standing in the way of women's suffrage in the United States was the legal doctrine of covertures. Under this idea, a married woman was legally one with her husband, and therefore, his vote *was* her vote. An unmarried woman could make contracts and own property, and many did, but voting was often prohibited. There were states that allowed women to vote before the 19th Amendment was passed but their vote was insecure and often overruled.

One of the earliest and longest-serving champions of a women's right to vote was Susan B. Anthony. Born in 1820, she was a staunch abolitionist from a deeply religious family; one of her brothers moved to Kansas to bolster the anti-slavery forces during the period of fighting that preceded the hanging of John Brown.

In mid-life, she developed a lifelong friendship with another reformer named Elizabeth Cady Stanton. The two of them worked tirelessly on the issues of women's suffrage and temperance in the following decades. Temperance, the term for the abolition of alcohol, was linked to suffrage because if a woman was married to an alcoholic who ruined the family finances, the woman had no recourse.

In 1873, Anthony was put on trial for trying to exercise her right to vote in New York. She responded forcefully in her defense. When she was convicted and ordered to pay a one hundred- dollar penalty, she hissed "I shall never pay a dollar of your unjust penalty," and she didn't. To prevent the proceedings from going any further, the judge never ordered her taken into custody. She never paid the fine and died in 1906, years before the passage of the 19th Amendment that guarantees women the right to vote.

By World War I, eight states had passed laws allowing women to vote, but the service of women in the war effort gave new life to federal law, and the Susan B. Anthony Amendment gained traction. In 1920, the name was changed to the 19th Amendment, and it was ratified by enough states to become the law. The right of women to vote would never be infringed upon again.

There would be other cultural changes that would result in legislation and Constitutional amendments in the future, but before the extension of further rights could manifest, the nation would endure two more trials by fire to finally emerge as the world's preeminent global power. The final sprint to the top had arrived.

From the 1919 film titled The Speakeasy. Movies and media began to influence the way American saw themselves and the world.

SECTION 7: CRASH

British Prime Minster Churchill, US President Roosevelt and Soviet Premier Josef Stalin meet at in February 1945 to discuss the pending end of the war in Europe

"So, first of all, let me assert my firm belief that the only thing we have to fear is…fear itself — nameless, unreasoning, unjustified terror which paralyzes needed efforts to convert retreat into advance." — Franklin Roosevelt

"There are no innocent civilians. It is their government and you are fighting a people, you are not trying to fight an armed force anymore. So it doesn't bother me so much to be killing the so-called innocent bystanders." — Gen. Curtis Lemay

"I am only the child of a small, poor family and had to fight my way by work and industry. When the Great War came, Roosevelt occupied a position where he got to know only its pleasant consequences, enjoyed by those who do business while others bleed."
— Adolf Hitler in a speech declaring war on the United States

The first twenty years of the 20th century brought technological miracles and miraculous wartime disasters to the world, and each period granted rich opportunities to the United States. The American industrial machine that had taken off after the Civil War was now delivering a level of affluence to more people than ever before. Money was circling around and finding a home in new and innovative corporations that were publicly owned through the purchase of stock, or shares in the company.

The United States grew economically from 1920 to 1929 as immigrants poured in, new cities developed in the middle of the country, and older cities constructed roads to the farmland surrounding them to create a new kind of living arrangement called the suburbs. It was a grand time for many, but the bursting American economic bubble that soon followed would leave millions in destitution. A bloodied and resentful Germany would rearm and resume where they left off at the end of World War I. The island nation of Japan would quickly build a colonial empire of stunning brutality. In Soviet Russia, tens of millions of people would die of starvation and wartime violence. All of these events combined to clear the United States' path to dominance.

THE ROARING TWENTIES

As wars so often do, the end of the First World War ushered in a time of intense commercial activity and creativity around the Western world. President Warren G. Harding stated that the 1920s "brought to normalcy" a world that had been abnormally miserable in recent years. That sentiment was nonsense, of course– the world had changed radically and was about to change further– but it embodies the feeling that the period between 1914 and 1920 had involved an abnormal amount of misery and people were ready to engage in furious building and fun when that period finally ended.

The party of the 1920s occurred in the United States under the umbrella of the 18th Amendment, which prohibited the manufacture and sale of alcohol. This period is known as Prohibition and the desire to ban alcohol had been growing for some time as the result of activist organizations such as the Women's Christian Temperance Union. Congress passed the amendment in 1917 and it was ratified by the states in the following year. The ban took effect in 1920. Many Americans didn't drink alcohol, so the amendment was either supported or of limited concern, but in major cities where the Roaring Twenties were redefining businesses and culture, the 18th Amendment created 'speakeasies,' a type of establishment that served alcohol illegally. These businesses purchased alcohol illegally from merchants under the control of criminal organizations known as the Mafia. After 13 years, the 18th Amendment was repealed by the 21st Amendment, and to this day, it is the only amendment ever annulled. However, while Prohibition ended, the Mafia and organized crime did not.

The real action was in economics and the unpredictable shifts in culture that drove America in new directions.

A burst of literature came forth and redefined the Great American Novel and the way American men saw themselves. "The Great Gatsby" by F. Scott Fitzgerald is one of the most enduring novels from this period and offers a portrait of the era, often referred to as the Jazz Age. In both "The Great Gatsby" and "The Sun Also Rises," written by World War I veteran Ernest Hemingway, the leading male characters have flaws and weaknesses that motivate them throughout the novel. This type of story, which centers on the interior landscape of a man's mind, was a radical departure from stories about the stoics of the frontiersman or cowboy era, and it gained prevalence during the time that an Austrian doctor named Sigmund Freud published theories that people were motivated by their inner and subconscious desires. The interior mental landscape of the human being emerged in this period as a new sort of frontier.

New forms of art emerged in fashion and dance, coinciding with the rise of new music, news of which spread through an increasingly popular press. Women cut their hair short and dressed in looser fashions, preferring to dance in ways that were far removed from the stiff European waltzes that had defined formal dancing. These developments were interesting to some and deeply scandalous to others. In this period, a dividing line in worldview grew between the young and old, the city and country, the experimentally minded social explorers and pastorally minded traditionalists. Explorations of the mind were producing wildly different notions on the purpose of human life that had previously been focused on survival.

This rift in worldview occurred not only in the United States; it spread through Europe, notably in Germany. After the loss in World War I, the Kaiser, Wilhelm, had been forced to abdicate and a republican form of government had taken its place. The new government's first assembly had taken place in the city of Weimar, so the German government that existed between 1918 and 1933 is referred to as the Weimar Republic. The shift in culture during this period is referred to as Weimar Culture.

Weimar Culture was as radical as the emerging culture in New York and London. It had a strong visual aesthetic that was captured by the German Expressionists, and the art movement known as Dada. A movement called Bauhaus defined the commercial design of the era, and the Bauhaus architectural forms influenced modern architecture then and now. Music and theater, with their emphasis on experimental character forms and cabaret acts, were popular among many, but, as in the United States, wildly unpopular with others, among whom was an artist-turned-politician named Adolph Hitler.

Hitler loved the traditional 19th century German masters, but was especially fond of Germanic music; he revered Wagner and operas that called upon the mythic German past. Weimar art forms became linked in his mind to Jews, whom he believed wished to undermine traditional German culture and unity. Many of the Jews from the Weimar period realized the undercurrent of anger towards them in Germany long before it manifested as Nazi rule, and those that could leave Germany did so, many coming to the United States. This influx of people was another boon to the United States. Many of the brightest minds in both the arts and sciences fled Germany before the cabaret music stopped and the next war grew closer. That group included such diverse talents as scientist Albert Einstein, film director Fritz Lang, actress Hedy Lamarr, and composer Arnold Schoenberg.

DEPRESSION AND ROOSEVELT

The tribal cultures that were common in the Western hemisphere for many millennia, and were still common in the Americas before the arrival of the Europeans, did not have economies in the modern sense. Resources were distributed along tribal or familial lines, with tribal resources like food commonly shared. There was trading, but an economy is an abstract term for the aggregate amount of exchange taking place; to have a modern economy, there must be money to speed up transactions, banks to hold and loan money, a steady and reliable supply of money so that people view it as a store of value, and goods and services that people want to buy and sell. Civilized societies have diversification of the workforce and money to facilitate the exchange of the fruits of that diversified labor force. An economy is an interlinking web where no node of the web is perfectly whole or independent.

Pastoral and Colonial America had economies that engaged in all manner of trading, but as the nation industrialized, and as the banking system centralized, given the US government's increased supply of currency in circulation, the economy in aggregate grew and diversified. It also grew in financial sophistication, and the market for stocks and bonds grew with the frequency of trading and the number of people participating. Most people didn't engage in any economic activity outside of going to work, being paid, and trading their money for necessities such as food, or making payments on the things they borrowed money to buy, like a house. But in the Roaring Twenties, there was a rapid expansion in investors who wished to survive strictly on the rising price of assets in the expanding economy. This class of investor is sometimes referred to strictly as a speculator, who has no interest in the business invested in, but only the price to invest. Some think of speculators as parasites, but they put their hard-earned money down just like any other investor, and businesses use that money to expand their operations. As a system, even with speculators trying to profit strictly on the velocity of the economy, it worked well in the 1920s for many, including some members of the middle class.

When the country was primarily agricultural, Americans were isolated somewhat from the financial shocks or variations in stock pricing. They only had to worry about what they bought, which was limited because so much of what they used, they made themselves. Milk prices don't create a concern when you own a cow, for example. But slowly, throughout the 19th century and in to the 1920s, markets, pricing, money, regulations, and investments began to link to form complex chains of economic activity. A miner in West Virginia who had a loan on his house was linked to the larger economy through the stocks and bonds that indicated the financial health of his employer, and the rate at which power plants were being built to use the coal he mined out of the ground was reflected in the price for coal. Shocks to any part of this system could suddenly affect the guy who simply went to work to get the coal out of the earth, even though he had no control over other parts of the system and no alternative if things went poorly because he no longer owned a cow or a farm.

In 1929, things went very poorly indeed. In the fall of that year, the world economy began to slow down and contract. On Tuesday, the 29th of October, the number of stock sellers drastically surpassed the number of buyers and so prices began to plummet. This day became known as Black Tuesday. Suddenly, jobs were lost as the demand for nearly everything fell. Even as prices fell, demand didn't rise, and that set of circumstances led to the Great Depression.

The actual cause of the Great Depression is still debated by economists. Since an economy is aggregate activity, what drives the aggregate has no one source and so, unlike in a war, a general slowdown can't be pinned to one event or person. Regardless of how it happened, it happened. By 1930, millions of Americans were unemployed and starving. In 1930 alone, economic activity had shrunk by nearly nine percent. There were "bank runs," where depositors would go to the bank and demand their money, but since the banks had lent the money out to people who could no longer pay it back, depositors went away empty-handed. Those loans couldn't be called in; the money had been spent buying and building new businesses that now had diminished customer bases. It was a vicious cycle that repeated itself in many industries. Thousands of banks failed in this period and their depositors lost everything.

By 1932, unemployment reached twenty-three percent. Nearly one in four people who needed a job could not find one; the Roaring Twenties were now very much over. Art and music radically sobered in content and tone. It was in this year that a presidential contest occurred in which the Governor of New York, Franklin Roosevelt, stepped forward to run for the Democrats.

Franklin Roosevelt was the fifth cousin of President Teddy Roosevelt but, the two men did not know each other. Franklin Roosevelt had been stricken with polio as a child and could not walk unaided, but in a pre-television era, Roosevelt commanded attention with his sonorous voice. His opponent was Herbert Hoover, a Republican, who had been president since 1929. Roosevelt attacked his political opponent by coining the term 'Hoovervilles' to describe the shantytowns that had filled with the desperate and unemployed Americans during Hoover's presidency.

Roosevelt promised that, if elected, he would bring government relief efforts to bear that would surpass anything previously seen, and the public elected him by a landslide. He took office in 1933 at nearly the same time that Hitler took control in Germany. These two men, who never met and were so unalike, both rose to power and died within weeks of each other.

When Roosevelt took office, the economy was in broad disarray. Congress passed a series of acts called the New Deal, which inserted the government into the economy in a manner that would have been unthinkable just a few years before. There were reforms in banking laws, in agriculture, in housing construction, in monetary policy, in debt relief, and in work programs that were sweeping in scope and had many long-term consequences. These acts passed in 1933, and their implementation in the following years pushed the United States government further into the economic affairs of the country than it had ever been before, establishing patterns that are still with us today. The Social Security Administration, for example, is still a colossal institution in the pattern of American life; every American child born still receives a Social Security number from the government. Before 1933, this system did not exist. Birth certificates, social security numbers and death certificates suddenly became primary documents in American life, because birth dates, age, and death were connected to the citizen's financial relationship with the federal government.

The economy did, in fact, begin to turn around after passage of the New Deal legislation. How much of that progress resulted from the New Deal and how much would have occurred naturally is, like the Depression itself, the subject of continued debate. There were many legal challenges to these new laws, but by and large, the Supreme Court allowed the laws to stand, and President Roosevelt was reelected in 1936, 1940, and finally in 1944 during the war.

THE DRUMBEAT OF WAR

For hundreds of years, the major events of European history were driven by kings and queens and popes and aristocrats. However, 20th century had the wider proliferation of media, the increased availability of education, and the economic prosperity driven by mass production, all of which was driven by the common man, who would rise to his place in the world. Lowly status at birth became less of a curse, and the opportunity to advance was a common promise made by many governments. The era of the divine right of Kings was over.

In the United States, many men, politicians like Abraham Lincoln, industrialists like John D. Rockefeller, and inventors like Thomas Edison rose from poverty to make enormous contributions to the world. In Europe, a similar situation played out, except that there, the common man often carried within him the same hatreds, rivalries, and pathologies of the aristocratic set, but such men were unrestrained by any sense of *noblesse oblige*. Joseph Stalin fit this mold, as did a man born in the town of Linz, in the Austro-Hungarian Empire, named Adolf Hitler. His unlikely rise and catastrophic fall paved the way for American dominance in the late 20th century. Hitler was that century's the unlikely Napoleon.

Adolf Hitler was born in 1889 into a somewhat chaotic family, where he fought with his strong-willed father. Both his mother and father, along with several siblings, died when he was young. By the time he was eighteen, he was free to pursue his dream of being an artist without the overbearing criticism of his family. However, as an artist, Hitler became a pastoralist and landscape painter in a time when modernism was taking over the art world. Already, he was out of step with the times, which were turning modernist in art, architecture, and music. Hitler admired order and classicism in art and life, and he detested the clashing modernism of the emerging art forms. He was a strong German nationalist and believed in the demands and structure of German traditions in both art and music. The Germans excelled in structure and order, and Hitler craved both.

After failing repeatedly to make any headway as an artist in Vienna, Hitler moved to Munich just as World War I was beginning. He joined the Bavarian Army, which was under German Imperial command, and served throughout the entire war. He was awarded the Iron Cross for bravery as a dispatch runner, where he seemed to have had a miraculous streak of good luck surviving amid so much death. For example, at the First Battle of Ypres, Hitler's regiment entered the battle with 3,600 men, only 611 of whom survived; one was Adolph Hitler. Despite participating in many of the biggest and deadliest battles of the war, he was never seriously injured. He was recovering from a mustard gas attack when he heard of the surrender of the German Army.

His wartime experience was the primary event that shaped his life up to that point. In the post-war years, as Germany struggled with debt and economic depression through the 1920s, Hitler spent ample time with other Army veterans, nursing their grudges and the belief that they had been betrayed. The Adolph Hitler the world was to know was born here.

Casual anti-Semitism was common throughout Europe in this period, but Hitler had not engaged with it thus far. A Jewish doctor treated his mother for cancer before she died, and young Adolf had written him a kind note with the final payment. Hitler's superior officer in the Army, the one that recommended him for the Iron Cross, had been Jewish. Hitler knew that one of his grandfathers might have been the Jewish patriarch in the house where his grandmother served as a housekeeper.

But in the period after the war, Hitler discovered that he had a talent for public speaking and he found that railing against the evil and conniving nature of the Jewish people seemed to get a great response, as did intense speeches about the greatness of the German people. Hitler entered politics in the same way he had entered art and soldiering; as a response to his intense and unfocused need for meaning and order. Art had been a complete failure, and soldiering had been a success, mostly because he hadn't been killed, but he never went beyond the rank of corporal. Hitler found his stride in politics, and in another stroke of incredible good fortune for him, he found a party he could remake as he saw fit; the National Socialists, known as the Nazi Party. After several lost elections, he ran for national office as the partner of the ailing, aristocratic, and ancient World War I General, Paul von Hindenburg.

By 1933, Hitler had maneuvered past all of the German governmental controls placed on politicians and assumed full and unrestricted power over Germany. Hindenburg died the following year as the former corporal began to defy the treaty conventions that had ended World War I, and rearm the nation for a war he was already running in his head.

THE SUN GOD

Meanwhile, on the other side of the world, an entirely different kind of conflict was brewing. The Japanese created an empire after having their ports forcibly opened by American warships in 1854. After exhausting the Americas, Spanish, French, British, and Dutch business interests moved into Asia. The island nation of Japan saw what the Europeans did to China and the Philippines, and they did not want any Western or Christian influence in Japan. Japan's leadership tried to isolate their island society from the rest of the world, but that had proven to be impossible, and so they aggressively switched tactics.

Once Japan opened up, they came out swinging and quickly built an empire of their own by invading Korea, China, and Mongolia, even engaging in a short war with Russia. They developed the Greater East Asia Co-Prosperity Sphere, which included all the territory they had come to dominate. The Japanese meant to push back against Western influence in Asia.

The Japanese had an Emperor as a leader, but also powerful military cabals that the Emperor only nominally controlled. The British Empire butted up against the territory that the Japanese Army was consuming throughout the 1930s, alongside claims from the Dutch, a few Portuguese holdings, French Indochina, and the Philippines, which had been claimed as a territory by the United States since the end of the Spanish-American War in1898. All of these powers were bound to come into conflict in such close and complex quarters, and eventually, they did.

In September 1939, British efforts to mollify Hitler and get Germany to return to its Treaty of Versailles obligations failed, and Germany invaded its neighbors. Austria fell, then Belgium, and then, in 1940, Hitler's Nazi Party and German military accomplished what the Imperial German Army of World War I could never do; they successfully invaded France, and German soldiers marched on Paris.

Germany, Italy, and Imperial Japan agreed to a Tripartite Pact in 1940, which was an agreement not to engage in war with each other, and allow each signatory to dominate their spheres of influence. This created the Axis powers and set the stage for the giant conflict to come.

In the United States, President Roosevelt was inaugurated just as Hitler was reaching high office in Germany. As Hitler began to invade surrounding European countries, Roosevelt extended aid to American allies, mainly the British who now stood alone in Western Europe against the Nazis, without officially joining the war. The Japanese dragged the United States in to the war, however, in the American territory of Hawaii.

PEARL HARBOR

On the Sunday morning of December 7, 1941, Japanese warplanes swarmed over the Hawaiian island of Oahu, and began coordinated bombing and strafing runs targeted at the American Navy base called Pearl Harbor, plus a few other outlying airfields. By the time they departed, a total of 353 aircraft launched from six different Japanese aircraft carriers stationed offshore participated in the attack. The results were devastating for the unprepared Americans. Eight battleships were damaged or lost, including the *USS Arizona*, which went down with 1,177 men inside. Many cruisers, destroyers, several other ships, and squadrons of aircraft that never got off the ground were also damaged or destroyed. In the end, the attack killed 2,403 Americans and launched the United States into World War II.

Within hours of the attack on Pearl Harbor, the Japanese attacked military positions in the American-held territories of the Philippines, Guam, and Wake Island, and the British-held territories of Hong Kong, Malaysia, and Singapore. The following day, December 8, President Roosevelt asked for and received a formal declaration of war against the Japanese. The Japanese responded in kind. Roosevelt's speech following Pearl Harbor came to be known as the "Day of Infamy" speech, and it opened with Roosevelt saying:

> *"Mr. Vice President, and Mr. Speaker, and Members of the Senate and House of Representatives: Yesterday, December 7, 1941, a date which will live in infamy, the United States of America was suddenly and deliberately attacked by naval and air forces of the Empire of Japan."*

He went on to commit the Americans to victory:

> *"No matter how long it may take us to overcome this premeditated invasion, the American people in their righteous might will win through to absolute victory."*

The lead-up to the attack on Pearl Harbor was full of intrigue and rising tensions over Japanese efforts to expand their empire and prevent the American Navy from aiding US allies in Europe. Japanese predations in China were well known and brutal. Throughout the 1930s, while Hitler was consolidating power in Germany and preparing for invasions across Europe, Japan invaded territory after territory in Asia. In China, their occupation was particularly grim and ghoulish, with mass rapes and pyramids of human heads on display.

In response, the Americans and British began to embargo supplies to Japan, the most critical of which was oil. Negotiations to smooth relations and resume trade began, but while these were going forward, the attack on Pearl Harbor was planned by Japanese Admiral Yamamoto, who, along with several other military leaders, convinced the Emperor Hirohito that war with the Americans, British and French was the only way to save Japan's territorial holdings in mainland China, Manchuria, and Korea. This two-track plan– negotiations while planning a sneak attack– is what prompted Roosevelt's 'Day of Infamy' language.

And so, with no plan for how to restrain the massive United States after attacking them, the Emperor and his forces set in motion a military strike on two of the largest and most powerful nations on earth, the United States and the British Empire. If the trade negotiations had succeeded, perhaps this conflict could have been avoided, but it was not. The Japanese chose war, and they got it.

Of course, war with Japan meant war with Germany as well, given the conditions of the Tripartite Pact. The attack at Pearl Harbor brought Adolf Hitler into military conflict with the United States, though he was already in a war with the massive Soviet Union which he had ordered invaded by the German Army in June of 1941. It was a foolish position to be in for the young Japanese Emperor and the aging German Führer. Hirohito was well-traveled and urbane, but Hitler never traveled outside of continental Europe in his lifetime, and while he may have held a low view of Americans, Hitler knew of the United States and its makeup. His only surviving sister, Paula, stated that as a child Adolf liked to play "Red Indians" with his friends, so even in 1890s Austria, the American Western legend had permeated. Young Hitler was play-acted the fate of the Native Americans at the hands of the army he now faced. And yet there he was, having cast his nation's lot on a 1,000-plus mile front in Soviet Russia and, courtesy of the Japanese, in conflict with the very nation whose mass mobilization of fighting men in World War I had sealed Germany's fate.

The United States did not enter the war late, as had happened in World War I; it had only been going for about eighteen months when the Americans were drafted. What followed was a massive change in the country, its place in the world, and the final destruction of whatever power, prestige, and influence Europe had left.

The strategic facts and low likelihood of victory should not have been lost on Hitler, and yet he pressed forward with his agenda anyway. No European monarch had ever acted more foolishly. Hitler knew fairly early that Germany would not win the war, but he was determined that the Jews would not survive in Europe either. He and thousands of his followers set in motion a purpose-built killing apparatus that drew in nearly all the Jews of Western and Eastern Europe. This was the Holocaust, the deliberate murder of six million Jews, as well as millions of others. The names of the industrial killing centers, known as concentration camps, ring down through the years; Auschwitz, Dachau, Bergen-Belsen… European claims to civilizational superiority ended in the ovens of these death factories. No tribesmen had ever acted so savagely.

World War II destroyed Germany, demoralized France, sidelined Spain as a power, bolstered the monstrous Soviets after claiming twenty-six million of its people, and further crippled the fading British Empire. When the fires finally went out in Europe, the United States emerged victorious and free, and, in a sense, alone.

The USS Arizona burns after the attack on Pearl Harbor

D-DAY

World War II was a complex affair involving millions of combatants. It brought war and privation to hundreds of millions of civilians. What happened on the Eastern Front alone, where the Nazis fought the Soviets, is a tale of incredible human endurance and brutality combined with acts of superhuman sacrifice and bravery.

The American involvement was deep and equally as complicated on both sides of the world. What the American Marines did at places like Guadalcanal ring down through the generations for good reasons. It was the American strategy to invade, or ignore, certain islands in the Pacific on the way to mainland Japan. Invading islands where the Japanese had dug in was costly, brutal warfare, and Guadalcanal, which was one of the Solomon Islands, was particularly brutal and costly for both sides. The Marines lost 1,600 men directly from combat, and thousands more died of disease. The Japanese lost a total of 24,000 men from combat, disease, and starvation.

After the war, American troops were stationed permanently in Europe for the first time, where they remain to this day. They entered Western Europe through the beaches of France, specifically along the coastal areas of Normandy. This once-in-a-lifetime event marks the beginning of the permanent presence of US forces on the continent that fostered its beginnings, resulting in one of the most consequential and enduring military alliances of all time.

Throughout the early years of the war, the Soviets had requested that the Allies invade Europe and create a Western Front in order to force the Germans to fight a two-front war. British and American troops engaged the Germans in North Africa, Sicily, and finally on the Italian mainland. But rather than take a route through Italy and cross over the Alps, it was decided that the allies should launch an amphibious assault on the French coast and cross the flatlands of northern France, the same territory that had been scarred by the trenches of the First World War, to reach Germany as quickly as possible.

Plans were drafted in 1943 and the operation, code-named *Overlord*, was set into motion. Several landing points were considered, but Normandy was chosen because, if the invasion succeeded, there was a broad plain beyond the beaches with open roads in several directions, including a great egress straight into Germany. Thirty-nine allied divisions were selected to participate, which included over one million men, with twenty-two divisions coming from the US, twelve divisions of the British, three Canadian, one Polish, and one French. Command was under the British General Bernard Montgomery.

The German battle order was large, and the German forces were under the command of Erwin Rommel. In the weeks leading up to June 6, 1944, many efforts were made to trick the Germans into thinking that an invasion would come at other locations, and these plans worked for the most part.

The weather was poor for the June 6 target date, but the delay would mean a lack of surprise, so, at midnight, bombardments from battleships off the coast began. Minesweepers came through, then paratroopers began to fall behind the German lines, and then finally, at first light, the amphibious assault vehicles full of men arrived and deposited them on the beaches.

A furious and deadly fight ensued as German machine gunners poured fire over the men on the beaches below. The same scene played out on the code-named Utah Beach, Juno Beach, Gold Beach, Omaha Beach, Sword Beach, and Pointe du Hoc. By the end of the first day, the Allies had moved 160,000 men to France at the cost of 10,000 wounded and 4,414 dead. By the end of June, another 875,000 soldiers had entered France, and the long march to free the French of Nazi rule, and the even longer march to enter Germany and end the rule of Hitler, was well underway. Hitler would be dead in less than a year, joining the over 1,000 German soldiers lost in the first day of the Normandy invasions.

By October, Field Marshall Erwin Rommel would die by his own hand. Rommel and many other German officers, including several that had seen the invasion at Normandy, and knew beyond all doubt that the war was lost, participated in an attempt on Hitler's life by planting a bomb where he reviewed maps with his staff. They believed that Hitler's death was the only way to stave off the now-imminent disaster of a total loss. If Hitler was killed, a negotiated settlement like the one that ended World War I was possible.

The assassination attempt failed. Hitler proved that he still had the good fortune that had followed him from the trenches in World War I, and, though his clothes were shredded in the bomb blast, he was fine. A dragnet to find the conspirators was tossed and eventually, Rommel was found out. He was given several choices, all of them fatal, but was told that if he committed suicide, his family would be spared, and he would be given a state funeral. He was given a cyanide capsule and driven into the countryside, where he bit on the capsule and died. He was given the state funeral, as promised, and any hope of a negotiated surrender for Germany was buried as well. Germany would fight on to a complete and final defeat.

In the east, millions of angry Soviet soldiers were closing in on Poland and the German heartland. From the west, hundreds of thousands of Allied troops, including the Americans, were closing in as well. Victory was certain, but the path to that victory would be bloody and uncertain. Unknown to the soldiers entering Germany, or the Marines island hopping in the Pacific, was an experiment being conducted in the desert of New Mexico on a weapons system the likes of which no one had ever seen.

American soldiers land on Omaha Beach. Photo by Herman Wall

I AM BECOME DEATH: THE MANHATTAN PROJECT

Albert Einstein was born the son of a salesman in 1879 in the German Empire. He moved to Switzerland in 1895 to attended college, specializing in math and physics. In need of money, he took a job at the Swiss patent office while he worked on his Ph.D. at the University of Zurich. He had been an exceptional math and physics student as a child, though not a savant; some subjects did not come easy to him.

Nevertheless, he worked well on his own, and in 1905 he published four groundbreaking scientific papers. They described a universe of far less certainty and predictability than was previously thought. His theories on relativity had the unfortunate effect of undermining the layman's understanding of Newtonian physics, which had described the world in neat linear equations. Einstein wrote and studied the relativity of time, gravity, light, and things that most people took to be stable and reliable. His work was a key part of how the 20th century departed so violently from the relatively stable and predictable Victorian era. Quantum mechanics seemed more like philosophy to most, and a godless one at that. Many of Einstein's findings had to be described in odd ways by Einstein and other scientists, using terms like "spooky action at a distance" and "the undead cat."

Einstein was visiting the United States in 1933 when Hitler assumed full power, and being a Jew that lived in Berlin, he saw what was coming and refused to return. He stayed instead, and became an American citizen in 1940.

As war approached, many of Einstein's colleagues encouraged him to write President Roosevelt to warn that German scientists might be well along in developing an atomic bomb, the possibility of which was the result of much of Einstein's research. Einstein penned this letter to Roosevelt, who in turn assigned the first committee to look into the possibility of building a bomb whose destructive capacity would be based on the rapid release of nuclear energy. Such a bomb, in theory, would be far more powerful than any conventional bomb.

British and American scientists compared notes, and it was found that the British were further along in the development of such a warhead, but as the war began and the German menace grew, the project to build a nuclear bomb was transferred to the US Army under the supervision of a General named Leslie Groves. The scientific division would be directed by an Jewish American, Robert Oppenheimer. This secretive endeavor was called the Manhattan Project and it involved hundreds of scientists in Tennessee, Washington State, and at the Los Alamos Laboratory in New Mexico.

While this work went on, the Americans relentlessly pushed towards Japan, fighting from island to island against fanatical Japanese troops. American ships bombarded these islands with heavy guns, and then Marines went in to clear the islands at a heavy cost in American and Japanese lives.

As Japanese resources dwindled, they began to send out squadrons of suicide planes to attack American ships. These one-way attack planes were directed by Kamikaze pilots who flew directly into American ships and they took a toll on American assets. The Kamikazes, however, could not stop the inevitable, and eventually, Americans were in range of the Japanese mainland. Wave after wave of American heavy bombers flew over Tokyo and other Japanese cities, and they released incendiary bombs which caused massive fires that killed hundreds of thousands of Japanese civilians.

In Europe, a similar process was playing out as the Soviets closed in on Berlin. American and British bombers flew unfettered over German cities. In February 1945, American and British bombers attacked the ancient wooden city of Dresden with incendiary bombs, which created fires so intense that they sucked the oxygen out of the air and suffocated or incinerated thousands of German civilians.

The final days of the German Reich were a sad and horrific affair that carried on in Berlin, block after block, upon the arrival of Soviets forces in April of 1945. In the final battle, the Soviets lost 81,000 men and the Germans over 100,000. Hitler had retreated to his bunker in January of 1945 and remained there until April, surrounded and receiving terrible news that foretold a total German defeat. By late April, he could hear the bombs falling outside of his bunker. There was no rescue, no retreat, and nowhere else to turn. On April 29, he married his long-time girlfriend, Eva Braun, and on April 30, he took his own life with a pistol shot to the head. His military guard burned his body in a shallow bomb crater outside the bunker.

The Nazi Reich surrendered a few days later and the war in Europe was over. Sadly, President Roosevelt did not outlive Adolf Hitler, having died of a cerebral hemorrhage on April 12, and his vice president, Harry Truman, took office. The decisions that happened next fell to Truman during his first weeks as president.

The German surrender did not change the course of the war in the Pacific. The Japanese refused to give up, even though the Americans were closing in on their homeland. It was anticipated that the invasion of the Japanese mainland would cost hundreds of thousands of lives and that the Japanese, who were already using suicide attacks, would fight to the last man, woman, and child. On the tiny home island of Okinawa, the Americans got a preview of what invading Japan was going to be. Japanese forces fought to the death, and whole families of civilians committed suicide rather than face American occupation. Forces were being transferred around the world as the fighting in Europe ended, but the fighting in the Pacific continued and accelerated since the Japanese leadership showed no signs of surrender.

J. Robert Oppenheimer at Los Alamos

Truman was facing this situation when he was informed of the Manhattan Project and the type of weapon it intended to produce. In the New Mexico desert, scientists led by Oppenheimer were ready to test the new bomb. In the early morning of July 16, at a site code-named Trinity, the test was launched and the desert lit up with the brilliance of the sun from the weapon the men had created. The blast melted the sand under the test site. The yield was twenty-two kilotons; nuclear weapons were now a reality. Oppenheimer had witnessed this blast and he later wrote that a short quote from an Indian religious text came to mind as he watched the mushroom cloud rise: "*Now I am become Death, the destroyer of worlds.*" The country in possession of this new kind of bomb faced an implacable enemy who was already resorting to suicide attacks, and so its use was inevitable.

President Truman was notified of the Trinity test while in Berlin, where he was attending a conference with the victorious Allied forces. He now had a tough decision to make; should he use a nuclear warhead on the Japanese? If he did, should he give them advanced warning of the attack? He only had two bombs, and it would be a while before enough fissile material would be available to produce more.

Truman decided to use the weapons with the hope that it would to shock the Japanese into surrender. On July 26, 1945, the Americans issued a formal demand for surrender, which the Japanese government refused. And so, on August 6, an American B-29 high altitude bomber called the Enola Gay dropped the first bomb on the city of Hiroshima, leveling nearly every building and killing 140,000 people. Japanese military radio lost contact with Hiroshima, and they learned why when President Truman announced the strike to the public a few hours later. Said Truman:

> *"If they do not now accept our terms they may expect a rain of ruin from the air the like of which has never been seen on this earth. Behind this air attack will follow sea and land forces in such numbers and power as they have not yet seen and with the fighting skill of which they are already well aware."*

Japanese scientists went to Hiroshima and confirmed what had happened, but the government was too stunned and in disarray to respond. Since there was no indication of Japanese surrender, Truman decided to drop the other bomb that was on hand. On August 9, 1945, an American B-29 called Bockscar dropped a bomb on Nagasaki, creating similar devastation.

The Emperor met with his council and finally decided to surrender. He went on the radio on August 15 to make the announcement, saying

> *"Should we continue to fight, not only would it result in an ultimate collapse and obliteration of the Japanese nation, but also it would lead to the total extinction of human civilization."*

The war was over.

THE AFTERMATH

The New Testament tells the story of Jesus within the framework of the Hebrew experience under Roman rule. The Romans ruled as other empires did, with force and threats, but for the subjected peoples, cooperation had benefits. The Romans lived with the law and brought order to many chaotic lands, including the Jewish homeland of Judea and Israel. During the period of Roman occupation, there were many factions of Jews, including those that wanted to wage war on the infidel Romans and force them out of greater Israel. These were the Zealots and they believed that Jews should be ruled by God and no other earthly power. Other Jews wanted to focus on their worship and let the Gentiles do the hard work of administering the law and defending the territory. The Kingdom of God, they claimed, was not a temporal administration. These were the Pharisees and other establishment figures.

The biblical story of Jesus ends before the outcome of this intra-Jew conflict reached its apex in 70 A.D, when the Zealots waged a war with the Romans that they disastrously lost. In retaliation for defying Roman rule, the Romans destroyed Jerusalem, knocked down the Temple built by King Solomon, and the Jews who survived became members of a Diaspora that spread across Europe.

In the centuries that followed, the Jews thrived in every country where they landed, but always as a persecuted minority. When allowed, they rose to public office or accrued wealth, but this was an exception to the rule. Mostly, they were poor merchants and craftsmen, such as tailors and jewelers. They concentrated on these trades because the skills they acquired were portable, and if there was a pogrom, which was the term for an organized effort to kill and expel Jews, they could flee with their skills, since goods would often have to be left behind. The Jews of old Europe tended not to own factories or land because those stores of value were not portable and Jews were often on the run.

From the period of the Jewish Diaspora under Roman rule in 70 AD, until Nazi rule, some 1,900 years, Jews lived and thrived in Europe. The Holocaust, the sad moniker for the deliberate targeting of the Jews of Europe, brought that long period to an end. The "Final Solution", as it was euphemistically called, fundamentally destroyed Jewish life in Europe. It was, in nearly every respect, a successful destruction of Jewish communities throughout the continent. Towns that had known the Rabbi and the Jewish Quarters for centuries were depopulated of Jews completely. Their homes, their art, and their property were all distributed. At the end of the war, concentration camps like Auschwitz and Dachau entered the popular lexicon as locations of industrial murder. It was a genocide of particularly stunning effectiveness.

Who was responsible for this landmark atrocity? It was made possible by the rise of Adolf Hitler, but there is no record of him personally killing any Jews. His signature is not on any documents that authorized the Holocaust. He was erratic in his leadership style and he often met with subordinates at night, only indicating what he approved of, and left the details to his inner circle. Those men organized larger groups of men to accomplish the construction of the camps, and then they arranged the transportation to populate them. The Holocaust took the efforts of thousands of people who did what they were told, perhaps they thought it was under orders, but Hitler did not lead the Poles, or Ukrainians, or many other nations and peoples that participated in the round up and murder of Jews. The Holocaust was a pan-European project that unleashed and gave body and motion to a latent anti-Semitism that was already there, and had been there for centuries.

The shock of what had happened in the death camps made the survivability of the Jewish people an open question, and so the weakened British, in the waning days of their long empire, worked with the newly established United Nations to create a Jewish homeland. This place would be called Israel after the long tradition of the Jewish people in the land of the Bible which was, as the result of World War I, under British control.

The Arab majority in the region rejected the formation of this new nation from the start. Fighting over land began shortly after the war in Europe ended, but tough Holocaust survivors, Jewish fighters from Europe who resisted the Nazis, the Jews who still lived in the area, and Jews from other countries around the world flooded into the region to fight for the new Jewish homeland. In 1948, the nation of Israel was formally recognized. The Holocaust had brought into being the new incarnation of the Jewish nation in the land of the Torah.

To many, Israel was a miracle after the horrific disaster of the Holocaust. Many of the Arabs who lived in the land they referred to as Palestine, fled and began a long campaign of warfare and terror against the Jewish state. The United States recognized the new Jewish nation and became a staunch ally and arms supplier, but the creation of Israel plunged the Middle East into years of conflict and warfare that many subsequent US Presidents have tried to resolve without success.

Around the same time, Britain completed its withdrawal from India after nearly a century of colonial rule. In the aftermath, the majority Hindu population and the millions-strong Muslim population began to murder each other in staggering numbers. The country was partitioned, with the Muslims pushed east and west and the Hindus retaining most of India. Those eastern and western territories became the nations of

Pakistan and Bangladesh. The partitioning claimed up to two million lives in riots and counter riots between the warring factions. India remained a nation of celestial chaos for many decades, but years of British rule had planted the seeds of democracy which in time has grown to be the world's most populated democratic nation. Remarkably, the United States, the modern world's oldest democracy, and India, the largest, have never faced military hostilities against each other.

World War II brought the Japanese occupation of China to an end, and weakened the British hold over any part of the mainland. But the end of the war plunged China into a long and deadly civil war between the communist forces, led by a peasant named Mao Zedong, and the republican forces led by General Chiang Kai-shek. The Chinese Civil War was a horrendous affair that claimed millions of Chinese lives. In the end, the communist forces won in 1949 on the mainland, and the Nationalist forces were forced to retreat to the island of Taiwan, where they remain to this day.

The victorious Chairman Mao, like Stalin, tried to consolidate and modernize China in the same way Stalin had; by force and terror. Neither man had any checks on their power and so ruled by whim and decree. Mao's plans were responsible for mass starvation and further hideous atrocities carried out in a country that had not known order or unity in modern living memory. China, under Mao, lost more people than China under the Japanese. When Mao died in 1978, his successors began the laborious process of opening up the Chinese economy without changing the Chinese political body. The China of today is the result.

By 1950, the midpoint of the 20th century, the world had an unstable but functional international governing framework in the United Nations. A Jewish homeland rose in the Middle East, the Soviets developed their own nuclear weapons, China grew into a formidable communist power, and India was a chaotic, but democratic, free state. Germany and Japan were stripped of any military power of their own and instead housed American military forces, and so were free to focus on rebuilding and economic development. At this time, the United States was responsible for one half of the entire world's economic output.

The conditions that would define rest of the 20th century were in place after a war-torn and murderous first half drew to a violent conclusion. For the United States, and the rest of the world, the difference between the balance of powers in 1850 and 1950 was enormous.

However, the United States was about to discover that being the world's leading national power included as many responsibilities and limitations as it had rights and privileges.

The atomic burst over Hiroshima on August 6, 1945 signaled the end of the war and the beginning of US dominance

SECTION 8: CALCULATIONS

US General Douglas McArthur observes the Inchon Landing in Korea

"But once war is forced upon us, there is no other alternative than to apply every available means to bring it to a swift end. War's very object is victory, not prolonged indecision. In war there is no substitute for victory." — General Douglas McArthur

"For this is what America is all about: It is the uncrossed desert and the unclimbed ridge. It is the star that is not reached and the harvest that is sleeping in the unplowed ground." — President Lyndon Johnson

"We have also come to this hallowed spot to remind America of the fierce urgency of Now. This is no time to engage in the luxury of cooling off or to take the tranquilizing drug of gradualism. Now is the time to make real the promises of democracy."
— Martin Luther King

At the end of the Second World War, Europe lay in ruins, financially and spiritually exhausted. Asia was in the same condition; Japan was ruined, and China had entered a new phase of brutality. Soviet Russia was triumphant in the war but lost twenty-six million of its citizens. The Middle East was still mostly tribal, but it was about to experience a fantastic boom in wealth which would not bring widespread prosperity, but prolong and intensify the conflicts between its many warring factions. The British Empire was a tattered remnant of its former self, and the once dominant entity was shrinking into an island nation once again.

Only the United States remained unaffected economically and materially after the war. The realization of Manifest Destiny had made the country safe in its North American fortress, and both the population and economic growth of the period were riding on waves of fantastic inventions that remade human life. The prosperity brought by that economic boom allowed for the contemplation of the rights and privileges of American citizens in a way that no one would have considered one hundred years back. The country was economically strong and culturally confident.

But the US would experience what other winners had come to know; getting to the top and staying on the top are different skill sets, and being in charge comes with enormous costs. Success is a terrible teacher, and an internationally successful United States was going to be quite different from the surging and striving United States that defined the period between 1776 and 1945. The US was about to learn the limits, both external and self-imposed, to its enormous power.

COLD WAR

Few of the poisonous fruits of World War I were quite as costly to the world and the United States as the Russian Revolution that brought about the Soviet Union. The USSR, which stands for Union of Soviet Socialist Republics, stood in stark contrast to the United States, which practiced a governmental democracy which included free markets and managed capitalism. These two behemoths were bound to come into conflict. Once the Soviets mastered the nuclear bomb, which they did in 1949, a war between the two antagonistic countries became a potentially existential crisis for humanity. Avoiding a nuclear missile exchange was the preeminent priority. The war avoiding doctrine of MAD, Mutually Assured Destruction, was developed at this time.

The Soviet economic system was based on the theories put forward by a German named Karl Marx who thought that economies should be managed by governmental central planning. His ideas had been published in several books including one titled *The Communist Manifesto*. In theory, the state and its economies existed for the good of the lower classes of people, called the proletariat, but in practice, the Soviet system had some distinct flaws, such as regular shortages of necessities the lower classes needed to buy, like food, an entrenched party driven by a privileged political class, and a heavy-handed state security system that operated labor camps in the eastern wilderness where dissenters would be sent to be punished. All orthodox communist countries have developed an oddly monarchal ruling class and if a dictator had sons, they would often be groomed for top positions. Mercifully, Stalin in Soviet Russia and Mao in communist China had no sons to inherit their power.

Over hundreds of years, the Russians managed to conquer many other countries and claimed millions of square miles as part of their territory, and so by the time the Soviets formed a government and took control of new lands in the aftermath of WWII, the Soviet Union covered a similar "sea to shining sea," as the United States except those seas were the Baltic to the west and the Pacific to the east, with the Arctic Ocean to the north. The Soviets after WWII controlled a sixth of the total landmass of the earth, but unlike the United States, which shared a border with two countries, the Soviets had borders with eleven countries, many of which were hostile. The Soviets never enjoyed geographic or strategic security like the United States, and that was made evident when the Germans and their allies invaded the Soviet Union in June of 1941. The long years of fighting and massive frontlines of the Soviet/Nazi military conflict are considered to be the largest mechanized battlefront of the 20th century, and possibly the most brutal battlefront in the history of human warfare. This experience was seared into the Soviet mind, and would motivate them for the decades to follow. What Westerners call World War II, they call The Great Patriotic War, placing the Soviet struggle at its center.

After the war, the bloodied but victorious Soviets claimed and held much of the territory their army invaded, including most of Eastern Europe, among other lands to the south and west. They intended to have client states that would act as a buffer between the Russian heartland and any invaders. The Soviets developed nuclear weapons soon after the United States, in part due to espionage. They quickly developed the means to deliver warheads to the West as well; Soviet aviation was very advanced.

And so it was this country, a nation that had lost millions of people and still not sued for peace with the Nazis, a nation that controlled a sixth of the earth's landmass, a people who could develop atomic weapons and the means to deliver them, and a country that had leadership unconcerned about the next election, that the United States faced in the years following WWII. The Soviets were poised on the edge of Western Europe and clearly, the French and British would not be able to stop them if they pressed west. Only the United States could do it, and this reality linked the US with Europe in a way that no period in the past had managed. Previously, the US would pull back after a war, but not this time.

The United Kingdom, greatly diminished after the war and decline of its empire, was perched furthest west in Europe, and was also very aware of the Soviet menace that followed on the heels of the Nazi menace. Keeping the Americans engaged in Europe was now a pressing British priority. In 1946, the former British Prime Minister Winston Churchill travelled to the United States to advocate for the "special relationship" between itself and its former colonies in order to keep the Soviets and their communist states at bay. Churchill spoke at Westminster College in Fulton, Missouri while President Truman sat behind him and listened intently. The plucky wartime hero warned that an "*iron curtain*" had descended in Eastern Europe and that the Soviets were looking for weakness from the Western powers.

Churchill's speech marks the beginning of the Cold War between the US and its allies on one side, and the USSR on the other. Both powers were armed with enough nuclear power to annihilate each other and pollute the atmosphere with dust and radiation for decades to come, so the pressure not to let the war turn hot was enormous. Still, a sort of war was waged on every continent in the form of proxy wars and clandestine activities such as espionage and sabotage.

In 1949, the Soviets delivered their first nuclear bomb test. The test worked. The US government knew that the Russians now had the atomic bomb. At the same time, the United States entered into a defensive security pact with most of Western Europe, called the North Atlantic Treaty Organization (NATO), that pledged that an attack on one member country would be an attack on all, and all would be required to spring to the defense. In 1955, the Soviets responded with the Warsaw Treaty Organization (WTO), which became known as the Warsaw Pact. It bound Eastern Europe into a similar co-defense arrangement with the Soviets.

From the end of World War II until the end of the Soviet Union in 1991, these two massive security organizations had the whole arsenal of modern warfare perched and ready to deploy if another war broke out in Europe. A new war in Europe never came, given the high costs, but many conflicts broke out elsewhere around the globe. In nearly every instance, Americans became involved if the Soviets did as well.

It did not take long before the first proxy war between Soviet-backed forces and Americans began. In June of 1950, the Soviet-backed communist government of North Korea launched a surprise attack on South Korea, using first and foremost giant Soviet tanks. The South Korean military could not stop these tanks or the North Korean troops following behind them. American forces stationed in Japan were put into motion. The first hot action of the larger Cold War was on.

KOREA

In May of 1945, when the Nazis officially surrendered and the war in Europe ended, the Soviets sent troops to the Far East to fight the Japanese. It was clear to the American war strategists by that time that the Soviets had no intention to leave any territory they occupied, so they requested that the Soviet forces pouring down the Korean Peninsula stop at the 38th parallel, which they did.

Three weeks later Soviet forces were met by the American military who had accepted the surrender of Japanese troops in Korea. It was in this haphazard way that the 38th parallel became the border between one people in two hostile nations. Technically, Korea was free in that it was no longer occupied by the Japanese or the Chinese, but in reality, a communist government had been stood up in the Soviet-occupied zone to the north, led by Kim Il-sung. A democratically elected government was set up in the south, resulting in the Republic of Korea (ROK). At that point, both Soviet and American military forces withdrew from the peninsula leaving behind two hostile Koreas. The 38th parallel was now a border for two diametrically opposed methods of governance with one ethnically identical people. In many instances, Koreans had family members on opposite sides of the border.

North Korean Premier Kim Il-sung in 1950

Kim Il-sung consulted with both Stalin and Mao, the new leader of the communists in China, before he launched an attack on South Korea. At the crack of dawn on Sunday June 25, 1950, North Korean forces crossed the 38th parallel. Kim Il-sung rightfully thought that the members of the army of the Republic of Korea would not be at their post after a typical Saturday night. North Korean troops, backed by Soviet T-34 tanks, crossed the line of demarcation after a shelling barrage and the war was on. The ROK army folded quickly and Seoul, its capital, fell to the communists.

The North Korean forces ran down the peninsula rapidly, while American forces in Japan scrambled to respond. When deciding what to do, President Truman weighed several factors. First and foremost, he feared triggering a wider war with the Soviets that might spill into the tense European theater, where so many wars had been fought before. Second, he had the Chinese to consider; North Korea shared a long border with the sympathetic communists. Finally, he faced a much-dwindled American military, and an American public with no appetite for the enormous national sacrifice required for yet another worldwide military conflict. But, if he did nothing and Korea fell, Japan would be isolated. In the new world in which the United States was the global counterweight to the communist mega-powers, allowing an ally to fall or be surrounded was unacceptable.

And so it was decided. The United States would fight, but within limits. For the first time in American history, a legal basis for war was sought from a source other than Congress. The US delegation to the newly formed United Nations pushed for and received Resolution 83, which authorized member nations to defend the Republic of Korea. Truman ordered American military commanders to lend aid to the South.

The initial response was a disaster; many lightly-armed American soldiers died or were taken prisoner upon their first contact with the North Koreans and their Soviet super tanks. The Americans were pushed to the very tip of the Korean peninsula and were in danger of being overrun. General Douglas MacArthur engineered an amphibious landing above the North Korean forces at Inchon, which allowed the allies to cut North Korean supply lines, and finally, with the help of overwhelming US airpower, the tide of the battle began to turn. The North Korean forces were pushed back above the 38th parallel, in poor shape and with a fraction of the troops or tanks with which they began.

Here, we come to a great hinge of history so common to the American experience. War had defined the country in so many ways: internal wars, wars with neighbors, wars in Europe, and wars around the world. The United States had prevailed in all of these conflicts. But now, President Truman, the same man who had decided to drop nuclear bombs on Japan just a few years earlier, was looking at the possibility of a land war in Asia with poorly defined combatants and no clear path to victory. The rewards were scanty, but the risks were real enough; the smaller conflict in Korea could spark a larger conflict with the nuclear-armed Soviets.

These diplomatic issues were not the concerns of General MacArthur, who was a military man charged with winning battles and wars. MacArthur demanded that the North Koreans surrender, and when that was not forthcoming, he requested permission to press into China over the Yalu River to disrupt the staging grounds for future attacks.

At this point, the defeated North Koreans looked to the Chinese for help, and they received it. Chinese soldiers joined the fight out-of-uniform and moved into Korea under cover of darkness. It did not take long for the allied forces, primarily the Americans, to discover that they were actually fighting the Chinese, so General MacArthur organized a plan to win that entailed seeking a total victory over China, not just the North Koreans. To win, MacArthur wanted to "unchain the lightning" and use tactical nuclear weapons against Chinese bases in Manchuria. And further, MacArthur thought that the decision to use nuclear weapons should be that of a General in the field rather than the president.

President Truman was being pressured to normalize the use of nuclear weapons against a new enemy, but this he would not do even though hundreds of thousands of Chinese soldiers shifted the balance of power on the ground. The US and UN forces were pushed back from the Yalu River in a series of tactical defeats. When MacArthur protested that politics had supplanted military strategy, Truman fired him.

The push back from the Chinese border to the 38th parallel came at enormous American expense in blood, but Truman did not want a proxy war in Korea turning into a massive land battle with a communist country allied with the Russians. Containing the conflict and limiting the possibility of a nuclear exchange between rival powers was a driving priority for President Truman. This was a new development in American military history and showed the world the limit to American willingness to use its now-dominant military power. These limits would not be the last the country would face.

Around the 38th parallel, the war devolved into a stalemate. Chinese and North Korean troops took heavy losses when the US and its allied powers brought massive conventional firepower to the field; artillery and airpower blunted the numerical advantages of the Chinese. In 1951, armistice talks began, but Truman would not be able to see them through. World War II hero General Dwight Eisenhower took office as the President in 1952, and while heavy shelling and intense fighting continued, peace talks carried on through that year and into the next, until a complete armistice was reached and signed in July of 1953.

Finally, the 38th parallel fell quiet. The war had lasted three years, and yet the borders between North and South Korea, between communist and non-communist, remained the same. The North did not achieve its strategic goals and the South had survived. Some 37,000 American soldiers died to secure South Korea, and yet their victory did not end in an enemy surrender, which had been the American way of war since the Continental Army accepted British surrender at Yorktown in 1781. Nuclear weapons and high-power confrontations were driving the United States into limited wars and alliances in the way European powers had once been forced to manage their affairs.

This new position in the world put the United States at the center but did not allow the country to fully command global outcomes. As had happened to so many powerful nations that came before, the surging and confident United States was now reaching its limits.

Great power, it seems, came with many boundaries and responsibilities.

THE BOOMERS AND THE EMPIRE OF RIGHTS

While the United States stood triumphant at the end of the Second World War, the country was no more in control of its culture than any other time. In the fifties, the massive and transformative cultural conflicts to come were all in their formative stages. The decade is now associated with static conformity, but it was a busy decade in which a general optimism about the future began to manifest.

The most important of these changes was the "Baby Boom" that followed the end of World War II. Through the high-watermark of the Baby Boom, a child was born every seven seconds in the United States. The naming of any generation is often the work of journalists and writers reporting on the findings within demographic reports and the social sciences. The rough boundaries of the Baby Boom generation, later referred to simply as the Boomers, are those born between 1946 and 1964. This generation can be divided further into two groups: the 38 million boomers born between 1946 and 1955 that came of age during the Vietnam War, and the trailing 38 million who were born from 1956 to 1964 that came of age during the malaise period of the 1970s.

The boom in babies was repeated in many countries throughout the world including China, which encouraged the formation of a large family at the time. In most countries, the government didn't have a child policy, and so the boom was the product of individual choices. Many of these choices were made by returning soldiers who had put off marriage and children because of war, or because of the Great Depression that had preceded the war. American cities were sprawling into the suburbs, expanding to accommodate wider roads and larger homes more conducive to larger families. The American government provided the GI Bill, which was an initiative that paid a returning soldier's tuition if he or she wanted to go to college. Many soldiers took advantage of this proposition and university enrollment dramatically increased. Pent-up demand made for a booming retail market, and, the Korean War notwithstanding, the relative peace around the globe gave couples a sense of confidence and optimism about the future. That kind of confidence signaled that it was safe to have more children. At the peak of the boom, the global birthrate reached 3.7 children per woman.

Even after World War II, when the American armed forces were present in dozens of countries, the United States declined to behave like an empire. The American military had mostly withdrawn from the countries that had been invaded, and even the defeated Axis powers from World War II that were still occupied by the American military weren't colonial possessions in any traditional sense. The American relationship to Europe was not mercantile as the European relationship to the colonies had been. If the country had become an empire by holding the remnant Spanish territories, and then conquered the territories that had been invaded during the World Wars, perhaps the cultural history of the country would have been much different. There would have always been a frontier out there in the world somewhere, some rebellion to put down, and that frontier would have required hardy men to defend it. The baby boom would have provided those men to the mission and the industrial power of the United States would have provisioned those men. By declining to expand past the Manifest Destiny of conquering North America, the United States instead opened a new frontier of rights for its citizens, and, in the prosperous years of the 1950s, this frontier began to rapidly expand.

Universal suffrage allowed women the right to vote, and World War II had given many women exposure to the industrial workplace. With so many men in uniform and overseas, war production fell to women who worked heavy machinery as well as traditional tasks previously performed by men. Many did not forget this experience and stayed in the workforce after the war.

The term feminism is credited to a French writer in the 1830s, but by the time the term reached the United States, it was associated with the effort to secure suffrage for women, a period later characterized as first-wave feminism. Second-wave feminism centered around women in the workplace, with a broader emphasis on their options beyond the household, and this trend accelerated in the post-war years. Several books were published that supported the second wave, including the 1963 title "The Feminine Mystic" by Betty Friedan. The book asserted that there was widespread unhappiness among American women despite their material comforts. This was, she wrote, "the problem that has no name" that was created when women lost their personal identities to the expectations of becoming wives and mothers. The solution to the problem, Freidan wrote, was for women to look beyond these roles for fulfillment, which meant they would enter the workforce in greater numbers. In the coming years, that's exactly what they did, and the expectation that women would have professional careers became the default for American women. Friedan was one of the founders of the National Organization for Women, which formed in 1966.

Concurrent with the expansion of the rights and ambitions of women was the landmark Civil Rights movement that fought for the civil liberties of black Americans across the country. After the Civil War, the still-belligerent southern states had been occupied by Federal troops, and state governments remained under federal supervision. But when this period, the Reconstruction, ended in 1876, the former Confederate states fell back under the control of the local populations, and nearly all began to pass laws that segregated the population by race. These were known as the Jim Crow laws and they were often simply obnoxious, such as the law in Montgomery, Alabama that mandated black people had to give up seats on the public buses to white people, to the democratically detrimental, such as the poll taxes and literacy tests that were meant to keep black people from voting. Collectively, Jim Crow laws were meant to segregate the population from birth to death, from the maternity ward to the cemetery. By and large, these laws were common practice across the United States, including in the US military, which was dominated by southerners and remained segregated through World War II.

President Truman ended segregation in the US military, and the Korean War was the first fought by an integrated military; there were no longer designated black fighting units set aside and given special duties. This trend towards integration was just the beginning. Since the military is under the command of the president, it could be integrated by presidential order. Integrating the thousands of other institutions, however, would take far-reaching legal action and a corresponding cultural movement to accomplish. This was the work of the Civil Rights Era, and it would remake US institutions that had little to do with the ethnic relationships in the country.

MARTIN LUTHER KING AND THE MONTGOMERY BUS BOYCOTT

The issue of slavery had been unable to find a legal or negotiated path towards abolition, and the subsequent Civil War was a horrid national disaster. Had the courts, including the Supreme Court, had a case that came before it that could have pointed to a legal remedy, or given the slaveholding states some acceptable moral and legal direction on slavery, perhaps a negotiated settlement could have been worked out. If the court had ever ruled that slavery was unconstitutional, for example, maybe the states could have come up with a payment scheme for the slaves or a path to freedom that would allow for compromise politically. The courts, however, did not take such action on any case that came before them. In the cases that did, such as *Dred Scott v. Sandford*, the legal system upheld slavery as an institution and offered no path towards abolition. War was the only alternative. Segregation, however, was resolved through legal pathways in the period after World War II when the country was optimistically looking forward and the spirit of equality found a voice. The legal system was instrumental in finding a path out of danger in this instance.

A drinking fountain on the county court house lawn in Halifax, North Carolina, 1938

Segregation and the Jim Crow laws had been tested in the courts previously and found to be constitutional. In 1890, Homer Plessy, a man who was one-eighths black, entered the whites-only rail car at a train yard in New Orleans in violation of the Separate Car Act which segregated rail cars in Louisiana under the doctrine of "separate but equal." This doctrine was a loophole that all segregated communities used to enforce segregation without violating the 14th Amendment, which states: "No State shall make or enforce any law which shall abridge the privileges or immunities of citizens of the United States; nor shall any State deprive any person of life, liberty, or property, without due process of law; nor deny to any person within its jurisdiction the equal protection of the laws." Politicians narrowly tailored segregation laws to achieve their purposes, but not trigger a constitutional violation. Plessy sued the state over the Separate Car Act on the grounds that it was unconstitutional, but he lost. He eventually appealed to the Supreme Court, which took up his case. The judge who ruled against him in Louisiana was John Ferguson, so the case reached the Supreme Court docket as *Plessy v. Ferguson*. Plessy lost in the higher court as well and this set the standard for segregation laws which proliferated afterward. The court ruled seven to one that separate but equal did not violate the 14th Amendment. The Democrat-controlled southern legislatures quickly enforced the segregation of hospitals, lobbies, railways, schools, buses, and virtually everything else.

By the Fifties, many legal scholars thought that segregation was ripe for legal testing again, and so new cases were filed that challenged the separate but equal legal doctrine. Lawyers decided that schools should be the testing ground to see whether the *Plessy* ruling would still stand.

The US legal system can't act on its own like a legislature; it can only rule on cases that are brought forward when legal actions are filed. In 1951, the Brown family in Topeka, Kansas filed a suit against the local board of education that refused to allow their daughter to go to the closest school, which was for whites. She was directed to go to the school further away that was for black children. While it was a class-action lawsuit filed on behalf of the Brown family and twelve other black families, it is referred to as *Brown v. the Board of Education of Topeka*. It was filed in federal court since the legal theory was that the school board's treatment of Brown was a violation of the 14th Amendment. They lost the case in federal court in Kansas which ruled against them on the basis of their supposed adherence to the "separate but equal" doctrine.

At this point, the Browns turned to the NAACP, the National Association for the Advancement of Colored People, to appeal the case to the Supreme Court. They were represented by a black attorney named Thurgood Marshall. Marshall was the descendant of slaves on both sides of his family and was born in 1908 in Maryland. He went to Frederick Douglass High School, and later, after much encouragement from his father, he attended Howard University to study law. Howard University was chartered in 1867, right after the end of the Civil War, to educate black clerical students. The university was named after Oliver Otis Howard, a white Union Army general. Marshall graduated from Howard in 1933 at the top of his class and began his career in Maryland representing black clients in racial discrimination cases.

Marshall had worked with the NAACP for years, so the organization brought the *Brown* case to him. The NAACP shaped and funded the case as it worked its way through the legal system. The *Brown* case was a high-stakes gambit for Marshall because if he lost, segregation would be reaffirmed by the courts and no one could know when another such case would be able to reach the high court again. However, he didn't lose; the Supreme Court ruled by an unopposed vote in May 1954 that "separate educational facilities are inherently unequal," ringing the death knell for segregated schools across the country. The case of *Plessy v. Ferguson* was specifically repudiated in the *Brown v. Board of Education* case, which called for schools to be desegregated with "all deliberate speed." However, the ruling offered no specific timeline and failed to address the many other forms of segregated life throughout the country. Nevertheless, the case proved that segregation was an unconstitutional practice that was vulnerable in the courts, and cases that made it to the Supreme Court could win.

In Montgomery, Alabama, civil rights leadership was paying attention to what was happening in Kansas. Montgomery had been the capital of the Confederacy for a short time, and the city had strict segregation ordinances that went even further than other southern cities. One of the most hated provisions was the bus seating laws which stipulated black riders would fill in from the back and white riders would fill in from the front and when the two groups met, the black riders would give way to the white riders. They shared seats until the seats ran out and then the white riders had preference. This was a law, not a practice, and violations of this law would result in arrest.

The local NAACP chapter in Montgomery was led by Edgar Daniels Nixon. He was a train car porter and therefore insulated against local job retaliation. While he lacked a formal education, he had leadership skills and was a good networker. He had a core group of supporters in Montgomery, one of whom served as the NAACP's secretary. She was a local seamstress named Rosa Parks. Also in Nixon's circle of friends was the Gray family, which included a newly minted black attorney, named Fred Gray. These three and others were trying to get black voters registered, which was difficult but not impossible, and Gray represented black defendants in court.

One of Gray's defendants was a member of the NAACP Youth Council named Claudette Colvin. Colvin went to Booker T. Washington High School and rode the bus every day. In March 1955, she was asked to give up her seat for a white passenger and she refused. She was subsequently dragged from the bus and arrested; her father contacted Gray, who represented her in court. Two charges were dropped by the court, but she was convicted of assaulting a police officer. More importantly, however, she gave Gray, Nixon, and Parks the inspiration to challenge the bus ordinances. On December 1, 1955, Rosa Parks calmly boarded a bus and was arrested for refusing to give up her seat exactly as Claudette Colvin had, and this event set the stage for the next battle in the Civil Rights era, which was a continuation of the long fight against tyranny, and for racial equality and civil liberties.

Parks was arrested on a Friday and over the weekend word went out to the black community in Montgomery that they should boycott the buses come Monday morning. The time had come to address the odious practice of racial discrimination in Montgomery transportation. On Monday, the buses were mostly empty when Gray appeared in court with Parks.

The Montgomery Improvement Association was created to maintain the boycott on the buses and rally support for the cause. Over the years factions had developed in the black community of Montgomery and so, to garner the widest possible support for the boycott, the Montgomery Improvement Association chose a leader that was new to town. This newcomer was the pastor of the Dexter Avenue Baptist Church, and his name was Martin Luther King.

Over the coming months, King made several important speeches, some of which were broadcast on radio and TV, and all of which were covered by journalists far and wide. His mastery of rhetoric launched King to national prominence. The boycott lasted over a year, but in December of 1956, the lawsuit filed by Gray referred to as *Browder v. Gayle* (Browder was another black rider and Gayle was the Mayor of Montgomery) was affirmed by the Supreme Court, and federal marshals served Gayle papers instructing him to desegregate the bus system in Montgomery. Yet another brick in the wall of segregation had been knocked out.

In the entire Civil Rights era, there was no one legal case that could settle the issue of segregation and racial discrimination against black people, since cases are disputes between specific parties and therefore must apply specific and local legal remedies. To address the historical injustices of slavery would require the political system, as well as the legal system. Political action was coming, but in the Fifties, the cultural case for ending discrimination against black Americans finally breached the national conscience and became a sort of Manifest Destiny of rights. The movement had the effect of finally formally criminalizing the horrendous practice of lynching, which led to its eventual end.

In the purest sense of the word, lynching has nothing to do with ethnicity or race and refers to the practice of punishment without any sort of due process. Many kinds of people, nearly all men, were subjected to mob justice, but in practice, nearly all lynchings were in the former Confederate states and the overwhelming majority of the victims were black men accused of a variety of crimes. These were ugly public affairs in which a black man would be paraded in public with a noose around his neck, and then hung from a tree or post, and the body burned or shot and left in place for a time. Sometimes these murders were committed in coordination with law enforcement and sometimes not. There were many cases in which white Sheriffs used deadly force to protect black defendants, but there were also paramilitary forces, such as the Ku Klux Klan, that used deadly force and lynching to deny black defendants any due process. The purpose of denying due process was to humiliate and terrorize the black population and deliver a separate tier of unequal justice. The exact number is unknown, but modern estimates suggest that at least 4,000 black Americans were murdered in the period between the end of the Civil War and the Civil Rights Movement.

All levels of government perpetuated and participated in the abuse of black Americans. The attorney for the Montgomery Improvement Association, Fred Gray, later represented men who had been the subjects of the Tuskegee Syphilis Study, which was a poorly designed effort to study what untreated syphilis did to black men. This study was done under the supervision of a federal agency called the Public Health Service, and for fifty years, hundreds of men were enrolled in the study under false pretenses. Lists detailing these men were circulated to other health services, including local doctors, with the instructions *not* to treat them for syphilis so that the study could determine the path of the disease all the way to death. It wasn't until Peter Buxton, an employee whose parents had fled the Nazis in Europe, heard about the study and questioned its ethics that the program was stopped and even then, Buxton had to turn documents over to the press in order to pressure the government to act. Fred Gray represented the survivors until a settlement was reached. In 1996, President Bill Clinton issued a formal apology.

THE END OF THE BRITISH EMPIRE

The world wars had squandered the lives of millions of European men, including nearly a million from the United Kingdom in just the first war. This loss of manpower hurt the British Empire. The British had adopted a strategy of colonization similar to the Romans and left the cultures of colonized nations intact. This had worked for a time, but in the wake of World War II, the importance of national identity took hold, and no nation was going to accept rule from London or answer to a British monarch. By 1945, the British were in no position to impose their authority by force.

And so, the sun set on the British Empire after World War II, starting with the loss of India and other territories around the globe. But still, the old imperial impulse was present in British politics and when the British entered negotiations with Egypt over control of the Suez Canal, which linked the Mediterranean with the Indian Ocean, they came into conflict with the prototypical new nationalists in Cairo, Egypt who were led by Gamal Nassar.

The Egypt of the Bible had been a great power with Pharaohs ruling the land under royal authority and they left behind many spectacular monuments. For a time, the area was under the control of the Romans. Many other powers occupied Egypt, including the French, and then after World War I, the British. In 1869, the Suez Canal was created with European help and this strategic waterway, which cut through Egyptian territory, gave the Egyptians real leverage in the region for the first time in centuries. World War II and its aftermath gave Egypt a new sense of national pride and Nassar was a nationalist to the core. He sensed weakness in the British, and strength in the newly created nation of Israel and he wanted to both drive the British out and isolate the nascent Jewish state. To that end, in 1954 he ordered all British troops to leave the Canal Zone within twenty months, and in response, after a breakdown in negotiations, the British coordinated an invasion with the aid of the Israelis and the French. The British and French learned the hard way just how much the world had changed; after a tough and costly invasion, they found themselves isolated from nearly every other nation, including the United States. The United States had been selling oil to the British as well as propping up the pound sterling, Britain's national currency, and President Eisenhower threatened to stop American aid unless the British withdrew their forces.

And so, the same military that had burned Washington and the Presidential Mansion in 1814 and ruled over India and sent hundreds of thousands of men into battle in both World Wars withdrew their reduced forces from the Suez region on the order of its former colonial possession. What this move signaled could not have been any clearer.

In the coming years, the British granted independence to nearly all of its remaining territories without warfare. The formal ceremonies were attended by smiling British officials, including the new Queen, Elizabeth II, who gave formal sanction and good wishes to the departing territories. The British maintained a trade association, called the Commonwealth, and participated in a larger trade association called the European Union until recently. Trade unions, however, are not colonial arrangements. In the 1950s and the 1960s, the sun set on the British Empire as it had set on the Spanish Empire. The long European era of conquest which began with Columbus was over.

TELEVISION AND CELEBRITY

Thomas Edison and many other inventors had discovered how to capture image and sound in a durable medium that could be enjoyed and distributed to the American people. This new form of media led to the rise of famous actors and musicians, whose popularity went far beyond what was possible when these artists had to be experienced in person. The movies made celebrities out of certain actors and even the people who made the movies, but the invention of television drove the popularity of show business to new and dizzying heights.

Television evolved from a complex technical history; early versions of images moving on a glass screen were available in the 1920s, but the medium exploded into widespread use in the 1950s when the devices could be purchased for the home and networks to broadcast the content were established nationwide. Previously, radio networks established ways to communicate sound waves across the nation. President Roosevelt utilized the radio to reach the nation in his own voice during the Depression, and later during the war. Television extended that reach to include visuals, which altered the dynamic between citizens and political leadership. Moving images also pushed the public awareness and adulation of actors and musicians to new heights as shows, plays, and musical events came to dominate the television screen which was right in the home where all family members could see it, day and night.

It is difficult to conceive of any previous generation becoming so involved with people they had only experienced via the media. The colonial people had the dirty work of surviving to do, and the frontier generations were busy walking west, defending themselves, and eking out a living. Industrialization and the ever-expanding media gave people both the time and the means to become involved in the lives of actors, whose life stories were filtered and manipulated by the press. Television took these trends and normalized them in a variety of ways, eventually extending them into the political realm.

Early television programs became events that were watched from the home but experienced simultaneously around the country. *The Ed Sullivan Show* was one such an event.

Ed Sullivan worked in media his entire life. He was born in New York in 1901 and began to work as a newspaper reporter at a young age. In the years around World War II, he moved into radio, and, by 1948, was positioned nicely for the transition to television. By the time his show peaked in popularity, it was a destination all popular entertainers wanted to reach, including musicians.

Elvis Presley promoting his film Jailhouse Rock in 1957

One such musician that appeared on the Ed Sullivan Show in 1956 was Elvis Presley. Presley had grown up poor in Mississippi and spent a portion of his youth around black musicians who played blues and other primarily black musical forms, but he also heard a great deal of traditional country music. He eventually fused these forms into his own brand of rock n' roll music which, combined with his good looks and distinct dancing style, was uniquely popular. He found his way onto the radio, then into the newspapers, then into a thriving touring business, and even into the movies. His television appearance took his already thriving career to new and unprecedented heights. Interest in Elvis *the person* surpassed Elvis *the artist* and he reached a cult-like status, which was unique in the American experience. Millions of young girls found him to be an irresistible beacon, and black music performed by a white musician took black music to places it otherwise wouldn't have been. Even when Elvis was drafted and entered the US Army, his celebrity status didn't wane. All of this, of course, had a substantial effect on Elvis, a poor kid from Mississippi, since he was suddenly granted wealth and fame, and the power that came with those things. He grew more and more isolated and eccentric over time, and died of a drug overdose in his mansion in 1977 at the age of 42.

Another poor kid who reached the dizzying heights of celebrity was Marilyn Monroe. Elvis Presley kept his actual name his entire short life, but Marilyn Monroe was born Norma Jeane Mortenson in 1926. She was a native of Los Angeles, the center of movie production and later television production. Her turbulent early life was spent moving from home to home across Southern California. The identity of her father is unknown, and her mother had intermittent custody of Norma Jeane through her early years. Norma married and divorced in her teens, and after a while, she turned her good looks into work as a model. She was a young model in the movie capital of the world, and eventually plain Norma Jean became glamorous Marilyn Monroe. Marilyn bleached her brown hair blond and began to land acting jobs in film and television shows. She was successful as an actress, but also became known as a sex symbol. Her public perception was not based on her artistic excellence but was built on her persona as a fantasy sexual object as perceived through the media. As with Elvis, interest in her image was far greater than her as an artist, and she appeared in the press and on television as herself most often, as opposed to any fictional screen character. Her relationships and marriages were constantly in the press, as was speculation about details of her personal life. She was married to a famous sports star, a bookish playwright, and later in her life, was linked in the press to both President John F. Kennedy and his younger brother Robert. Like Elvis, Monroe died of a drug overdose at age 36 in August of 1962.

JFK

In May of 1962, just three months before her death, Marilyn Monroe traveled to New York to sing 'Happy Birthday' to President Kennedy, who was turning 45. The event was a Democratic fundraiser held at Madison Square Garden with over 15,000 people in attendance and more than 40 million Americans watching the event on TV. Monroe gave a sultry rendition of Happy Birthday to Kennedy while wearing a dress that concealed very little, and then a giant birthday cake was wheeled on to the stage. It was a made-for-TV event, but Monroe's ability to constantly hold, shock, and amaze people served the new president's glamorous image. Television was indeed very good for John F. Kennedy.

John Kennedy, or JFK as he later came to be known, was a departure from the model of previous presidents. He was far younger than any previous president and was sworn into office at the age of 43. He took over from the fatherly hero, General Dwight Eisenhower, who had taken over from the spectacle-wearing tough guy Harry Truman, who had taken over from the patrician and secretly disabled Franklin Roosevelt. Kennedy was a departure from the 20th century norm and his family arrived at politics with a substantial mystique that would only grow in depth over the coming years.

Kennedy's father had been involved in politics and he wanted his sons to reach high office. Joe Kennedy was from a wealthy family in Boston, but they were Irish Catholics and had been subjected to substantial anti-Irish and anti-Catholic sentiment over the years, which they never forgot. Joe was a natural businessman and prospered in shipbuilding and alcohol sales, with a short stint in Hollywood. He was a skilled Wall Street stock investor and an inside player who knew how to pull the levers of power.

Over time, Joe Kennedy grew to be close friends with Franklin Roosevelt, so Roosevelt appointed Kennedy to several important positions, including the American ambassador to the United Kingdom. When Kennedy made pessimistic comments about the British ability to stand up to the Nazis, his career in politics was over, but he passed down his ambitions to his sons.

Joe had nine children, and the oldest boy was Joe Kennedy Jr. Joe had hoped that Joe Jr. would enter politics, but his son was killed in 1944 during World War II as part of Operation Anvil, which was a plan to fly heavy explosive-laden aircraft into German installations. The aircraft carrying Kennedy exploded prematurely over the English Channel and he was killed instantly. Joe Kennedy Sr. then turned his attention to his next in line, young and good-looking John Kennedy.

John nearly didn't survive the war years either. Since the whole family had grown up on the waters off Boston, John Kennedy entered the Navy and was assigned duty as the commander of a small attack vessel called a PT boat. After officer training and a short time patrolling the waters off the east coast, Kennedy was transferred to the Pacific, where the PT boats were used to harass and attack Japanese shipping. In August 1943, Kennedy's boat, PT-109, was hit by a Japanese destroyer, cut in half, and sunk. Kennedy and the other survivors swam to a nearby island. In the days to follow, Kennedy swam great distances in the open ocean to reach help. For his actions, he was awarded several commendations and he became a genuine war hero.

After the war, Kennedy entered Congress as one of the House Representatives from Boston under the close supervision of his father. He was a Democrat who adhered to the standard Democratic policies of the period, which generally meant a preference towards expanding governmental benefits and supporting the formation of unions. In 1953, Kennedy became the junior senator from Massachusetts; Joe Kennedy had him right where he wanted him, positioned for a run at the presidency in 1960.

The presidential contest in 1960 pitted the glamorous Kennedy against the Republican Richard Nixon, who was quite the opposite of Kennedy. Like Kennedy, Nixon had served in the Pacific during World War II and entered Congress in 1947, but his commonalities with Kennedy stopped there. Kennedy was from a wealthy family in Boston; Nixon was from a poor family in California. Kennedy was Catholic; Nixon was a Protestant. Kennedy was a drinker; Nixon was not. Kennedy went to Harvard; Nixon went to Whittier College. Nixon married a high school teacher he met at a local theater while Kennedy married Jackie Bouvier, the daughter of a Wall Street broker and wealthy socialite. Kennedy left the House of Representatives to become a senator, as did Nixon, but Kennedy stayed in the Senate while Nixon became Eisenhower's dutiful vice president. One of Nixon's daughters married one of Eisenhower's grandsons. These two men, John Kennedy and Richard Nixon, were different in stature and tenor; Kennedy was all rhetorical flourish while Nixon was folksy and practical.

So, the contest in 1960 was a distinct choice between two very different candidates, and for the first time, the presidential debates were held on television, and it was on this platform where Kennedy trounced Nixon. Kennedy had what Nixon did not which was a sort of star power that Nixon could not develop no matter how many hours he was on television. The vote was still very close, but in the end, Kennedy won and became the 35th President of the United States, with Texas Senator Lyndon Johnson as his vice president.

CUBA

JFK entered office in the middle of a cold but deadly conflict between the United States and the Soviet Union. A war could be triggered between the two nations at any moment based on their differing views about the best way to organize a society. Competing visions about society and conflicts over resources drove many military confrontations throughout US history, from the desire to be free of British rule to the eradication of the land's native people. The Soviets had a competing political vision and, as an acquisitive and ambitious power, they were willing to take risks without concern for possible casualties.

Everyone understood that a direct war between the two nations would not be a clash between competing militaries that was isolated from civilian populations. Aerial bombardment of civilians had been the goal, the point, and the policy of both countries during World War II, so naturally military tacticians on both sides viewed civilian populations to be legitimate targets for irreversible nuclear bombardment. Both sides had nuclear missiles and both wanted to place their arsenals as close as possible to the other so that warheads could be launched at a moment's notice and over at the target in the shortest possible time.

It was in this environment that President Kennedy received intelligence that the Soviets had managed to position nuclear-tipped missiles in Cuba, just 90 miles south of the United States mainland.

Cuba had been a very early Spanish possession, and it was from Cuba that Hernán Cortéz departed to conquer Mexico in 1519. The US forced the Spanish out of Cuba in 1898. Cuba became its own nation under the influence of the United States, but the nation eventually entered a revolutionary phase led by a communist adherent named Fidel Castro. Rather than invade directly, the United States employed covert means to rid the island of Castro and used exiled Cuban paramilitary groups as a ground fighting force. These efforts failed, but Castro still feared he would be overthrown by the Americans and so he turned to the Soviets for help, agreeing to allow Soviet military bombers and missiles to be based on the island in exchange for military protection.

It did not take long for the Americans to find out. Thousands of Cubans in Miami spoke to their relatives on the island, and they reported seeing trucks pulling long cylindrical objects through the small towns. Spy planes were sent up to take reconnaissance photos, which confirmed that Soviet missiles and attack bombers were on the island.

Kennedy weighed his options. He could invade directly, as his predecessors surely would have done, or he could stop short of war. On October 22, 1962, he gave a televised address: *"To halt this offensive buildup, a strict quarantine on all offensive military equipment under shipment to Cuba is being initiated. All ships of any kind bound for Cuba, from whatever nation or port, will, if found to contain cargoes of offensive weapons, be turned back."*

In the following two weeks, the Americans and Soviets exchanged angry cables while the American military prepared for the possibility of nuclear war, should the Soviet Union strike to counter an American invasion of Cuba. Kennedy did not keep these plans and considerations secret from his Soviet counterparts.

Eventually, after some very close calls between US and Soviet ships and aircraft, the Soviets agreed to withdraw their missiles from Cuba and the United States forswore an invasion of the island. So, Cuba would not be a forward operating base for the Soviets, but it would remain a poor communist nation right off the American state of Florida long after the Soviet Union ceased to exist some 30 years later.

An American Navy SP-2H Neptune aircraft flies over a Soviet freighter in October 1962

ASSASSINATION

John Kennedy became the president just as media was coming to dominate the American mind. He was the first celebrity president in that sense. As such, it's difficult to evaluate the man separate from his image, and his violent and public death added to the legend of the Kennedy years put forward by his widow and others as being Camelot, the idyllic kingdom of Arthurian myth.

Kennedy's war record and heroism are not in dispute; he was brave. He was a patriot and in his inaugural address, he called his fellow citizens to love and serve the nation. His short speech includes this passage:

"Let the word go forth from this time and place, to friend and foe alike, that the torch has been passed to a new generation of Americans—born in this century, tempered by war, disciplined by a hard and bitter peace, proud of our ancient heritage—and unwilling to witness or permit the slow undoing of those human rights to which this nation has always been committed, and to which we are committed today at home and around the world. And so, my fellow Americans: ask not what your country can do for you—ask what you can do for your country."

By 1963, Kennedy turned his attention to his reelection campaign. Despite having a vice president from Texas, he performed poorly in the state in 1960, and so a trip was planned to campaign for the 1964 vote. By that time, the Democrats faced an electorate in the South that was growing more conservative than other elements in the party.

On Thursday, November 21st, Kennedy arrived in Texas and made a series of speeches in San Antonio and Houston. His itinerary would take him to Dallas, then to Austin, after which he was scheduled to spend the weekend with his vice president at Johnson's ranch. On Friday November 22ND, Kennedy made a speech in Fort Worth and then flew aboard Air Force One the short distance to Dallas, where he was to participate in a parade and make a lunchtime speech. The weather was clear, and so it was decided that the limousine he was to travel in would not have its bubble-top installed. Kennedy rode in a 1961 Lincoln limousine with Texas Governor John Connelly sitting in front of him and his wife at his side.

The parade route had been publicly announced, and so everyone knew which roads the motorcade would travel. Lee Harvey Oswald likely learned that the President would pass by the building where he worked by reading about it in the local newspaper.

Oswald was a troubled man who defected to the Soviet Union in 1959 but returned to the United States a few years later. His father died a month before he was born, and his early life had been chaotic. He lived with his mother and sometimes with his half-brother, whom he admired. Oswald had been in the US Marines, where he became a qualified marksman despite twice being court-martialed over weapons violations. After a short period, he was released from the Marines early and defected to the Soviet Union, where he married a Soviet girl, and after a short time the couple returned to the United States. The Soviets knew him to be unstable.

In early 1963, Oswald traveled to several places including New Orleans and Mexico City, and sought to return to the Soviet Union but they were not interested in his return. The FBI knew of him and his activities, and they questioned his wife about him on occasion. He bought a rifle via mail order under a fake name and in April 1963, shot at a conservative US General, Edwin Walker, through a window in Walker's home. The bullet nicked the window frame and missed Walker, but the bullet fragments were later examined and determined to have come from the same rifle used to assassinate President Kennedy.

In October 1963, Oswald took a job at the Texas School Book Depository as an order filler, earning minimum wage. He was working there when the newspapers published Kennedy's parade route, and that day he had a friend take him to the Depository building with a long package that he claimed contained curtain rods, though it probably contained the rifle he used to shoot at General Walker.

On Friday the 22nd of November, Oswald used book boxes to conceal his position from anyone else on the 6th floor of the Depository building. He had a rifle, a concealed position in an elevated space, and the President was going to drive right passed him. Oswald's abortive attempts to be a man of importance were about to reverse themselves. Infamy was his to claim. At 12:30, the motorcade passed by the Depository building, and Oswald fired three shots in quick succession. Two of those shots hit the President, with the second hitting Kennedy in the back of the head. Blood, bone, and brain splattered his wife sitting next to him and others in the car. The last shot was fatal.

At 1:00 PM, John Kennedy was declared dead at Parkland Hospital. His body was put in a casket and loaded onto Air Force One. At around 2:30, Kennedy's vice president, Lyndon Johnson, was sworn in as president before leaving Texas for the capital. Kennedy's wife Jacqueline stood next to him still wearing the blood-splattered Chanel suit from earlier in the day.

What happened next was an odd and unfortunate twist of events that are still confounding. The next morning, Saturday the 23rd, as Oswald was being moved from the Dallas Police headquarters to the county jail, he was shot at close range by a nightclub owner named Jack Ruby. Television cameras carried the event live for millions of Americans to witness. Oswald was declared dead at Parkland Hospital a short time afterward.

Jack Ruby was found guilty of murder in his subsequent trial. He claimed he had killed Oswald for killing Kennedy, and to save Mrs. Kennedy the pain of having to return to Dallas for a trial. President Johnson convened a commission to look into the assassination of Kennedy and the report that the committee published, called the Warren Report, determined that Oswald acted alone, as had Ruby.

In 1967, Ruby died of cancer at Parkland Hospital.

EARLY DAYS OF VIETNAM

The French Revolution put an end to the long Bourbon Dynasty in France, but it did not end the French impulse for a monarchy, or end the European appetite for colonial possessions. As such, in the late 19th Century, France acquired, via war with the Chinese, an interest in Indochina, which is the region below China that runs from Vietnam through to Thailand.

Relations between France and Vietnam were complex. French Indochina was a classic colony and was designated a *colonie d'exploitation* (a colony of economic exploitation). French rule was tough on the native population. For a time, the Nazi-backed government in France, called Vichy France, backed the Japanese who had brutally taken over China and parts of Vietnam. After World War II, the French reasserted themselves in Vietnam, and their presence inspired Vietnamese fighters under the leadership of Ho Chi Minh to resist the French with military force. Minh's fighters eventually defeated the weakened French forces in 1954 and a conference was called in Geneva to settle the fate of the country. The United States was already the dominant power in Asia by then and so participated in the conference. The country was divided into a northern and southern sphere with the idea that it would be united as one country again after a vote to be held in 1956. That vote never came and so the country slipped into a Cold War pattern similar to Korea; communist forces to the north backed by the Soviets, non-communist forces backed by the United States to the south.

The government in South Vietnam was neither popular nor effective. Its only redeeming virtue to the United States was that it was cooperative and not backed by the Soviets. In backing the South Vietnamese government, the United States had fallen into a similar pattern that had happened since in Indochina, Central

America, and in the Middle East. President Roosevelt summed up the problem succinctly in describing the strongman Anastasio Somoza in Nicaragua, who was corrupt but still backed by the United States: *"He may be a son of a bitch but he's our son of a bitch."*

Over time, the same forces that had fought the French re-formed into the Viet Cong, and they were trained and supplied by Ho Chi Minh in North Vietnam. War was creeping forward in South Vietnam with all the characteristics of modern warfare: hit and run attacks, assaults upon civilians, assassinations, torture, soldiers out of uniform, and military confrontations with no fixed battlefront.

President Eisenhower had done little to address the situation in Vietnam. Kennedy had shown no appetite for introducing American troops into the conflict, but when he was killed, President Johnson took over American involvement in Vietnam and Johnson was of the mind to get tough, using the American military to swing the balance towards the South Vietnamese. American advisors and troops swarmed into the region and the battles grew in size and intensity. Consequently, the list of American dead began to grow.

At least two things had changed, however, since the dominant performance of the Americans in World War II. First, there were no more takers for direct military conflict with the United States. All had seen what happened to the Japanese when they provoked the mighty Americans and faced them directly. But second, all had seen what had happened in Korea when the Americans had declined to throw the full weight of their power in a drive to final victory. The Americans would negotiate if the blood became too thick and further, the American public could now see firsthand the violence overseas through their televisions. The Vietnamese developed the strategy employed by others since: avoid direct conflict, harass the US military on the edges, kill a few soldiers here and there, terrorize the local population so they won't cooperate, and use the American media to swing the American public away from the war. This strategy was pioneered by the North Vietnamese in the Vietnam War. They employed classic guerrilla warfare techniques. Guerrilla is the diminutive form of the Spanish word for war which is guerra, and the Vietnamese kept their forces and attacks small with the intent to slowly wear down the Americans.

Vietnam War Protest in Washington, D.C. by Frank Wolfe, October 21, 1967

1968

By 1968, the leading edge of that demographic bump called the Baby Boomers were reaching adulthood. The Cold War was in full swing, and President Johnson had dedicated a record number of US troops to South Vietnam. Many of those troops were Baby Boomers who had been drafted and sent to the war against their will. It was also an election year. 1968 was a watershed year from start to finish as growing trends coincided with historic events in twelve meaningful and tragic months.

In January, the North Vietnamese launched a direct offensive against the forces in South Vietnam, which included the Americans stationed there. It was to coincide with the Lunar New Year celebration and was called the Tet Offensive, in reference to the festivities. Throughout the war, the North Vietnamese had developed a system of trails that ran across Vietnam which allowed them to sneak in thousands of fighters and supplies deep into the south. In January, these forces coordinated in the offensive which involved over 80,000 fighters attacking in hundreds of towns all across the country. These attacks engaged American forces, which inflicted overwhelming casualties on the North Vietnamese at substantial costs to themselves. More importantly, the Tet battle plan included attacks in Saigon, the South Vietnamese capital. Attackers hit the American Embassy, where a few Viet Cong blew a hole in the fence and rushed the building. They never gained entry to the building and were quickly killed, but the sight of the North Vietnamese at the American Embassy had a galvanizing and negative effect on the American public, which began to surmise that the war in Vietnam had no path to victory. An American photographer, Eddie Adam, captured a photo of a South Vietnamese policeman executing a Viet Cong officer with a pistol shot to the head. This shot looked remarkably like photos that had emerged of Nazis executing civilians during the Holocaust, and when it was run in US newspapers, attitudes towards the war began to turn hard and fast. A war with no front against an enemy with no uniform in defense of a nation without shared values was not one Americans could support, and not one they wanted American soldiers to die in.

By March of 1968, the first primary votes in the election were cast, and they revealed how weak President Johnson was with voters, mainly because of the war. Seeing the weakened state of the sitting president, John Kennedy's brother Robert, Joe Kennedy's third son, entered the race for the Presidency. In the meantime, students were protesting in American cities and universities and taking over school buildings and issuing lists of demands. In early American history, universities had been places for the children of the elite to learn how to govern and lead, and thus not been the location of revolutionary rioting. That had clearly changed; universities had become places where middle class kids were often turned into activists.

On April 4, Martin Luther King was assassinated in Memphis. In the years since the Montgomery Bus Boycott, King had been involved in the Civil Rights movements and had largely triumphed by virtue of his inspiring messages delivered in his distinct style. He called on his supporters to reject violence and he called on American leaders to live up to the promise made in the Constitution to treat all equally. The Civil Rights movement had succeeded wildly in King's time and culminated in the Civil Rights Act of 1964, which prohibited any form of legal discrimination in federal law which would supersede any action by the states. Racial discrimination against black citizens past that point was no longer encoded in American law. King worked towards greater economic advancement for black Americans until his death. Eventually, his assassin was caught in London trying to flee to South Africa and it was revealed to be James Earl Ray, another three-name misfit who affected the course of American history. King's death was followed by days of rioting across the United States.

In June, Robert "Bobby" Kennedy was killed by an assassin's bullet in the kitchen of a hotel in California. He had entered the Presidential race late but was gaining traction against his primary opponent Eugene McCarthy, a senator from Minnesota. Kennedy was in Indiana when King was assassinated, and he called for non-violence in response. In a sense, Robert Kennedy was far more like King and the new Democratic party than the older more conservative party of his brother John. After winning the California primary and making a short victory speech, he then took a shortcut through the kitchen of the Ambassador Hotel in Los Angeles where he was shot by Sirhan Sirhan, an Arab who opposed Kennedy's support for Israel. Kennedy died twenty-six hours later, and his death is considered to be one of the first shots in the war between the Americans and the Muslims of the Middle East.

In August of 1968, Soviet forces sent in troops and tanks to demonstrate to the youthful protestors in Czechoslovakia that a rebellion would not be tolerated. Young people in Soviet-backed countries had similar impulses to their western counterparts and had initiated the Prague Spring, which was a call for further political liberalization and freedom within their nations. The Soviets responded with 750,000 soldiers and 6,500 tanks. This show of force would become significant in later years, especially when the Soviets failed to respond accordingly in 1989.

Also in the hot summer of 1968, riots broke out in Chicago, the city where Democrats held their convention. After Johnson had bowed out and Robert Kennedy had been killed, the party chose Hubert Humphrey, Johnson's pro-war vice president, to be their nominee. Anti-war protesters descended on Chicago and battled against the Chicago police for days.

In November, Humphrey lost the election to the Republican Richard Nixon of California, who had been revived politically. After losing the 1960 election, Nixon ran in the 1962 gubernatorial race in California and lost yet again. But in 1968, he ran for president, winning the Republican nomination, and prevailing in the general election to become the 37th President of the United States.

There were many other important events in 1968. For example, American troops had massacred hundreds of Vietnamese civilians in March at Mai Lai, an event that came to light in 1969. The confusing and frontless battle with no end was bringing out the very worst in the American soldier, as it had in the battles with the western natives in North America. Public knowledge of the event further hardened the American position on the war in Vietnam.

The cultural and scientific transformation of the country carried forward at breakneck speed. A radical feminist tried to assassinate the pop artist Andy Warhol. The zombie classic *Night of the Living Dead* premiered in the United States. The Apollo program sent American astronauts out of Earth's orbit and humans got the first-ever look at the dark side of the moon. There were multiple breakthroughs in the development of computer technology. Newspapers and TV news reports kept the breaking news stories coming to a stunned American public.

But mostly in 1968, there were the wrenching birth pains of a new world about to be born.

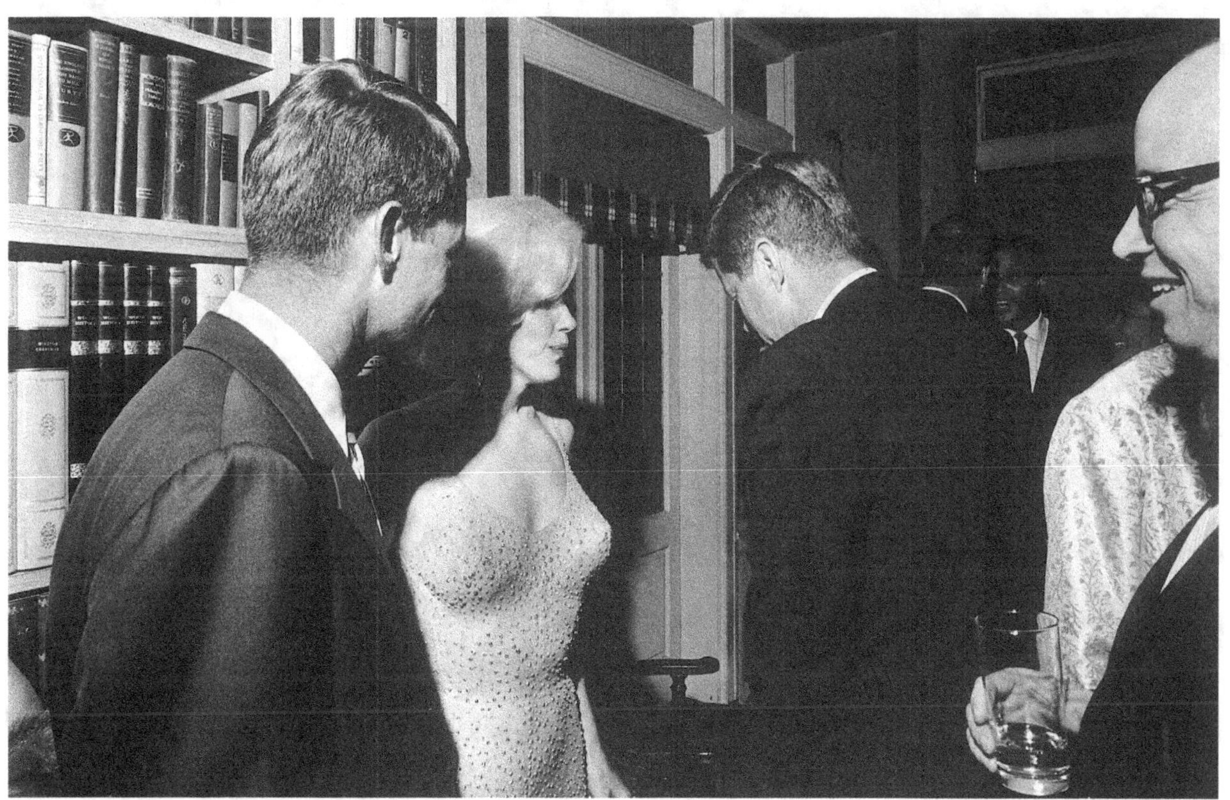

Marilyn Monroe pictured with President Kennedy and Robert Kennedy in 1962. The Kennedy years brought the mix of media and politics together

SECTION 9: CIRCUMSPECTION

"Freedom is a fragile thing and it's never more than one generation away from extinction. It is not ours by way of inheritance; it must be fought for and defended constantly by each generation, for it comes only once to a people. And those in world history who have known freedom and then lost it have never known it again." — Ronald Reagan

The United States held zenith-like power for only a brief moment. The country had become the world's dominant power in part because so many other countries entered suicidal wars, which allowed for the US to advance. The country enjoyed the benefits of defensive geography, having secured its territory early and with great ruthlessness and determination. The stalemate in Korea, the loss in Vietnam, and the profound changes to the culture and structure of society were shaking the foundations of America even as the nation progressed to greater achievements. These benchmarks would not create a greater national identity, determination, or cohesion; quite the opposite was underway. The forces pulling the country apart began to assert themselves even as global disorder continued to cede benefits to the US. The ever-shifting yin and yang of history began to weigh on the Americans while they enjoyed the fruits of 200 years of labor.

THE MOON LANDINGS

The rivalry between the United States and the implacable Soviet Union was played out in many ways and places, sometimes symbolically and sometimes in deadly real-world terms. The American idea of individual liberty conflicted with the Soviet ideal of goods distributed equally in a classless society. Because of this clash, competition between the two nations played out on every field, notably within the sciences.

The Soviets believed their society could advance the scientific frontier better and faster than the decadent West, and they meant to prove this superiority by launching an artificial satellite, a man-made object that would orbit the earth.

Since the end of WWII, each country had developed powerful rockets that could deliver bombs over long distances far better than vulnerable aircraft could. With each passing year, these rockets grew larger and their weight-carrying capacity became greater. A rocket launched from one country could be loaded with a nuclear weapon and sent to another country in a way that fundamentally could not be stopped. In theory, Washington and Moscow could both be utterly destroyed at any moment. Modern rocketry made this possible.

It was in October of 1957 that the Soviets launched an artificial satellite into orbit named Sputnik. The Sputnik satellite was a ball that weighed only 180 pounds with radio antennas poking out in several directions. After it achieved orbit, radio operators around the world heard the steady and oddly terrifying beeps it transmitted.

The American reaction to Sputnik proved to be even more historic than the satellite itself. President Eisenhower launched a series of initiatives in response to Sputnik, including the creation of the National

Aeronautics and Space Administration, forever known as NASA, which was tasked with developing an American space program. NASA seized upon its work with vigor and began to implement a series of rocket and satellite launches.

In 1961, President Kennedy asked Congress to commit NASA to put a man on the moon. In 1962, he made an address at Rice University in Houston calling space *"the new frontier"* of American exploration. *"We choose to go to the Moon in this decade and do the other things, not because they are easy, but because they are hard,"* Kennedy spoke, just fourteen months before his death in Dallas.

The Apollo program was the name of the missions meant to place an American man on the moon in less than a decade. Apollo was the Greek and Roman god of the sun. The program developed increasingly larger and more powerful rockets for its missions, aided by the leader of the Nazi rocketry program, Werner von Braun. Among others, he directed the efforts of the Apollo missions, which culminated in Apollo 11, the actual landing on the moon. On July 20, 1969, two men, Neil Armstrong and Edwin "Buzz" Aldrin, landed on the moon and planted a US flag in its dusty soil. The American reaction to the Sputnik shock was complete.

There were other American missions to the moon, but after a few years, the last mission landed and returned and no permanent American presence was established. The frontier of space was explored, but very little was found.

The high of seeing a man on the moon faded as Vietnam again became the focus of the American news and the transformation of American culture continued apace. In August of 1969, just a few weeks after the moon landing, a huge music festival was put together near Woodstock in upstate New York. It attracted tens of thousands of young adults, and their music epitomized the counterculture generation. The 'peace' of Woodstock replaced the science of the moon landings in short order. The monumental fulfillment of a human longing thousands of years old faded from the news as Americans returned to the concerns of the moment while the tumultuous 1960s drew to a close.

The decade to come would offer no respite.

WATERGATE

The 1970s was a pivotal decade in the history of the United States. The country celebrated its bicentennial in 1976 in the showdown of the turmoil of the 1960s. Two centuries of growth and development had passed since the country's founding. What had begun as an uprising against a monarch on a distant throne had turned into a military colossus with enough firepower to destroy the entire earth, powered by an economy that represented an enormous percentage of the global output. The United States had triumphed at just about everything.

And yet, the 1970s were a time of national deflation and disappointment; nearly every year brought a new set of frustrating disasters. The early years were dominated by Vietnam, where American soldiers were still dying in large numbers without a victory celebration in sight. Combat deaths had declined since the horrendous years of the late sixties, but the American news was full of reports on the ongoing fighting, and President Nixon was trying to negotiate a ceasefire that would allow US forces to withdraw short of a complete defeat. The less-than-victory standard from Korea had morphed into a less-than-defeat strategy.

Richard Nixon had triumphed in the '*annus horribilis*' of 1968 in part on a pledge to end the war in Vietnam with honor, if such a thing were possible. He tried to achieve this first and foremost through a process called 'Vietnamization,' which was the term for transferring the fight to the South Vietnamese, to win or lose on their own. The South Vietnamese forces were built up and the American forces were drawn down while Nixon's secretary of state, Henry Kissinger, began direct talks with the North Vietnamese to reach a cease-fire agreement.

Nixon ran on a message to end the war in 1972 and was reelected easily, defeating the Democratic candidate, George McGovern, who was aligned far to Nixon's left and promised to withdraw immediately from Vietnam regardless of the consequences.

Nixon's lopsided victory meant he would continue the bombing campaign in North Vietnam, and Vietnamization would continue apace. Negotiations finally reached a conclusion in January 1973 with the signing of the Paris Peace Accords. American troops quickly withdrew after many long years of combat even though it was clear that the South Vietnamese military still depended on US support. The military weakness of the South, along with the virulent opposition to the war in the United States, did not escape the notice of the communists in the North.

Nixon and his wife leaving the White House in 1974

However, by the time the last American troops left Vietnam, President Nixon was involved in a scandal that prevented the celebration of this landmark achievement. In June 1972, during the presidential campaign, five people broke into the headquarters of the Democratic National Committee at the Watergate Hotel complex. They were later caught, and their financial records lead to the Nixon campaign.

Once the press found out about the connection between the break-in and the president, the story which came to be called simply 'Watergate' was covered extensively in the media. The Democratically-controlled Congress had many members that were aligned with the new youth movement and they passionately hated Richard Nixon. Watergate gave them a reason to use their platform in Congress to press for subpoenas and public hearings. There were investigations and counter investigations involving all of the top-level leadership within the Nixon White House, including the Attorney General and Nixon's Chief Counsel. Congress appointed a Special Counsel to look further into the accusations and the Senate established a complete Watergate Committee.

The newspapers carried daily stories on the affair, which enraged Nixon to no end and possibly undermined his judgment. Leaks from inside the government were printed in the news regularly, a new journalistic trend that would grow in the coming years. All three major networks broadcast the Senate hearings day after day. For weeks, there was nothing else on television except Watergate when the hearings were in session.

In February 1973, not long after the Paris Peace Accords ended the war in Vietnam, it was revealed that the Nixon White House had a covert taping mechanism installed in the Oval Office. A federal judge ordered the tapes from White House meetings to be turned over to investigators. Nixon refused to release the tapes and tried to fire Archibald Cox, the Special Counsel hired by his own Attorney General, making the affair a constitutional issue. His own Attorney General, among others in his administration, resigned or refused to carry out the order. Nixon became increasingly isolated in the White House and his political support melted away.

Based on Nixon's refusal to cooperate and the evidence assembled, a Washington DC Grand Jury began issuing criminal indictments to Nixon Administration officials. The tapes made in Nixon's office were eventually released with an unexplained eighteen-minute gap, and the public heard a foul-mouthed Nixon on those tapes that they did not know. The tapes included recordings of Nixon speaking about the break-in during a period in which he had claimed ignorance of the event. Nixon made speeches to the public, trying to distance himself from the scandal, but to no avail. Articles of Impeachment were being drafted in the House when he abruptly resigned in August of 1974, the first American president to do so.

Vice President Gerald Ford took office and pardoned Nixon in due course for any wrongdoing, which shielded the former President from any further legal repercussions. The exact purpose of the break-in was never established.

Other members of the Nixon Administration who knew of the break-in, or denied involvement under oath, were not shielded from prosecution and their trials carried on well past the bicentennial in 1976. Those legal proceedings were overshadowed by a greater tragedy that resulted from Nixon's sudden fall; in April of 1975, the American public and the newly promoted President Gerald Ford watched in impotent silence the violent end of South Vietnam.

THE FALL OF SAIGON

The Army of the Republic of Vietnam, known as ARVN, had advanced equipment and sufficient numbers, but it relied heavily on US support to remain viable. Nixon's Vietnamization plan began to turn the fighting over to ARVN in 1970, so US combat deaths began to decline as planned. But for ARVN, the death toll shot up astronomically. Thousands of South Vietnamese died to save their country, but ARVN was just not an effective fighting force.

The South Vietnamese government was led by Nguyen Thieu, who had participated in a coup against the government in 1963 but was then democratically elected President in 1967. His leadership of the ARVN, especially in its final days, never received high marks, nor did his reputation for fighting endemic corruption. Whatever quality that was needed to organize a society to resist the communists was not transferred to his government during the long years that the United States fought in Vietnam, but the Northern leadership never wavered in its commitment to conquer the South. If the war in Vietnam was a contest of wills, the North had the greater will, possibly because of their experience fighting the French and their unwavering commitment to their goals.

Thieu opposed the Paris Peace Accords and knew that his benefactor was looking for an exit, which the Accords provided. Along with everyone else, he was aware of the anti-war protests in the United States. Once American forces left the country, ARVN faced the North alone and the strategists in the North kept the pressure on Thieu.

After 1973, the communists in North Vietnam did not need to fear US bombers and so could plan logistically without needing to hide. They only feared re-engagement by the United States. Congress helped in that regard by passing several laws which restricted the president from using the military without congressional authorization. All sides knew that authorization was not forthcoming.

When Nixon came under investigation for Watergate, the fate of South Vietnam was sealed. Congress decreased financial support for South Vietnam, and the North began to move their regular army, not guerilla fighters, along the borders and then into the country. When Nixon resigned, the green light flashed for the North; there was nothing to stop them from taking the South after decades of fighting, because under no circumstances were the Americans coming back. The treaty obligations were not a consideration.

The communist army moved south in 1975 at breakneck speed as ARVN units fled in terror or surrendered en masse. By April, they were at the gates of the southern capital, Saigon, and the only thing the US military could do was try to evacuate its people, who had been allies and would now surely be killed by the triumphant and vengeful communists.

American planes and helicopters began to ferry people to American military ships at sea as Northern forces enclosed the city. Vietnamese citizens took to the open ocean in rickety ships in a desperate effort to escape before the purges began. On April 30, in front of a TV audience around the world, the American Ambassador to Vietnam, Graham Martin, lifted off from the embassy roof in a helicopter with the Marines assigned to protect the building. The embassy grounds were covered in disappointed and fearful civilians who had nowhere else to turn. The Northern army was just a mile away and that army invaded and ransacked the embassy shortly after.

The Vietnam War was now over and the United States had lost. President Ford watched with the rest of the nation as Vietnam fell to the communists and 57,000 American deaths were rendered meaningless. It was a stunning blow to American morale and impacted how Americans saw their country in many ways. The bicentennial year that followed occurred in the shadow of Vietnam, which was long and dark.

HOSTAGE

In addition to being the bicentennial, 1976 was an election year and it offered Gerald Ford the opportunity to face American voters. He triumphed over Ronald Reagan, a former actor and the Governor of California, to secure the Republican nomination.

The Democrats nominated a new kind of Southern Democrat, unlike the fierce segregationists they had put forward in the past, or the radical northern leftist they put forward in 1972. Jimmy Carter was the former Governor of Georgia, a soft-spoken man with a lilting Southern accent that reassured the rattled American public. Ford had the power of incumbency on his side, but in 1976, televised debates were reintroduced to the contest for the first time since Kennedy and Nixon had faced each other in 1960. Carter was able to make real progress with the televised audience while Ford made some awkward errors. In the end, Carter won the 1976 contest by less than a percentage point in the popular vote, and with the bare minimum in the Electoral College.

Carter took office in January 1977. On his first day, he pardoned all who had evaded the draft during the Vietnam War via executive order in an effort to move the country forward. However, many of the events that would define Carter's term in office, and had nothing to do with Vietnam, were already in motion. A new series of setbacks and difficulties for the United States was underway by the time Carter arrived, and his reaction to them was not effective. The flashpoint of the world was moving from Southeast Asia to the Middle East.

By 1973, American oil production had declined, and, so the majority of oil used to fuel transportation and industry was imported from the Middle East, where the oil was easy to extract and abundant. However, the countries in the Middle East that exported oil had placed an embargo on selling to the United States as a result of US support of Israel. This precipitated a spike in the cost of nearly all forms of energy. Oil underwrote the production of nearly everything else, and so high oil costs resulted in rapid inflation for nearly everything Americans purchased.

Since the advent of central banking under the control of regulators, the answer to higher inflation was to raise interest rates, and so the cost of borrowing money began to rise as well. High-interest rates for borrowing, when combined with high inflation, gave Americans a new economic term to ponder: the misery index.

In 1979, President Carter made a speech directed at the American public about the economic condition of the country. This speech came to be called the "malaise" speech by the press, and the term stuck to Carter and came to describe both the condition of the country and his response to it. What unfolded next in Iran drove home the idea of American powerlessness.

The United States had long had trouble dealing with foreign tyrants that ruled their countries in manners that diverged from the ideals of Western liberalism. The *"he's our son of a bitch"* problem articulated by

Roosevelt persisted. To cooperate with or oppose these governments was not an easy issue to resolve, but the practice had been to interact with whatever government was in power in a way that promoted the American interests. How those governments came to power, or how they used that power, was secondary; the United States had to deal with the world as it was and not how it might be.

President Carter had different ideas about dealing with foreign tyrants, and as such, wavered in supporting the Shah of Iran at a critical moment when many in Iran were turning to Islamic religious leaders to purge the country of what they saw as un-Islamic Western influences. The world of Islam had been turning to the West and growing more liberal for decades, but that trend began to turn back as nationalists like Gamal Nasser took office in Egypt, and in turn, were beginning to be supplanted by new Islamist leadership unseen in the region for centuries.

United States policy had long been to support the various Middle Eastern monarchies, many of which had been put in place by the British after World War I, so that it could secure stable supplies of oil, but Iran was wracked by a series of violent public protests in 1979, and the Shah of Iran received little American support. He was then forced into exile. These events occurred with little reaction from Carter, even though Iran had been a steadfast US ally in the volatile region.

With the fall of the Shah, a new breed of firebrand religious leaders took over in Iran and converted the country into a theocracy of politically oriented imams who held a deep animus towards the United States. This Iranian Revolution was not opposed by Carter until November of 1979, when a group of alleged students overran the American Embassy in Tehran and took 52 Americans as hostages.

President Carter took military action off the table at first, declaring that the safety of the hostages prevented American retaliation. Economic sanctions were placed on Iran and the Carter Administration attempted multiple diplomatic ploys to gain the release of the hostages, but days turned to weeks and then months and the Iranians still did not cooperate. The American press covered the drama continuously as Carter barricaded himself in the White House and worked on the situation to the exclusion of all else. All the while, the election year of 1980 grew closer.

In April of 1980, while his reelection campaign was in full swing, Carter ordered a military rescue mission, called *Operation Eagle Claw*, but it failed spectacularly when two helicopters collided in the desert staging ground and the entire mission was scrubbed. The plan had been to fly US operatives to the American Embassy in Tehran to grab the hostages, bus them back to the coast, and then fly them out to ships waiting in the Persian Gulf. It failed before really getting started. Images of Iranians dancing on the wreckage of the abandoned American helicopters were broadcast around the world. The Iranians dispersed the hostages afterwards so rescue attempts became impossible.

It was with this crisis, with the failed rescue mission hanging around his neck, that Carter ran for reelection in 1980. He was running against an actor-turned-politician named Ronald Reagan who had almost stolen Ford's nomination in 1976. Reagan was a fierce conservative and a compelling speaker. He conveyed confidence and certainty, while Carter had displayed timidity in the eyes of the public.

The result was a definitive win by Reagan. The Iranians released the American hostages minutes after Reagan's inauguration in January 1981. The disastrous 1970s, a decade which began with the resignation of the president, continued with the fall of Vietnam, and ended with punishing inflation and military humiliation, was finally over.

REAGAN

Ronald Reagan was a unique figure in American history. He grew up poor in Illinois, where he attended Eureka College before moving to Hollywood during the Great Depression. While Kennedy had youthful glamour, Reagan had been an actual movie star before and during World War II. He moved into television during the 1950s and was the president of the Screen Actors Guild, later becoming the Governor of California from 1967 to 1975. He triumphed over a weakened Jimmy Carter in 1980 and was reelected by a wide margin in 1984.

Reagan governed as a conservative. He was an uncompromising foe of communism, and even though he had been the president of a union, he supported anti-union legislation. When the union for federal air traffic controllers went on strike, which violated a federal law forbidding federal employees from using strikes in negotiations, Reagan gave the strikers forty-eight hours to get back to work and fired all 11,000 of them when they didn't return.

Reagan's economic policies were oriented towards limited taxation and governmental oversight, but in a predictable pattern, limits on taxation failed to restrain the growth of the federal government, which had built its spending powers into the charter of various agencies. This transfer of political power to the various administrative agencies had been upheld by the courts and was becoming common practice. It had the benefit of protecting Congress from blame, but it meant that the gap between what the government took in through taxation and what the government spent would be covered by borrowing money through the sale of bonds or by minting more money. The theory was that economic growth would allow the government to generate more money with lower taxes on a larger economy, and while economic growth was strong in the Reagan years, taxes never kept up with spending. Debt was inevitable.

In March of 1981, barely weeks into his presidency, Reagan was shot by a deranged man trying to impress celebrity Jodie Foster. This was yet another odd crossing point between the media and the American political establishment. Reagan was rushed to the hospital to have the bullet removed from his chest, and he became the first American president to survive an assassin's bullet. His survival and smiling countenance afterwards became part of his message that it was "morning in America" again.

The Democrats controlled Congress during the Reagan presidency and had been seeking for some time to limit the executive powers to wage war without Congressional authorization. Both the Korean and Vietnam Wars had been conducted without the declaration of war that Roosevelt had sought after Pearl Harbor. In the Reagan years, there were still proxy Cold War battles around the globe, including a brutal contest in Nicaragua, and Congress had passed specific laws against the government funding or otherwise becoming involved in these conflicts.

By this time, however, significant ambiguity had crept into the federal government's definition of what constituted declaring war, conducting a war, or funding a war. The Central Intelligence Agency, created for gathering intelligence and conducting covert operations, was under the direction of the president, but was funded through Congress. Who really funded, controlled, or directed this organization and its many far-flung operations? What controls applied to a covert agency, and did it conduct operations that could be defined as a war? These questions snared the Reagan presidency in its second term and revealed how much of the federal government was being operated outside of the electoral political system.

Adjacent to Iran is the nation of Iraq. The British-installed monarch of Iraq had been deposed and over time, a brutal and psychotic general named Saddam Hussein came to power. Hussein sensed weakness in Iran's Islamic Revolutionary era, and so in 1980 he directed his forces to attack the country. This conflict devolved into a stalemate quickly and was characterized by trench warfare and masses of dead. It was an ugly war with a strong element of Islamic religious conflict, since Sunni Muslims ruled the Iraqi population and Shia Muslims ruled the Iranian population. This was a religious division with ancient hatred on both sides.

President Ronald Reagan with British Prime Minister Margaret Thather in 1984

The Iran-Iraq War was a wonderful opportunity for the United States to play both sides against the middle and as long as it continued, as deadly as it was, that was good for US interests. The government began to sell arms to the Iranians, the same people who had held Americans hostage just a few years earlier. Worse yet, elements within the executive branch of government used the proceeds from these sales to direct weapons to the Contra fighters in Nicaragua that were fighting a typical Cold War battle. Through the machinations of the American government, the sale of weapons in an ethno-religious war in the Middle East funded the purchase of weapons for a war between communist and capitalist fighters in Central America. American voters did not sanction American involvement in either conflict.

This event came to be known by the press as the Iran-Contra Affair and was the subject of intense public hearings. Media attention had converted Congress into a semi-investigative agency that was, at least in part, show business meant to smear political opponents. Nixon's fall made Congressional hearings a political weapon that would be used over and over by both political parties. Reagan denied knowledge of the transactions, but there were indictments and convictions among his staff.

After eight years, Reagan's vice president, George H.W. Bush, was elected as his successor. Bush had been an oilman and a congressman from Texas; he was the son of privilege, with a father that had been the US senator from Connecticut. Bush was a pilot in the US Navy during World War II and was shot down while carrying out attacks on the Japanese. He was much more like Kennedy than Reagan in many respects, but he had been a loyal VP under Reagan and was rewarded with Reagan's support.

The transition to Bush took place in 1989. Reagan went back to his ranch in California, making a few speeches in the following years and eventually announcing that he had developed dementia and would cease public appearances. His final years were spent in a mental darkness until his death in 2004.

THE MIDDLE EAST WARS

President Bush could attest that the history of the world turns in unpredictable ways. Bush was a one-term president whose reputation for fairness and decency did not translate into electoral success despite an impressive resume: he was the son of a senator, a war hero, an innovative businessman in the oil industry, a congressman from Texas, the Ambassador to the United Nations, the Ambassador to China, and the director of the CIA. He was a stable married man with several children. Bush presided over a lopsided American victory in the Middle East and was in office when the most dangerous adversary in US history disintegrated.

And yet, he lost the 1992 election to a Baby Boomer who was the governor of a poor southern state with a well-founded reputation for womanizing. Bill Clinton's many faults were apparent in 1992, but he took down an incumbent president with perfect credentials.

Under George Bush, the United States military had the opportunity to demonstrate that it was not the same force that lost in Vietnam or bungled the Iran hostage situation. It began when Saddam Hussein, the volatile dictator of Iraq, ordered his military to invade Kuwait, a tiny nation to the south. Iraq owed billions to Kuwait as the result of loans related to the Iran-Iraq War. There were many economic and historical tensions between the countries, made worse by a major diplomatic blunder on the part of the US Ambassador to Iraq, April Glaspie, who used vague language to describe the US position on Iraq and Kuwaiti relations. Iraqi military forces invaded Kuwait in August of 1990. Iran had been the first neighbor invaded by Iraq, followed by Kuwait, and now it appeared that an American ally and oil stalwart, Saudi Arabia, was next in line. This was not acceptable to the Americans

President Bush condemned the invasion and demanded that the Iraqi forces withdraw. Hussein refused, in part due to his strategic confusion regarding the American reaction, and in part due to his need not to be perceived as weak to his culture and countrymen. The Saudis opened their Muslim nation to foreign troops and the US began to progress towards war as the method to dislodge the Iraqis from Kuwait. President Bush, who had been the ambassador to the UN, used the functions of the UN to authorize the military buildup and give any subsequent actions a patina of international legitimacy.

For months, military forces poured into the area. Most were Americans stationed in Saudi Arabia. After giving Hussein a final warning in January 1991, joint international forces began a sustained bombing campaign that demonstrated something new: American bombs and missiles were no longer metal devices dropped from planes and driven by gravity. Often flying at treetop level, these new American missiles were targeted through cameras on the nose of the rocket, or Global Positioning Satellites, or American lasers, and they were so accurate that they could be directed at any window on a particular building. They were outrageously precise. American military planners could take out infrastructure like power plants and bridges and limit the impact on civilians. Using these weapons, the infrastructure of Iraq was being ground to dust by American military air power.

And then the ground campaign began. As American soldiers poured into Kuwait, the Iraqi soldiers who had been bombarded by American missiles marched forward to meet them with their hands in the air. No one wanted to fight. In that sense, the Iraqi soldiers gave back what the Vietnamese soldiers had taken from the American military. The US was winning again, big time.

After allowing more of his soldiers to be ruthlessly killed, Hussein ordered his military to set the Kuwaiti oil fields alight and leave. The fires could be seen from orbit. Eventually, to keep the joint militaries from marching on Baghdad, he surrendered and accepted peace terms that kept him in power.

Sadly, American involvement in the Middle East conflicts was not over, and Hussein would be heard from again, but it would be the belligerent namesake son of President George Bush who would initiate the next steps. In just over a decade, Hussein would find himself at the end of a rope.

THE SOVIET EMPIRE FALLS

Vladimir Lenin was the primary architect of the Soviet Union. Lenin was a committed socialist with a strong authoritarian streak who ruled under a modified sort of government control called Leninism. When he died in 1923, he was succeeded by Joseph Stalin, who died in 1953. Stalin was succeeded by Nikita Khrushchev, who was forced out of power in 1964 and replaced by Leonid Brezhnev, who died in 1982.

In the period from 1917 to 1982, the Soviets only had five leaders, with an average tenure of thirteen years. The next guy, Yuri Andropov, lasted only fifteen months, and the guy after that, Konstantin Chernenko, lasted only thirteen months. All seven of these men had been alive during the Russian Revolution in 1917; the Soviet leadership had aged without passing the baton to a younger generation. By the 1980s, they had run out of elderly revolutionaries and now had no choice but to go with a younger leader. The man they chose next was different from the previous leaders of the Soviet Union.

Born in 1931, Mikhail Gorbachev was from a poor family and worked on a collective farm in the Stalin years. He was an affable person and a good student, however, so he attended university and slowly made friends throughout the Communist Party. In 1978, he was appointed Secretary to the Central Committee, and therefore had access to the Soviet leaders at the highest echelons of power. He was close to Yuri Andropov, who had groomed Gorbachev for leadership, and after both Andropov and Chernenko died within months of being appointed, the stunned Party leadership picked Gorbachev, a man with no military background or history with the secret police, a man with no ties to the revolution, and no memory of the Tsars or Bolshevik civil wars, a man who had never served time in a gulag, as the leader of the Soviet Union.

It was apparent from the beginning that Gorbachev was a different kind of leader. In addition to being younger, he was far less opaque and gangster-like. He talked of reform and better relationships with the West, the United States in particular, and he met with President Reagan many times. Reagan seemed to like Gorbachev, and the two talked about limits on US and Soviet missile stockpiles at length.

In April 1986, a nuclear power station at Chernobyl in the Ukraine exploded and spread radioactive dust across the Soviet Union and into Europe. The Soviets said nothing, but the radioactivity was eventually picked up hundreds of miles away, and the Soviets could not deny that a major nuclear meltdown, the worst the world had ever seen, had occurred. This disaster further convinced Gorbachev that the country needed deeper reforms.

Most significantly, Gorbachev obliquely stated on a few occasions that the Soviets would not use force to quell rebellions in Eastern Europe, as they had done previously with brutal efficiency in Hungary and Czechoslovakia. The Hungarians went into open revolt in 1956. In response, fearing the loss of a key satellite state, the Soviets sent in tanks and soldiers that killed thousands of Hungarians. In 1968, several nations of the Warsaw Pact invaded Czechoslovakia to crush the Prague Spring uprising, and the results were identical: dead civilians and no change in government.

By 1989, freedom movements began to grow in many communist countries, including China. China and the Soviet Union had a choice to make, the same one that their predecessors had been forced to make, which was whether or not to use military force against civilians seeking political liberation.

The Chinese communists had no problem choosing force. They did not tolerate the construction of a "Goddess of Democracy" in a public space in the capital during the spring of 1989 and crushed the brief pro-democracy movement at Tiananmen Square in June. It was a bloody and uncompromising rejection of any pro-democracy movement in China that killed unknown thousands.

However, similar movements in East Germany, Bulgaria, Poland, and many other communist countries did not receive a similar Soviet response. Gorbachev seemed to waffle on what had been a key element of the communist world since the Nazis had been defeated; if you rebel, the Soviets will crush you. Young people in those countries took notice, as did their emergent leadership.

In Poland and Hungary, elections were held and won by the reformers. The Soviets did nothing. In November 1989, the East Germans broadcast a statement that the hated wall separating East and West Germany would be opened to allow for unrestricted movement between the segregated parts of the country. This statement was carried over radio and soon after, people began to crowd the border stations. The nervous guards, who had not been informed of any change in plans, faced growing and demanding crowds, and they eventually opened the gates. Thousands of East Germans walked freely into West Germany after forty-four years of forced partition. Crowds on both sides of the border began hacking at the wall, publicly tearing down this hated symbol of communist oppression, again with no response from the Soviets.

In December 1989, a violent revolution broke out in Romania and crowds rushed the government plaza, driving Nicolae Ceausescu, their out-of-touch and hated dictator, to the countryside where he was captured. On December 25, 1989, Ceausescu and his wife Elena were given a two-hour trial, declared guilty of genocide and other crimes, and then taken outside for immediate execution. Images of their lifeless, bullet-ridden bodies were broadcast on state television, yet the Soviets still did not react with a show of force.

Finally, in 1990, the wobble began in the Soviet Union itself. Hard-line communists began to push back against Gorbachev, but he pushed onward with changes to the government that would privatize some businesses. Inexplicably, actual elections were held. Gorbachev became a celebrity outside of the Soviet Union, but a controversial figure within it, driving the country towards a decision about its government.

In 1991, the remaining hardliners in the Communist Party staged a coup, but the tide was not with them. Gorbachev's ally Boris Yeltsin rallied people to the streets where they swarmed the tanks in Red Square, and while there was conflict within the streets of Moscow, it did not include the mass slaughter of civilians seen in the Chinese response to rebellion two years earlier. There was chaos amidst some firing and shelling, but in August of 1991, the coup plotters were put down, the ruling body referred to as the Supreme Soviet suspended activities, and the tricolor flag of Russia, the one before the Revolution, was hoisted above the capital. The Soviet Union had officially collapsed, and the Russian Revolution had run its course.

The Cold War with the Soviets was over. The conflict that created two massive wars (Korea and Vietnam) and thousands of smaller conflicts across the globe had come to an end. The Americans won, to the degree that undeclared wars have victors. The United States was now the sole superpower on earth.

THE CLINTON YEARS

Bill Clinton was elected the 42nd President of the United States in 1992 when he defeated the sitting president, George H.W. Bush. The US economy had gone into a short recession in 1990 and the perception of a bad economy aided Clinton, as did the strong third-party candidacy of another Texan, Ross Perot.

By 1992, thirty-two years had passed since the first "GI Generation" president, John F. Kennedy, had been elected, and George Bush was an aging representative of that era. Clinton was a boomer with strong opinions and experience in the Vietnam War protest movement and the Civil Rights era, both of which were priorities for the younger generation.

The Clinton campaign had to contend with many revelations about Bill Clinton's alleged extramarital affairs, what one of his staffers referred to as "bimbo eruptions." The American public either did not believe the allegations or did not care, because Clinton was elected, despite the stories of affairs having been well known and widely reported.

In 1994, the House of Representatives was taken over for the first time in forty years by the Republicans, and Clinton had to contend with a GOP majority in the House for the remainder of his presidency. No one knew exactly what this indicated in 1994. In 1996, the Republicans put up the aging Senator Bob Dole as their candidate, whom Clinton triumphed over easily with his message of building the future and not looking to the past. The GI Generation finally ceased to be presidential material.

But then, several legal, cultural, and political trends suddenly converged. As the Governor of Arkansas, Clinton allegedly carried on sexual relationships with many women, and tried to initiate several more. His wife, Hillary Clinton, either did not know or did not care. One woman who had refused his advances was a state employee named Paula Jones. Jones was at a conference in Arkansas in 1991 where she was asked by a State Trooper to go to the Governor's hotel room. There she said Bill Clinton exposed himself and asked her to perform sexual acts. She refused and left, but later filed a lawsuit against Clinton for sexual harassment, a new legal violation at that time.

By the time Clinton was President, there were additional questions about his business dealings while he was the Governor of Arkansas, and so a Special Counsel led by the attorney Kenneth Starr was appointed to look into the matter. The Special Counsel had become a permanent feature of the relationship between Congress and the President.

Eventually, Starr came in contact with the Paula Jones lawsuit, and his investigators began looking at patterns in Clinton's behavior. The Special Counsel was given tapes that a civil servant had made of a young woman, Monica Lewinsky, describing in detail her sexual relationship with the President that had taken place in the Oval Office and surrounding offices. Lewinsky was an intern and thirty years younger than Clinton. On the advice of a friend, Lewinsky had kept physical evidence of the affair, but when she was approached by the office of the Special Counsel, she refused to cooperate. However, Starr and his team revealed that they had recordings of her talking about the relationship, and so Lewinsky was legally forced to cooperate and hand over the evidence.

The Special Counsel subpoenaed Clinton, who was forced to testify on the Lewinsky matter. Starr conveyed to the Clinton legal team that he had irrefutable evidence of Clinton's sexual relationship with Lewinsky, and that Clinton should not perjure himself by denying the affair with Lewinsky, which he had done publically. Clinton did it anyway.

Clinton's denial of the affair, combined with the tapes and the physical evidence, was a clear-cut case of perjury that the Republican House of Representatives used to deliver Articles of Impeachment to the Senate for a trial. The American public did not wish to see Clinton removed from office because of his dalliance with Lewinsky, which they deemed a private affair, and the Senate refused to remove Clinton from office for lying under oath about an affair. It looked bad, but did not rise to the constitutional definition of "high crimes and misdemeanors."

And so, Clinton survived to serve out his term, but, with the arrival of the Boomers to high office, things had changed. John Kennedy was alleged to have carried on affairs with many women secure in the knowledge that the press would protect him. If that was true, those days were over. The private and personal were now political. Nothing was off the table.

Left: President Bill Clinton and his wife Right: Monica Lewinsky in 1997

THE INTERNET

The Cold War inspired the development of many technologies, and none have had as far-reaching consequences as the development the internet. Its foundations were established by the Department of Defense in the 1960s around the idea of sharing computational resources across a network.

The computer itself had started as a semi-mechanical device used to crunch numbers and aid in code breaking, but in the decades following World War II, computers grew in power and shrunk exponentially in size and cost. Breakthroughs in transistor technology, and new methods to create electronic pathways onto preprinted boards, had opened up the burgeoning computer industry to new uses through the use of coded instructions for the computers to execute. Machines that had formerly been limited to doing mathematical work for humans could now execute routines involving complex computations and word processing. The internet proposed to link these machines together so that humans could communicate through them and do as yet undreamt things.

The first version of what would become the internet was called ARPANET and in October 1969, not long after the moon landings, it linked a computer at UCLA in Los Angeles to another computer in Menlo Park, California. More connections were made to ARPANET but most importantly, standards were developed that allowed for the expansion of the connections and the sharing of information.

It was inevitable that the growing power of computers, and their decreasing size and cost, would influence the rapidly proliferating growth of the companies dedicated to bringing computers into contact with each other. Home computers began to show up in stores in the 1980s that were dedicated to games and simple tasks like word processing. Big companies like IBM got into this market, as did new startups like Apple Computer.

As more homes installed computers, the first companies dedicated to creating a computer network entered the marketplace. For a time, this market was dominated by America Online. By installing the America Online software on a home computer and using a home phone line, a computer suddenly opened up to a world of available tools which only existed in a "third space" of computer software. By the mid-nineties, a whole new vocabulary entered the popular lexicon, which included terms like logging on, downloading, internet superhighway, and World Wide Web, among a host of others.

And then the computers began to take over functions that had been in other domains. News, for example, was distributed through newsrooms and subject to the editorial oversight of newspapers and TV channels. This monopoly on information began to break apart. In January of 1998, an online news website called The

Drudge Report claimed that Newsweek magazine was sitting on a story about Bill Clinton's affair with an intern. Newsweek was a traditional publication owned by the same group that held the Washington Post, which was the paper that broke the Watergate story. They could not break the Lewinsky scandal because the online news world did it first.

The Drudge Report was just the beginning. Within a decade, the entire printed news reporting business had moved into the far less regulated internet news business. Television was bound to follow. Music was completely colonized by the digitization and online distribution of audio, to the detriment of radio stations and record stores. Digital cameras replaced film photography, allowing for photos to be distributed to other devices through the internet. The inventions that allowed humans to capture sound, motion, and images were now subject to distribution for free in an instant anywhere in the world. The implication of these inventions is still being studied. Clearly, the internet is as important as the technologies developed by Thomas Edison and the Wright Brothers.

MEDIEVAL ISLAM

Just as the world was logging onto the internet to advance knowledge, the adherents of Islam were using the instruments of the 20th century, and the coming technology of the 21st century, to harm the United States. How these events would collide, and how they represented the new era of history, is as instructive as it is confusing.

In 1979, the Soviets decided to invade Afghanistan, a small country on their long and contentious southern border. Afghanistan had once been occupied by the British as part of their colonial holdings in India. After the British left in 1948, the country was ruled by a series of weak leaders, and by the late 1970s, rebel groups supported by Pakistan threatened to undermine the country's communist government. The possibility of a military coup and violence had become routine in the country, and yet the ailing Soviet Union stepped into this mess. Afghanistan devolved in to an unwinnable stalemate where Soviet troops were routinely ambushed. The Soviets had stumbled in to their own Vietnam, and the United States took full advantage. The United States funded rebel fighters called the Mujahedeen and one of their leaders was a wealthy Saudi named Osama bin Laden.

Right before its collapse, the Soviet Union withdrew from Afghanistan. Afghanistan quickly devolved into years of complex and unresolved civil war. Over time, a new type of Islam came to hold sway over the nation, one far more orthodox than the secular Islam that had developed in parts of the Ottoman Empire. This was 7th century Islam, but its adherents had 20th century weapons and 21st century technology.

Bin Laden was still in Afghanistan for much of this period as a new sect called the Taliban took hold. He had been appalled at Saudi Arabia's decision to allow the infidel armies of the United States, and other Western powers, to station in Saudi Arabia as part of the war to free Kuwait from Iraq, and he opposed US troops being in the same country as the holy sites of Mecca and Medina.

Osama bin Laden chose the route of terror to drive non-Muslims from the Middle East and spread Islam. From his base in Afghanistan, he founded an organization called al Qaeda, a stateless group of armed individuals dedicated to harming the West, specifically the United States. His group carried out several attacks in Africa, and other places that were of national interest to the United States, and he made public statements about being at war with America. Each situation that implicated al-Qaeda was complicated, and precluded a direct American response. A stateless actor had no armies or infrastructure to lose in an American missile attack.

The situation changed on September 11, 2001. A plot put together by al-Qaeda, planned both in person and over the internet, came to fruition. That morning, 19 terrorists, most of Saudi origin and all Muslim, hijacked four American airliners full of civilians. Two planes crashed into the World Trade Center in New York City, which burned and collapsed killing all inside. Another hit the Pentagon, killing all aboard and another two hundred people in the building. The fourth was likely headed for the White House. The civilians onboard found out through their cell phones that the other three planes had been deliberately crashed, and they would surely die if they didn't take control of the aircraft back from the hijackers. Several men, possibly led by a passenger named Todd Beamer, rushed the cockpit. A fight for control of the aircraft ensued. It crashed in rural Pennsylvania, killing all aboard but no one on the ground. In total, 2,977 people died in the attacks on September 11, more than had died in the Japanese attack on Pearl Harbor.

What would happen next fell to George W. Bush, son of George H.W. Bush, who had won the presidency by a narrow margin in the 2000 election. He dedicated his remaining term in office to responding to the attacks on 9/11.

The national response would push the American military further into the Islamic world, using the most advanced technology to monitor some of the least technological societies, and collect an unprecedented amount of information through the growing communication networks across the world. Much of that information was about American citizens. War and conflict would, yet again, show the depth and limits of American power.

The World Trade Center burns before collapsing on Sept 11, 2001

TWO MORE UNWON WARS

George W. Bush took over from the candidate that had defeated his father, Bill Clinton, after a disputed election in 2000 that went to the Supreme Court for arbitration. Bush had been well educated and successful in several ventures. After fits and starts in politics, he became the governor of Texas in 1994. His brother Jeb was the governor of Florida at the time of the presidential election in 2000, and it was the votes from Florida that were subject to the Supreme Court lawsuit.

The first year of the Bush presidency was not particularly notable for a middle-of-the-road Republican administration. Bush, or 'Dubya' as he came to be called, focused on tax cuts and a few reform initiatives. That all changed after 9/11/2001, when he was flown around the country on Air Force One as the government tried to figure out how many aircraft had been hijacked. He eventually made it back to Washington DC from Florida, where he had been visiting an elementary school, and his plans fell into place.

Suspicion fell on Osama bin Laden from the beginning. Flight manifests helped investigators to figure out the identities of the hijackers, all of whom were Muslims that had entered the country legally and many had taken piloting classes. The attack was a sophisticated plan that took money and time. It took al-Qaeda and Osama bin Laden, and it was no secret where he was: Afghanistan.

Within a month, American Special Forces were on the ground in Afghanistan. The use of Special Forces was a new development in which small units of soldiers would be dropped on the ground to coordinate the distribution of American firepower to whatever side of the conflict the Special Forces sided with. In Afghanistan, the US linked up with the rebel groups fighting against the Taliban, who had allowed bin Laden to use the country as a base for staging terror operations. Within a few months, the Taliban fell to the American military forces, and the US took nominal control of the country. Their control was nominal because unlike in Germany or Japan, the US did not have enough troops to stage a full occupation. They only had enough manpower to control a few cities. The new way of waging war, one that would ideally limit US military casualties, had a lighter footprint and utilized local forces. It was a sort of "pre-Vietnamization." This plan had downsides in Afghanistan, including the fact that much of the country was a lawless hideout. Unfortunately, the US failed to capture Osama bin Laden when it took control of the country. Bin Laden went into hiding.

The emergence of independent actors like bin Laden raised a new fear for the United States. What might happen if a non-state actor acquired a weapon of mass destruction? Having no territory or infrastructure to defend, the non-state actor could not be deterred, and in the case of radicalized Islam, it was believed that adherents did not value their own or anyone else's life above their religion.

It was in this atmosphere that Saddam Hussein reentered the picture. To stay in power, Hussein had agreed to several conditions at the end of the 1991 Persian Gulf War, one of which was to allow inspectors to view the weapons held at various military bases. It was well known that the Iraqis had been on a quest to acquire nuclear weapons; the Israelis had already destroyed a nuclear reactor built in Iraq in 1981. Over the years, the Iraqi government had violated many of the cease-fire agreements from 1991 and Hussein had refused inspections of the military facilities where it was suspected that weapons of mass destruction, including chemical, biological, and nuclear weapons, were hidden. Hussein's murderous rule, tyrannical family, continuous violation of the Gulf War agreements, constant warring, and the mass murder of his own citizens did not sit well in a post-9/11 world.

So in 2003, the Bush Administration took the agreements Hussein had signed in 1991 to the United Nations, noted how they had been breached by the government of Iraq, and asked for authorization to essentially restart the Gulf War and remove Saddam Hussein. Authorization was given from both the UN and Congress. In March 2003, a coalition of forces led by the United States invaded Iraq with a light footprint of troops and reached the capital of Baghdad within days. The Iraqi government was deposed, but Hussein and his family disappeared. The Iraqi Army was dissolved.

It did not take long for both Iraq and Afghanistan to turn into something like Vietnam, with a huge frontless war carried on with hit and run strikes against American soldiers and mass murder of civilians who cooperated with foreign forces. The United States pursued an accelerated policy of "Vietnamization" in both conflicts. Because there was never a large host of troops in either country, the number of American war dead never soared to that of the Korean or Vietnam War levels, but victory remained just as elusive.

The United States has thus far never been subject to another terrorist attack quite like 9/11. Saddam Hussein was eventually found and handed over for trial by the new government in Iraq. He was found guilty of mass murder and hanged. Video of his dead body was broadcast across the globe. As had happened to the Romanian dictator Ceausescu, Hussein had been cornered and killed. All Iraqis needed to see that he was dead. His hideous sons had been killed by the US Army's 101st Airborne Division and images of their lifeless corpses were shown on TV to ensure that everyone knew the Hussein family would not return to power.

In 2008, the US economy entered a horrifyingly deep recession. The presidency slipped back to the Democrats. In 2011, President Barack Obama ordered the strike on Osama bin Laden when bin Laden was finally located in Pakistan, living well in hiding near a Pakistani Military Academy. American Special Forces flew into Pakistan at night from Afghanistan, landed at the compound where bin Laden was living with a consort, and killed him. After scouring the compound for intelligence, they flew his body back to Afghanistan. Bin Laden was positively identified at an American military base, and his body was cast into the sea.

HISTORY MOVES ON

In 2008, the US economy was in recession and the war in Iraq was still raging onward with no sign of an ending strategy in place. As a result, George W. Bush left office with very low public opinion ratings. The Republicans nominated John McCain, a Vietnam War veteran, and the Democrats nominated a senator from Illinois named Barack Hussein Obama. The Democrats prevailed and thus America's first black president was elected.

Barack Obama was born in Hawaii to a white mother and a Kenyan father. His mother and father met at the University of Hawaii and were married for a short time before they divorced. Obama's father fled and young Barack rarely saw his father again.

Nevertheless, given his ancestry via his father, Barack Obama was able to run for public office as an African-American, which he was, only in the most literal sense. Given the long and torturous history of the descendents of slaves who were brought to the Americas in shackles, and labored for generations before freedom was granted via bloody warfare, and then worked at the bottom of the economic ladder for more generations, it is a historical irony that the first black president was in no way a part of that slave lineage. President Obama had no connection to the black slave experience in the United States, was not the descendent of slaves, and did not spend any of his life in the former Confederate states. He is black by his African father and that is all. His mother married a man from Indonesia after Barack's father departed, and so young Barack lived in Indonesia for a time, before moving back to Hawaii to live with his white grandparents. He has a half-sister from Indonesia as well as half-brothers in Africa sired by his wayward father.

After finishing high school in Hawaii, Obama attended college in Los Angeles and New York, and entered politics after settling in Chicago. He was elected to the Illinois legislature, like Abraham Lincoln, and then was elected as the senator from Illinois, an office sought after by Lincoln. As Lincoln had, Obama used his senatorial aspirations as a jumping-off point for the presidency, which he captured.

American politics had become very narrowly divided by 2008, and the Obama years, from 2008 to 2016, did little to make them any less poisonous. A closely divided Congress passed huge bills that were thousands of pages long, and many congressmen openly admitted that they had not read the bills they were voting on. President Obama eventually withdrew troops from Iraq, and Americans forces recently left Afghanistan after 20 years. Both wars ended far short of victory.

The recession of 2008 and 2009 began to lift after a time, and the economy improved, but radical advances in technology drove the gap between the richest Americans and the poorest even wider. The first 20 years of the 21st century were a tale of rapidly advancing computer technology doing to the human mind what the industrial revolution did to the human body; replacing it with superior machines. Incredible wealth has been both created and destroyed by advances in information and internet technology.

The internet gradually came to colonize ever-larger chunks of economic output. The industrial companies that drove the early days of the American economic expansion would often produce new jobs while machinery replaced farm work, but this next wave of innovation replaced American service jobs such as newspaper reporting, advertising, accounting, and even basic sales, but where these newly displaced workers were to go has not yet been revealed. The owners of the new companies benefitted greatly from the internet in the same way previous companies had benefited from railroads, military protection, and highways. Tech companies, however, produced far more wealth with far fewer people.

Apple Computer produced the iPhone, which quickly became a must-have device for every American. It has replaced the camera, the landline phone, the mail, the musical listening device, the alarm clock, the calendar, and much more. As a device, it is incredibly useful. There are very few areas of American life that are not dominated by the 'smartphone,' and in a short time, technology has turned millions of American youths, as well as everyone else, into tech addicts.

Amazon grew from an online bookseller to a company like no other. It has all the data it needs to position goods around the country that can be delivered to the home in record time. It is a retailer with unprecedented power, and its online sales comprise only one arm of the company. Amazon Web Services has monopolized a majority of the server and hosting needs for every other company in the world.

Google organized the world's online content into a library and made the Internet navigable. Its video services are unparalleled. It collects an unprecedented amount of data about its users, much of which is made available to advertisers. Google's ubiquitous search engine destroyed the once-mighty phone book and newspaper classified advertisements. Google search results are a sort of mind reading machine which captures the thoughts of billions of people via their search queries.

Finally, Facebook created a social content platform that people could customize as they saw fit. This further undermined the traditional press and allowed anyone to achieve a new kind of celebrity. Facebook and its subsidiary social media platforms have become an empire built on advertising sales, human vanity, and much more.

These four horsemen of the internet age, Apple, Amazon, Google, and Facebook, are American companies that are used by billions of people across the globe. Despite being founded in America, they are international companies with international loyalties and ambitions.

The Chinese have deliberately developed alternatives to each American tech giant. There are equivalent behemoths that serve the Chinese public and, in a pattern that has been repeated over and over, the Chinese have used the power of their consumer base to build companies that replicate US technology and remain loyal to the Chinese state.

Chinese technical process, population size, and will to power are the current focus of American concern. How the United States adjusts to the rise of the Chinese superpower is the current topic in the ongoing story of the American journey.

Steven Jobs, shown here in 2010, was a Boomer who founded
Apple Computer which gave the world the iPhone

EPILOGUE

A JOURNEY WITH NO DESTINATION

America has endured its most recent traumas and distractions, as it always has. It is difficult to tell at the moment what any particular event or idea will mean in the long sweep of history, but the meaningful events are always there. They are always there because the story never stops, particularly in the United States which, as a defining characteristic, has always been restlessness. The United States has been in physical and cultural motion from the beginning.

American values have also been in motion, as the country took up and discarded mythic archetypes. The founders gave way to the frontiersmen. The frontiersmen gave way to the cowboy. The cowboy gave way to the heroic soldier, who gave way to the scientist-astronaut. This evolution is captured nicely in the popular *Toy Story* movies, where the loyalties of an all-American kid named Andy are torn between a cowboy named Woody and an astronaut named Buzz. Their good-natured animosity is that between an old archetype and a new one. Woody's pre-recorded phrase is "There's a snake in my boot!" which is physical and immediate. Buzz's preprogrammed voice says, "To infinity and beyond!" which is abstract and open-ended. And so it goes, as both the country and culture of the United States morph to accommodate the times.

Can the United States remain both a coherent and competent country in the face of the world as it is, and as it will become? This is an open question, as it was in 1776 and 1860. The United States has certainly benefited from the wisdom of previous generations who saw the North American continent as a redoubt in a dangerous world of clashing national ambitions. The cultural imperative of Manifest Destiny drove the nation to push west regardless of cost. War was waged in the north in the War of 1812 and to the south in the Mexican-American War to ensure a defined border and peaceful relationships with Canada and Mexico. In short, Fortress North American was formed by steamrolling west, waging war, and keeping a wary eye on the old powers in Europe. This strategy of opportunism and belligerence worked.

Will it still work, and if so, will the United States continue to use it against new rivals and challenges?

China is an ethnocentric communist state unrestrained by both the Western legal traditions that guide world governance organizations, and the lack of any democratic consensus at home; consensus is what the Party says it is. China has a population larger than any other country except India. They are many, and they are ambitious. In many ways, they look like the early United States, and they have their own notions of Manifest Destiny. Can the dominant power coexist with a rising power? That has not happened in the past, but we shall see.

Demographics, as always, are destiny, and virtually every society on earth is getting older. The once belligerent Japanese are the oldest society on earth; clearly, they will not be a military threat in the future. The same demographic death spiral is happening in Europe. In Germany, Italy, and Spain, the average woman gives birth to only one child, which means the population will be cut in half with each succeeding generation. Four grandparents give birth to two kids who give birth to one child; the math is easy and uncompromising. These kids have no aunts or uncles or cousins; they are a single leaf on a withered family tree. In such a situation, schools close and churches empty, and graveyards fill and then are abandoned. European power of the past was built on its primary export, people who held Western ideals, and that day is over. Europe no longer exports people.

Just below Europe, across the Mediterranean Sea, is Africa which has some of the most youthful populations on earth. Already, immigrants pour across the Mediterranean Sea and walk to Europe through the East. These immigrant populations will come to dominate Europe in time. The same can be said about lightly occupied Russia with its gigantic empty east which abuts China with its gigantic population. Only Russian nuclear missiles keep the Russian east in Russian control.

In the meantime, China gets older with each passing year. How long will China remain a growing state? The same grandparent-parent-child math applies, and China may have fatally wounded itself during the 36 years it enacted a 'one child policy' which restricted most couples to only one child. Will its population inertia carry it forward no matter what its average age becomes?

Over the past 250+ years, the United States has bested every competitor that ever dared to defy the will of its incredible people. First were the British, and then there were the Mexicans. The nation defeated the break-away Confederates, and leveled the native tribes. The country defeated the remnant Spanish and ended their long career as *conquistadors*. American forces prevailed in two wars with the Germans, and they utterly defeated and destroyed the empire of the Japanese. After World War II, the United States outfaced the giant and malevolent Soviet Empire in a painful step by step confrontation that occupied American armies and navies all over the globe. The Koreans, Chinese, and Vietnamese could not best the US military in open confrontation. The country has fought back and won against many of the fanatical followers of Islam and dispatched their leaders regardless of how well hidden they were.

Further, there have always been forces tearing at the social cohesion of the nation. There have been great injustices in the United States, and this book could not cover them all. The history of American capitalism and its often violent confrontations with American labor could not be included, nor was there space for the telling of the many documented cases of corruption at all levels of government. The country is riddled with various social pathologies that are an ever-present reality for many Americans. Nevertheless, the United States has brought incredible innovation to the world, and advanced the rights of a greater variety of both groups and individuals than any society that has ever existed. The people of the United States are, as Abraham Lincoln described them, an *"almost-chosen people"* who do not wish for confrontation but are very experienced with it. We have confronted each other and the world, and often, come out the better because of it. There is strong reason to believe that this pattern of confrontation, compromise, and further development will continue.

The future is a country which you can only know once you get there, and you have no choice in the trip or destination. But the best predictor of the future is the past, and I hope this short book has given the reader a better way to understand where this journey is likely to go next. We will always be arriving in the tempest-tossed arc of history.

BIOGRAPHY

Tom Roush is a writer based in Houston, Texas. He holds advanced degrees in music, theater, communications, film, business, and computer science. He has worked for many of the leading companies on earth in media and technology and writing is a lifelong passion. He is the author of many news reports and magazine articles and this is his second book. His book of short stories about lonely and alienated men is called 'Loners,' and is available on Amazon.